Dick

I hope you find this useful

with warm regards

Bob

The Theory of the Cost-of-Living Index

THE THEORY
OF THE
COST-OF-LIVING INDEX

ROBERT A. POLLAK

New York   Oxford
OXFORD UNIVERSITY PRESS
1989

Oxford University Press

Oxford   New York   Toronto
Delhi   Bombay   Calcutta   Madras   Karachi
Petaling Jaya   Singapore   Hong Kong   Tokyo
Nairobi   Dar es Salaam   Cape Town
Melbourne Auckland

and associated companies in
Berlin   Ibadan

Copyright © 1989 by Oxford University Press, Inc.

Published by Oxford University Press, Inc.,
200 Madison Avenue, New York, New York 10016

Oxford is a registered trademark of Oxford University Press

Library of Congress Cataloging-in-Publication Data
Pollak, Robert A., 1938–
The theory of the cost-of-living index/by Robert A. Pollak.
    p.   cm.
Collection of 8 previously published and 4 unpublished papers.
Includes bibliographies and index.
ISBN 0-19-505870-4
1. Consumer price indexes.   I. Title.
HB225.P62 1989   338.5'28—dc19   88-23552   CIP

9 8 7 6 5 4 3 2 1

Printed in the United States of America
on acid-free paper

For Carol and Harold
And Sylvia and Morrison

Preface

My interest in the cost-of-living index developed during the academic year 1968–1969, which I spent working for the Bureau of Labor Statistics in the Office of Price Research. During my year at BLS I became involved in discussions of the practical problems that arose in constructing the Consumer Price Index (CPI). As a theorist, I approached these problems with the conviction that a well-developed theory of the cost-of-living index could provide practical solutions.

The twelve papers reprinted in this volume reflect that conviction. Their unifying theme is that, when suitably elaborated, the theory of the cost-of-living index provides principled answers to many of the practical problems that arise in constructing indexes of consumer prices. The title essay, "The Theory of the Cost-of-Living Index," completed in 1971, summarizes what was then known about the cost-of-living index and the closely related *preference field quantity index*. The paper provides a detailed discussion of the cost-of-living index and its bounds under the conventional assumptions of consumer theory. The remaining eleven papers elaborate the theory of the cost-of-living index under less conventional assumptions.

"Subindexes of the Cost-of-Living Index" (*International Economic Review*, 1975) was prompted by the observation that, although we often talk informally about price indexes for subsets of goods (e.g., "clothing," "footwear," "men's shoes"), the conventional theory of the cost-of-living index is the theory of a *complete* index. The paper defines various types of subindexes and investigates the relationship between subindexes and the complete index. "The Intertemporal Cost-of-living Index" (*Annals of Economic and Social Measurement*, 1975) extends the theory of the cost-of-living index from its traditional one-period framework to a multiperiod setting. It discusses both the complete intertemporal index and one-period subindexes. It also considers the implications of both *naïve* and *rational* habit formation for constructing these indexes. "Welfare Evaluation and the Cost-of-Living Index in the Household Production Model" (*American Economic Review*, 1979) examines the implications of the household production model for the definition and construction of exact cost-of-living indexes and various bounds on the exact index under alternative assumptions about household technology. "Welfare Comparisons and Equivalence Scales" (*American Economic Review*, 1979), coauthored with Terence J. Wales, examines the use of equivalence scales for making welfare comparisons between households with different demographic profiles (e.g., for answering the question "what expenditure level would make a family with three children as well off as it would be with two children and $12,000?"). We argue that such scales cannot be constructed on the basis of observed differences in the consumption patterns of households with different numbers of children because differences in consumption patterns provide only information about *conditional preferences* (i.e., preferences over goods taking family size as given) while interhousehold comparisons require *unconditional preferences*.

The next two papers discuss the construction and interpretation of indexes that measure the impact of price changes on the welfare of a group or population of households. "Group Cost-of-Living Indexes" (*American Economic Review*, 1980) discusses alternative extensions of the theory of the cost-of-living index from a single household to a group of households. "The Social Cost-of-Living Index" (*Journal of Public Economics*, 1981) explores a particular group cost-of-living index based on the Bergson–Samuelson social welfare function. "The Treatment of 'Quality' in the Cost-of-Living Index" (*Journal of Public Economics*, 1983) develops the implications of cost-of-living index theory for the treatment of *quality*. It considers both the *goods approach*, which treats each variety as a separate good, and two characteristics approaches, *L-Characteristics* (Lancaster's *linear and additive* specification) and *H-Characteristics* (Houthakker's *heterogeneous* specification in which the household consumes only a single variety of each product). The paper concludes by discussing the implications of the theory for index number construction and then relating it to the literature on *hedonic indexes*.

The last four papers in the volume "The Treatment of the Environment in the Cost-of-Living Index," "Consumer Durables in a Cost-of-Living Index," "Mortgage Interest Rates in the CPI," and "The Treatment of Taxes in the Consumer Price Index," were written in the early 1970s. They have been circulated in manuscript and cited in the literature, but they have not been published previously. I have included them in this volume to make them available to a wider audience.

All of the papers reprinted here were written with the support of the Bureau of Labor Statistics, which has had an ongoing commitment to index number research. I am grateful to BLS and to Joel Popkin, Janet Norwood, and Jack Triplett for their support. I am also grateful to the National Science Foundation and the National Institutes of Health for their support of my research. Finally, I am grateful to Franklin M. Fisher who provided much assistance and good advice along the way.

Seattle   R.A.P.
January, 1989

Contents

The Theory of the Cost-of-Living Index

The Theory of the Cost-of-Living Index

In this paper I summarize the theory of the "cost-of-living index" and the closely related theory of the "preference field quantity index." The first section is devoted to notation and preliminary background, and the second summarizes the theory of the cost-of-living index. The next two sections discuss upper and lower bounds for the index, and the preference orderings for which these bounds are attained. In section 5 I examine the effect on the index of the choice of a base indifference curve. Section 6 examines the form of the cost-of-living index corresponding to various specific preference orderings. In sections 7 and 8 I examine the preference field quantity index, a quantity index which is conceptually similar to the cost-of-living index. I show that it is equal to the expenditure index deflated by the cost-of-living index if and only if the preference ordering is homothetic to the origin. In section 9 I discuss the use of price indexes in empirical demand analysis and argue that the cost-of-living index is inappropriate for this purpose.

There are a number of areas of practical and theoretical importance which I do not discuss in this paper. No mention is made of quality change, goods provided by governments, or the treatment of the environment. Goods are assumed to be perfectly divisible and transaction costs to be zero. Inter-temporal aspects of the consumer's allocation problem are ignored, so the treatment of saving, interest rates, and consumer durables is not discussed. I have ignored these areas not only because they are difficult but also because a systematic theoretical attack on any of them must be based on a thorough understanding of the basic theory. A major purpose of this paper is to present a rigorous survey of that theory. The material in the first two sections should be familiar, but much of the material in later sections is new.

The discussion of bounds on the cost-of-living index in sections 3 and 4 emphasizes the importance of both upper and lower bounds. It is well known that the Laspeyres index provides an upper bound to the cost-of-living index based on the indifference curve attained in the reference situation, but little attention has been given to the corresponding lower bounds. In section 3 I establish upper and lower bounds, and in section 4 I characterize the preference orderings for which these bounds are attained.

It is well known that the cost-of-living index is independent of the base indifference curve if and only if the indifference map is homothetic to the

Research Discussion Paper #11, Research Division, Office of Prices and Living Conditions, U.S. Bureau of Labor Statistics, 1971; reprinted in *Price Level Measurement*, edited by W. E. Diewert and C. Montmarquette.

origin. In section 5 I consider several classes of nonhomothetic preference orderings and examine their implications for the relationship between the cost-of-living index and the base indifference curve.

In section 6 I consider a menu of preference orderings simple enough that they are suitable for empirical work and examine the cost-of-living index corresponding to each. Since computation of a cost-of-living index depends on estimation of an underlying system of demand equations, it is important to have some sense of what the possibilities are.

In section 7 I follow Malmquist in defining a preference field quantity index. In section 8 I show that use of a cost-of-living index to deflate the expenditure index does not yield this index unless the preference ordering is homothetic to the origin. This suggests that if one wants a quantity index, one must try to get it directly rather than by deflating expenditure by a price index.

The discussion in section 9 of the use of price indexes in empirical demand analysis suggests that the common practice of deflating prices and income by a Laspeyres index has no theoretical standing. It also implies that deflating them by the cost-of-living index would be little better. Furthermore, since the cost-of-living index cannot be computed until the unknown parameters of the system of demand equations have been estimated, a procedure which required deflation of price and income by that index would be of little practical value.

The literature on the theory of the cost-of-living index is of uneven quality. The most lucid general treatments are those of Samuelson (1947), Wold and Jureen (1953), and Malmquist (1953). A more recent survey is Afriat (1972). Fisher and Shell (1968) give a concise statement of the general problem and a detailed discussion of a particular type of quality change.[1]

1. PRELIMINARIES

An individual's tastes can be represented by a preference ordering defined over the commodity space. Let $X = (x_1, \ldots, x_n)$ and $X' = (x'_1, \ldots, x'_n)$ denote commodity bundles, and write $X \, R \, X'$ for "X is at least as good as X'." The binary relation R is a preference ordering. If R satisfies the usual conditions (completeness, reflexivity, transitivity, convexity, continuity), then there exists a real-valued function, $U(X)$, which "represents" the preference ordering in the sense that $X \, R \, X'$ if and only if $U(X) \geqslant U(X')$. We call $U(X)$ the *direct utility function* corresponding to the preference ordering, R, and we sometimes write it as $U(X; R)$ to emphasize the particular preference ordering, R, which the utility function represents. If $U(X)$ is a direct utility function corresponding to the preference ordering, R, then any increasing monotonic transformation of U is also a direct utility function representing R.

The *ordinary demand functions* are found by maximizing the direct utility function subject to the budget constraint. Let $P = (p_1, \ldots, p_n)$ denote the price vector, and μ total expenditure.[2] We denote the ordinary demand functions by $x_i = h^i(P, \mu)$ or $x_i = h^i(P, \mu; R)$, when we need to indicate explicitly the preference ordering from which the demand functions are derived. In vector form, $X = H(P, \mu)$ or $X = H(P, \mu; R)$.

We say that a system of demand functions exhibits *expenditure proportionality* if $h^i(P, \mu) = \gamma^i(P)\mu$ for all i. This is equivalent to requiring all income elasticities to be 1 or, equivalently, all income-consumption curves to be rays from the origin. We say that a preference ordering is *homothetic to the origin* if it can be represented by a utility function which is an increasing monotonic transformation of a function homogeneous of degree 1: $U(X) = T[g(X)]$, $g(\lambda X) = \lambda g(X)$. We often call the utility function itself *homothetic*. It is well known that a system of demand functions exhibits expenditure proportionality if and only if it is generated by a preference ordering which is homothetic to the origin.

The *compensated* or *constant utility* demand functions are found by minimizing the cost of attaining a particular indifference curve. We select a direct utility function to represent the preference ordering and denote the level of utility corresponding to the indifference curve by s; we denote the compensated demand functions by $x_i = f^i(P, s)$ or $x_i = f^i(P, s; R)$, or, in vector form, $X = F(P, s)$.[3] The role of s, the level of utility associated with the indifference curve, requires some explanation. The compensated demand functions depend on the particular indifference curve chosen but not on the particular utility function selected to represent the preference ordering. It would be more accurate to denote the compensated demand functions by $x_i = f^i(P, s; R, U)$ to indicate that the interpretation of a particular numerical value of s depends on the direct utility function selected to represent R. Usually, this elaborate notation is unnecessary.

The direct utility function represents preferences by assigning a number to each X in the commodity space. One collection of goods is assigned a higher number than another if and only if the first is preferred to the second. In a similar manner we define an indirect utility function which represents preferences by assigning numbers to *price-expenditure situations*, (P, μ): one price-expenditure situation is assigned a higher number than another if and only if the first is preferred to the second. The difficulty is that we have not yet defined what it means to say that one price-expenditure situation is preferred to another. The obvious meaning is that the best collection of goods available in the first situation is preferred to the best collection available in the second. Since $X = H(P, \mu; R)$ is the best collection of goods available at (P, μ), we say that (P, μ) is preferred to (P', μ') if and only if $X = H(P, \mu; R)$ is preferred to $X' = H(P', \mu'; R)$. We can use the direct utility function, $U(X; R)$, to assign numbers to price-expenditure situations and thus to define the indirect utility function $\Psi(P, \mu; R)$:

$$\Psi(P, \mu; R) = U[H(P, \mu; R); R].$$

Thus, the indirect utility function is the maximum value of the direct utility function attainable in a particular price-expenditure situation:

$$\Psi(P, \mu; R) = \max U(X; R) \quad \text{subject to} \quad \sum p_k x_k \leqslant \mu.$$

The ordinary demand functions are related to the indirect utility function by

$$h^i(P,\mu) = -\frac{\dfrac{\partial \Psi(P,\mu)}{\partial p_i}}{\dfrac{\partial \Psi(P,\mu)}{\partial \mu}}$$

This result is often called *Roy's theorem*; since we use it repeatedly, we sketch a proof. (1) Differentiate $\Psi(P,\mu) = U[H(P,\mu)]$ with respect to p_i, replace U_k by $-\lambda p_k$ (from the first-order conditions for maximization of the direct utility function), and replace $\sum p_k h_i^k$ by $-h^i$ (this follows from differentiating the budget constraint with respect to p_i). This yields $\Psi_i = \lambda h^i$. (2) Differentiate $\Psi(P,\mu) = U[H(P,\mu)]$ with respect to μ, replace U_k by $-\lambda p_k$, and recognize that $\sum p_k h_\mu^k = 1$. This yields $\Psi_\mu = -\lambda$. Hence, $-\Psi_i/\Psi_\mu = h^i$.

Finally, preferences can be represented by the *expenditure function*, $E(P,s)$, or $E(P,s;R)$, analogous to the cost function in production theory.[4] In production theory the cost function shows the minimum cost of attaining a given level of output or, equivalently, a given isoquant; in consumer theory it shows the minimum expenditure required to attain a given level of utility or, strictly speaking, a given indifference curve. The expenditure function is related to the compensated demand functions by $E(P,s) = \sum p_k f^k(P,s)$.

Alternatively, the expenditure function may be derived from the indirect utility function by solving

$$s = \Psi(P,\mu)$$

for μ. Since

$$\frac{\partial E(P,s)}{\partial p_i} = -\frac{\dfrac{\partial \Psi[P,E(P,s)]}{\partial p_i}}{\dfrac{\partial \Psi[P,E(P,s)]}{\partial \mu}} = h^i[P,E(P,s)]$$

we have

$$\frac{\partial E(P,s)}{\partial p_i} = f^i(P,s)$$

2. BASIC THEORY

The cost-of-living index is the ratio of the minimum expenditures required to attain a particular indifference curve under two price regimes. We denote the cost-of-living index by $I(P^a, P^b, s, R)$:

$$I(P^a, P^b, s, R) = \frac{E(P^a, s; R)}{E(P^b, s; R)}$$

The notation emphasizes that the index depends not only on the two sets of prices, P^a and P^b, but also on an initial choice of an indifference map or preference ordering, R, and the choice of a base indifference curve, s, from that map. One set of prices is called *reference prices*, and the other, *comparison prices*. If comparison prices are twice the reference prices, the index is 2; if they are one-half the reference prices, the index is one-half. In our notation the comparison prices are the first n arguments of the index function, and references prices the next n arguments. Interchanging comparison and reference prices yields a new index which is the reciprocal of the original index:

$$I(P^a, P^b, s, R) = \frac{1}{I(P^b, P^a, s, R)}$$

Either set of prices may be designated the reference set; a choice must be made, but it is a choice without substantive implications. Usually, we will denote comparison prices by P^a and reference prices by P^b. The reader is cautioned against calling the reference prices "base" prices; we reserve the term *base* to denote the indifference curve on which the index is predicated or the preference ordering to which it belongs.

Strictly speaking, the cost-of-living index depends only on the comparison prices, the reference prices, and the base indifference curve. It does not depend on the indifference map to which the base curve belongs. However, it is useful and realistic to imagine that the base indifference curve is selected by a two-stage procedure: First, a base map is chosen, and then a base curve is chosen from the map. Treating the base curve as part of a base map leads one to investigate the sensitivity of the index to the choice of the base curve from a particular map.

The logic of the cost-of-living index is best understood by interpreting it in the twin contexts of comparisons over time and comparisons over space. Features of the index that are easily overlooked in one context often stand out sharply in the other. This is particularly true of the role of the base preference ordering and base indifference curve.

For example, to construct a cost-of-living index to compare prices in Paris with those in Tokyo, we must specify the preference ordering on which the comparison is to be based. The Japanese government, considering how much to pay its diplomats in Paris, would presumably use Japanese tastes, while the French government would use French tastes. As is customary in discussing international price comparisons, we ignore differences in tastes within countries. But suppose the U.S. government wants to compare prices in Paris with those in Tokyo to decide on appropriate salary differentials for its diplomats. The comparison should be based on U.S. tastes. In principle, this is extremely important because it underscores the fact that the base preference ordering need not be one which is associated either with the reference prices or the comparison prices.

In intertemporal comparisons we often conceal the choice of a base preference ordering. To compare U.S. prices in 1970 with U.S. prices in 1969, it seems "obvious" and "natural" to use U.S. preferences. As a practical matter it seems likely that this would be appropriate in the majority of problems of this type although they would not be appropriate for the French government to use when deciding how much to increase the salary of its diplomats in Washington. The principal difficulty is that specifying "U.S. preferences" does not resolve the problem unless U.S. preferences are constant over time. Otherwise, it identifies a class of preference orderings from which the appropriate one still must be chosen. At first glance we have reduced the number of admissible preference orderings to two: U.S. preferences in 1969 and in 1970. But there is no reason why the comparison should not be based on U.S. preferences in 1971, 1958, or any other year. Fisher and Shell (1968) argue that current tastes provide a more appropriate indicator of the welfare effects of price changes than past tastes, but they are concerned only with the choice between 1969 and 1970 tastes and do not consider the possibility of basing the comparison on 1971 preferences.

The case of endogenous taste change is conceptually more difficult. If tastes change because of habit formation, as in Pollak (1970), then the appropriate base preference ordering may be a long-run pseudopreference ordering which generates the long-run demand function rather than any particular short-run demand function with its implied dependence on the historic time path of consumption.[5] Endogenous taste change has received little systematic attention in economic theory; if tastes are endogenous, the validity of individual preferences as a touchstone of social welfare must be reexamined.

We conclude this section by enumerating the properties of the cost-of-living index which follow directly from its definition and the properties of the cost function:

$$I(P, P, s, R) = 1 \tag{P1}$$

That is, if the comparison prices are equal to the reference prices, the value of the index is 1.

$$I(\lambda P, P, s, R) = \lambda \tag{P2}$$

That is, if the comparison prices are proportional to the reference prices, then the value of the index is equal to the factor of proportionality.

$$I(P, \lambda P, s, R) = \frac{1}{\lambda} \tag{P3}$$

That is, if the reference prices are proportional to the comparison prices, then the value of the index is the reciprocal of the factor of proportionality.

$$I(\lambda P^a, \lambda P^b, s, R) = I(P^a, P^b, s, R) \tag{P4}$$

If the comparison prices and the reference prices are multiplied by a common factor, the value of the index is unchanged.

$$I(P^b, P^a, s, R) = 1/I(P^a, P^b, s, R) \tag{P5}$$

If the comparison and the reference prices are interchanged, then the new index is the reciprocal of the old.

$$\text{If } P^{a'} \geqslant P^a, \text{ then } I(P^{a'}, P^b, s, R) \geqslant I(P^a, P^b, s, R) \tag{P6}$$

That is, if one set of comparison prices is higher than another, the index corresponding to the first is higher than that corresponding to the second. If the index is differentiable, we can express this monotonicity property as

$$\frac{\partial I}{\partial p_i^a}(P^a, P^b, s, R) \geqslant 0.$$

The strict inequality holds if all goods are consumed everywhere in a neighborhood of the initial price-expenditure situation. The property follows directly from the fact that an increase in any price cannot decrease the cost of attaining a particular indifference curve.

$$\min\left\{\frac{p_i^a}{p_i^b}\right\} \leqslant I(P^a, P^b, s, R) \leqslant \max\left\{\frac{p_i^a}{p_i^b}\right\}. \tag{P7}$$

The cost-of-living index for any base indifference curve lies between the smallest and the largest *price relative*, p_i^a/p_i^b. To prove this we set μ^b so that $\Psi(P^b, \mu^b; R) = s$ and, therefore, $\mu^b = E(P^b, s; R)$. It suffices to show

$$\min\left\{\frac{p_i^a}{p_i^b}\right\} \leqslant \frac{E(P^a, s; R)}{\mu^b} \leqslant \max\left\{\frac{p_i^a}{p_i^b}\right\}$$

or, equivalently,

$$\mu^b \min\left\{\frac{p_i^a}{p_i^b}\right\} \leqslant E(P^a, s; R) \leqslant \mu^b \max\left\{\frac{p_i^a}{p_i^b}\right\}$$

We now proceed with an overcompensation argument and an undercompensation argument. (1) If you give the individual $\mu^b \max\{p_i^a/p_i^b\}$, then he cannot be worse off than he was at (P^b, μ^b) because, regardless of what collection of goods he purchased at that price-expenditure situation, he can buy the same collection now with expenditure $\mu^b \max\{p_i^a/p_i^b\}$. In particular, this is true even if he consumed only one good, and that happened to be the good that experienced the largest price increase. (2) If you give an individual $\mu^b \min\{p_i^a/p_i^b\}$, then he cannot be better off than at (P^b, μ^b) because the new feasible set lies entirely within the old one except where they coincide at the vertex corresponding to the good whose price has experienced the smallest increase. These upper and lower bounds are important because they do not depend on knowing anything about preferences except that they satisfy the usual regularity conditions, and because they do not depend on knowing the quantities consumed in any price-expenditure situation.[6]

3. LASPEYRES AND PAASCHE INDEXES

The theory of the cost-of-living index provides no criterion for choosing either the base map or the base curve on which the index is predicated. The upper and lower bounds on the cost-of-living index expressed in P7

$$\min\left\{\frac{p_i^a}{p_i^b}\right\} \leqslant I(P^a, P^b, s, R) \leqslant \max\left\{\frac{p_i^a}{p_i^b}\right\}$$

represent the best that can be done without additional assumptions. In this section we examine the cost-of-living index corresponding to two "indifference map–indifference curve" combinations which stand out as "natural" or "obvious" ones on which to base the index, namely, those which correspond to the reference situation and the comparison situation.

Consider an individual with preference ordering, R^a, who, facing prices P^a with expenditure μ^a, chooses the basket of goods X^a: $X^a = H(P^a, \mu^a; R^a)$. Similarly, $X^b = H(P^b, \mu^b; R^b)$. The most suggestive interpretation is in terms of place-to-place comparisons. Suppose P^a and P^b denote prices in Paris and Tokyo, so R^a and R^b denote French and Japanese preferences. There are two "natural" or "obvious" indifference curves which stand out as candidates on which to base a cost-of-living index. If we are to use French tastes, it seems "natural" (although certainly not necessary) to consider the indifference curve attained by a Frenchman facing prices P^a with income μ^a. We define s^a by $s^a = \Psi(P^a, \mu^a; R^a)$. If we are to use Japanese tastes as our norm, it seems "natural" to consider the indifference curve attained by a Japanese facing prices P^b with expenditure μ^b: $s^b = \Psi(P^b, \mu^b; R^b)$. Thus, the two "natural" (s, R) combinations on which to base a cost-of-living index are (s^a, R^a) and (s^b, R^b). In the case of intertemporal comparisons the situation is identical. However, if tastes do not change over time, then $R^a = R^b$, and the two "natural" base indifference curves belong to the same preference ordering.

We have identified two "natural" indexes, $I(P^a, P^b, s^a, R^b)$ and $I(P^a, P^b, s^b, R^b)$. There are other indexes which have some claim to being called "natural", and the primacy attributed to these two may reflect no more than the fact that we have interesting theorems about them. Two other "natural" indexes are $I(P^a, P^b, s^{a*}, R^a)$ where $s^{a*} = \Psi(P^a, \mu^b; R^a)$ and $I(P^a, P^b, s^{b*}, R^b)$ where $s^{b*} = \Psi(P^b, \mu^a; R^b)$. The first is based on the indifference curve which could be attained by an individual with the map of the comparison situation facing comparison prices with the expenditure of the reference situation. The second is based on the curve attained by an individual with the map of the reference situation facing reference prices but with comparison expenditure.

The two indexes which we identified as natural are of special interest because we can establish better bounds for them than we could in the general case. To establish these bounds, we define a fixed weight index, $J(P^a, P^b, \theta)$,

$$J(P^a, P^b, \theta) = \frac{\sum \theta_k p_k^a}{\sum \theta_k p_k^b}$$

where $\theta = (\theta_1, \ldots, \theta_n)$. The fixed weight index is a ratio of weighted sums of prices, but we could, without loss of generality, divide through by $\sum \theta_k$ and interpret the index as a ratio of weighted averages of prices. We shall interpret the weights as quantities of the goods in a market basket, so the index is the ratio of the cost of that market basket at prices P^a to its cost at prices P^b.

A fixed weight price index provides little useful information unless the weights are carefully chosen. Two obvious choices of weights are X^a and X^b. The fixed weight index with weights equal to X^b is called a *Laspeyres* index:

$$J(P^a, P^b, X^b) = \frac{\sum x_k^b p_k^a}{\sum x_k^b p_k^b}$$

That is, the Laspeyres index is a fixed weight index with weights associated with the reference prices, P^b. We often write the Laspeyres index in the form

$$J(P^a, P^b, X^b) = \sum w_k^b \left(\frac{p_k^a}{p_k^b} \right)$$

where $w_k^b = x_k^b p_k^b / \mu^b$. That is, the Laspeyres index is a weighted average of the price relatives, p_i^a / p_i^b, where the weights are the expenditure weights of the reference situation. To show the equivalence of these two forms, we write

$$J(P^a, P^b, X^b) = \frac{\sum x_k^b p_k^a}{\mu^b} = \sum \frac{x_k^b}{\mu^b} p_k^a$$

$$= \sum \frac{x_k^b p_k^b}{\mu^b} \frac{p_k^a}{p_k^b} = \sum w_k^b \left(\frac{p_k^a}{p_k^b} \right)$$

We use the fact that X^b is the market basket purchased by an individual with preferences R^b with expenditure μ^b at prices P^b to establish an upper bound on $I(P^a, P^b, s^b, R^b)$.

Theorem.

$$\min \left\{ \frac{p_i^a}{p_i^b} \right\} \leqslant I(P^a, P^b, s^b, R^b) \leqslant J(P^a, P^b, X^b).$$

The lower bound is the one asserted in P7, but the upper bound is an improvement since

$$J(P^a, P^b, X^b) = \sum w_k^b\left(\frac{p_k^a}{p_k^b}\right) \leqslant \max\left\{\frac{p_k^a}{p_k^b}\right\}.$$

since the w's are nonnegative numbers which sum to 1. That is, the Laspeyres index is an upper bound on the cost-of-living index based on the indifference curve attained in the reference situation.

Proof. To show that $J(P^a, P^b, X^b)$ is an upper bound on $I(P^a, P^b, s^b, R^b)$ we write the latter as

$$\frac{E(P^a, s^b, R^b)}{E(P^b, s^b, R^b)} = \frac{E(P^a, s^b, R^b)}{\mu^b}$$

and the former as

$$\frac{\sum x_k^b p_k^a}{\sum x_k^b p_k^b} = \frac{\sum x_k^b p_k^a}{\mu^b}$$

It suffices to show that

$$E(P^a, s^b, R^b) \leqslant \sum x_k^b p_k^a$$

But this follows directly from the fact that the minimum cost of attaining s^b at prices P^a cannot be greater than the cost of X^b.

The Paasche index is the fixed weight index with weights equal to the market basket purchased at the comparison prices, P^a, with expenditure μ^a:

$$J(P^a, P^b, X^a) = \frac{\sum x_k^a p_k^a}{\sum x_k^a p_k^b}$$

It is the ratio of the cost of buying the market basket X^a at prices P^a to its cost at P^b. The Paasche index is a lower bound on $I(P^a, P^b, s^a, R^a)$, the cost-of-living index corresponding to (s^a, R^a).

Theorem.

$$J(P^a, P^b, X^a) \leqslant I(P^a, P^b, s^a, R^a) \leqslant \max\left\{\frac{p_i^a}{p_i^b}\right\}.$$

Proof. The upper bound is the one established in P7. To establish the lower bound, we must show that

$$\frac{\sum x_k^a p_k^a}{\sum x_k^a p_k^b} \leqslant \frac{E(P^a, s^a, R^a)}{E(P^b, s^a, R^a)}.$$

Since the numerators are equal, it suffices to show

$$\frac{1}{\sum x_k^a p_k^b} \leqslant \frac{1}{E(P^b, s^a, R^a)}$$

or, equivalently,

$$E(P^b, s^a, R^a) \leqslant \sum x_k^a p_k^b$$

But this follows immediately since the minimum expenditure required to attain (s^a, R^a) at prices P^b cannot exceed the cost of X^a at these prices.

To summarize: The Laspeyres index is a fixed weight index with weights corresponding to the market basket purchased in the reference situation. It is an upper bound on the cost-of-living index corresponding to the preference ordering and indifference curve attained in the reference situation. The Paasche index is a fixed weight index with weights corresponding to the market basket purchased in the comparison situation. It is a lower bound on the cost-of-living index corresponding to the preference ordering and indifference curve attained in the comparison situation. It is not true that the cost-of-living index lies between the Paasche and Laspeyres indexes. Instead, we have a lower bound on one cost-of-living index and an upper bound on another.

4. WHEN THE INDEX IS EQUAL TO ITS BOUNDS

In section 3 we established two important bounding theorems for the cost-of-living index:

$$\min \left\{ \frac{p_i^a}{p_i^b} \right\} \leqslant I(P^a, P^b, s^b, R^b) \leqslant J(P^a, P^b, X^b)$$

and

$$J(P^a, P^b, X^a) \leqslant I(P^a, P^b, s^a, R^a) \leqslant \max \left\{ \frac{p_i^a}{p_i^b} \right\}$$

In this section we investigate the preference orderings for which the cost-of-living index coincides with one or the other of its bounds.

4.1 When the Cost-of-Living Index Is Equal to the Laspeyres or Paasche Bounds

It is well known that if the preference ordering is represented by a *fixed coefficient* direct utility function

$$U(X) = \min \left\{ \frac{x_i}{a_i} \right\}$$

then the cost-of-living index $I(P^a, P^b, s^b, R)$ is equal to the Laspeyres index $J(P^a, P^b, X^b)$. To show this we make use of the fact that the expenditure-minimizing quantity of good i for attaining a level of utility s^b is given by $x_i^b = a_i s^b$. Hence, the cost of attaining s^b at prices P^b is given by $\sum x_k^b p_k^b = \sum a_k s^b p_k^b$ while the minimum expenditure required to attain s^b at prices P^a is given by $\sum x_x^b p_k^a = \sum a_k s^b p_k^a$. Hence, the Laspeyres index $J(P^a, P^b, X^b)$ coincides with the cost-of-living index $I(P^a, P^b, s^b, R)$.

The homothetic fixed coefficient case is not the only one in which $I(P^a, P^b, s^b, R) = J(P^a, P^b, X^b)$. Any preference ordering which does not permit substitution along its indifference curves implies a cost-of-living index, $I(P^a, P^b, s^b, R)$, which coincides with the Laspeyres index, $J(P^a, P^b, X^b)$. There is no need for the indifference map to be homothetic.

Theorem. The cost-of-living index coincides with the appropriate Laspeyres and Paasche bounds if and only if the preference ordering can be represented by a direct utility function of the generalized fixed coefficient form

$$U(X) = \min \{g^i(x_i)\} \quad g^{i'}(x^i) > 0$$

Proof. If the preference ordering is of the generalized fixed coefficient form, it is easily verified that the cost-of-living index coincides with the appropriate Laspeyres and Paasche bounds.

If the cost-of-living index coincides with its Laspeyres bound for all s^b, then

$$\Psi(P^b, m) = \Psi[P^a, \sum h^k(P^b, m) p_k^a]$$

for all m. Differentiating with respect to p_i^b and m, we find the ordinary demand functions:

$$-h^i(P^b, m) = \frac{\sum p_k^a \dfrac{\partial h^k}{\partial p_i^b}}{\sum p_k^a \dfrac{\partial h^k}{\partial m}}$$

Hence,

$$\sum p_k^a \left[\frac{\partial h^k}{\partial p_i^b} + h^i \frac{\partial h^k}{\partial m} \right] = 0$$

or, differentiating with respect to p_j^a,

$$\frac{\partial h^j}{\partial p_i^b} + h^i \frac{\partial h^j}{\partial m} = 0$$

This, of course, implies that the substitution effects are zero. We next show that the demand functions $h^2,\ldots,h^n$ can each be written as functions of h^1:

$$h^i(P,m) = \delta^i[h^1(P,m)]$$

We do this by showing that the ratios of the partial derivatives are equal

$$\frac{\dfrac{\partial h^j}{\partial p_i}}{\dfrac{\partial h^j}{\partial m}} = \frac{\dfrac{\partial h^1}{\partial p_i}}{\dfrac{\partial h^1}{\partial m}}$$

for all i,j. Equality of the partial derivatives follows from our characterization of the substitution effect; indeed, the common value of the ratios is h^1. Substituting these demand functions into the direct utility function yields the indirect utility function

$$s = \Psi(P,\mu) = U[h^1(P,\mu), \delta^2(h^1),\ldots,\delta^n(h^1)] = \delta[h^1(P,\mu)]$$

This implies $x_1 = f^1(P,s) = f^1(s)$, and, hence, $x_i = f^i(P,s) = f^i(s)$. This implies that the direct utility function is of the generalized fixed coefficient form where g^i is the inverse of f^i.

The Laspeyres (Paasche) index may coincide with the cost-of-living index to which it is the upper (lower) bound for a particular value of s, say s^*, but not for all s. This occurs if the indifference curve corresponding to s^* is of the fixed coefficient form. In another context Marjorie McElroy (1969) has provided an interesting example of such an indifference map; she constructed it by allowing the "necessary basket" of a linear expenditure system to coincide with the "bliss point" of an additive quadratic.[7] At the critical point, the Laspeyres and Paasche indexes coincide with the corresponding cost-of-living index.

4.2 When the Cost-of-Living Index Is Equal to the "Other Bounds"

In section 4.1 we showed that the cost-of-living index coincides with the appropriate Laspeyres or Paasche bounds if and only if the preference ordering is of the generalized fixed coefficient form. We now examine the two forgotten bounds: $\min\{p_i^a/p_i^b\}$, the lower bound of $I(P^a, P^b, \_, \Lambda^h)$, and $\max\{p_i^a/p_i^b\}$, the upper bound of $I(P^a, P^b, s^a, R^a)$. For what preference orderings do these cost-of-living indexes coincide with their bounds?

If the preference ordering can be represented by a linear direct utility function

$$U(X) = \sum a_k x_k$$

then the indifference curves are parallel lines, and all goods are "perfect substitutes." The minimum cost of attaining the indifference curve s is given by

$$E(P, s, R) = \min\left\{\frac{p_i}{a_i}s\right\} = s\min\left\{\frac{p_i}{a_i}\right\}$$

Hence, the cost-of-living index is

$$I(P^a, P^b, s, R) = \frac{\min\left\{\dfrac{p_i^a}{a_i}\right\}}{\min\left\{\dfrac{p_i^b}{a_i}\right\}}$$

The ordinary demand functions corresponding to this utility function are not single valued. If $p_1/a_1 = p_2/a_2 = \cdots = p_n/a_n$, then the budget line coincides with the indifference curve corresponding to $s = \mu a_i/p_i$, and the consumer is indifferent among all commodity bundles which exhaust his expenditure. For any other configuration of relative prices some goods will not be consumed.

Suppose that an individual's preferences are represented by a linear utility function and that when facing prices P^b with expenditure μ^b, he consumes all goods in positive quantities. Then

$$\frac{p_1^b}{a_1} = \frac{p_2^b}{a_2} = \cdots = \frac{p_n^b}{a_n} = r$$

so the cost-of-living index is given by

$$I(P^a, P^b, s^b, R) = \frac{1}{r}\min\left\{\frac{p_i^a}{a_i}\right\} = \min\left\{\frac{p_i^a}{a_i}\right\}\frac{1}{r} = \min\left\{\frac{p_i^a}{a_i}\frac{a_i}{p_i^b}\right\} = \min\left\{\frac{p_i^a}{p_i^b}\right\}$$

A similar result holds for the generalized linear direct utility function, $s = U(X)$, defined implicitly by

$$\sum \alpha^k(s)x_k = w(s)$$

where $\alpha^1, \ldots, \alpha^n$ and w are functions of s. The cost-of-living index is given by

$$I(P^a, P^b, s, R) = \frac{\min\left\{\dfrac{p_i^a}{\alpha^i(s)}\right\}}{\min\left\{\dfrac{p_i^b}{\alpha^i(s)}\right\}}$$

The indifference curves are linear, but they are not parallel; of course, they cannot intersect in the positive orthant, but there is no reason to rule out intersections of extensions of the indifference curves outside the commodity space. If all goods are consumed at (P^b, μ^b), then it is easy to show that $I(P^a, P^b, s^b, R) = \min\{p_i^a/p_i^b\}$. This is what one would expect since the relevant characteristic in our previous example is that the indifference curves are linear; whether or not they are parallel is irrelevant.

We emphasize that it was necessary to assume that all goods are consumed at (P^b, μ^b). Suppose $p_i^a = p_i^b$, $i = 2, \ldots, n$ and $p_1^a < p_1^b$. If x_1 were not consumed at (P^b, μ^b) because it was too expensive, then a small decrease in its price, all other prices remaining constant, will not affect the cost-of-living index; x_1 will still be too expensive and will not be consumed. Hence, the value of the index would be 1, not $\min\{p_i^a/p_i^b\}$.

Theorem. The cost-of-living index coincides with the appropriate "other bounds," $\min\{p_i^a/p_i^b\}$ or $\max\{p_i^a/p_i^b\}$, if and only if the preference ordering can be represented by a generalized linear utility function

$$\sum \alpha^k(s)x_k = w(s)$$

and all goods are consumed in positive quantities in the base situation.

Proof. We have already proved that if the utility function is of this form, then $I(P^a, P^b, s^b, R)$ coincides with $\min\{p_i^a/p_i^b\}$.

We now show that preference ordering corresponding to the generalized linear direct utility function is the only one for which

$$I(P^a, P^b, s^b, R) = \min\left\{\frac{p_i^a}{p_i^b}\right\}$$

provided that all goods are consumed at prices P^b with expenditure μ^b. We cannot vary the p_i^b's because such variations may invalidate the hypothesis that all goods are consumed. We can, however, vary the p_i^a's. If $p_1^a/p_1^b < p_i^a/p_i^b$ for all $i \neq 1$, then in a neighborhood of P^a the index depends only on p_1^a and is independent of $p_2^a, \ldots, p_n^a$. Hence, in that neighborhood $E(P^a, s^b)$ depends only on p_1^a and s. Since the compensated demand functions are the derivatives of the expenditure function,

$$f^i(P^a, s^b) = \frac{\partial E(P^a, s^b)}{\partial p_i^a} = 0 \quad i \neq 1$$

That is, only good 1 is consumed. This is the case in every price-expenditure situation unless there are "ties," and this implies linear indifference curves.

We now turn briefly to the index $I(P^a, P^b, s^a, R^a)$ and its upper bound $\max\{p_i^a/p_i^b\}$. If the preference ordering can be represented by the generalized linear direct utility function, then

$$I(P^a, P^b, s^a, R^a) = \frac{\min\left\{\dfrac{p_i^a}{\alpha^i(s^a)}\right\}}{\min\left\{\dfrac{p_i^b}{\alpha^i(s^a)}\right\}}$$

If all goods are consumed at (P^a, μ^a), then

$$\frac{p_1^a}{\alpha^1(s^a)} = \frac{p_2^a}{\alpha^2(s^a)} = \cdots = \frac{p_n^a}{\alpha^3(s^a)} = r$$

so that the cost-of-living index becomes

$$I(P^a, P^b, s^a, R) = \frac{r}{\min\left\{\dfrac{p_i^b}{\alpha^i(s^a)}\right\}} = \frac{1}{\min\left\{\dfrac{p_i^b}{\alpha^i(s^a)}\dfrac{1}{r}\right\}} = \frac{1}{\min\left\{\dfrac{p_i^b}{p_i^a}\right\}} = \max\left\{\dfrac{p_i^a}{p_i^b}\right\}$$

This result is precisely analogous to that obtained for $I(P^a, P^b, s^b, R)$, as indeed it must be.

The importance of the existence of preference orderings for which the cost-of-living index actually attains its "other bounds" lies in its immediate implication that these bounds are "best bounds." That is, if anyone claims to have found better bounds for the cost-of-living index, we can always find an admissible preference ordering whose cost-of-living index lies outside the proposed bounds. Although our "other bounds" may not seem as satisfying or as useful as the Laspeyres and Paasche bounds, our demonstration that they correspond to the generalized linear utility function shows that it is not our lack of ingenuity but the inherent logic of the situation which prevents us from finding better ones.

5. THE BASE INDIFFERENCE CURVE

In this section I examine how the choice of the base indifference curve affects the cost-of-living index.

5.1 Expenditure Proportionality and Homothetic Indifference Maps

If the preference ordering is homothetic to the origin, then the implied cost-of-living index is independent of the particular indifference curve chosen as a base. That is, if R is homothetic to the origin, $I(P^a, P^b, s, R)$ is independent of s. To prove this, we use the fact that if a preference ordering is homothetic to the origin, then it can be represented by a direct utility function homogeneous of degree 1; the implied demand functions exhibit expenditure proportionality; and the indirect utility function can be written in the form

$$s = \Psi(P, \mu) = \phi(P)\mu$$

where $\phi(P)$ is homogeneous of degree -1. Hence, the expenditure function is given by

$$\mu = E(P, s) = \frac{s}{\phi(P)}$$

and the cost-of-living index by

$$I(P^a, P^b, s, R) = \frac{E(P^a, s, R)}{E(P^b, s, R)} = \frac{\phi(P^b)}{\phi(P^a)}$$

which is independent of s.

The converse of this result also holds: The cost-of-living index is independent of the base indifference curve if and only if the preference ordering is homothetic to the origin. Instead of showing this directly, we first introduce what appears to be a roundabout way of specifying the base indifference curve from a given preference ordering R. We specify the base indifference curve as the one corresponding to a base level of expenditure, m, at reference prices, P^b. The level of utility corresponding to the base indifference curve is given by $s = \Psi(P^b, m)$. It is often convenient to write the index as a function of m rather than s. We write $I^*(P^a, P^b, m, R) = I(P^a, P^b, \Psi(P^b, m), R)$. The index $I(P^a, P^b, s, R)$ is independent of s if and only if $I^*(P^a, P^b, m, R)$ is independent of m.

The specification of the index as a function of m rather than s is more than a useful mathematical trick. In practice, it is a sensible, convenient and commonly used method of specifying the base indifference curve. That is, the base indifference curve is specified to be the indifference curve from a given base indifference map attainable by an individual with a particular expenditure at base period prices. In fact, we cannot interpret the index $I(P^a, P^b, s, R)$ without additional information which enables us to attach some meaning to the numerical value of s. To do this we need either the direct utility function, the indirect utility function, or the expenditure function. The cost-of-living index, $I^* = I^*(P^a, P^b, m, R)$, is defined implicitly by

$$\Psi(P^b, m) = \Psi(P^a, mI^*)$$

Differentiating with respect to p_i^b and m and making use of the assumption that $\partial I^*(P^a, P^b, m, R)/\partial m = 0$ yields

$$\frac{\partial \Psi(P^b, m)}{\partial p_i^b} = \frac{\partial \Psi(P^b, mI^*)m}{\partial \mu} \frac{\partial I^*}{\partial p_i^b}$$

$$\frac{\partial \Psi(P^b, m)}{\partial m} = \frac{\partial \Psi(P^a, mI^*)I^*}{\partial \mu}$$

Hence,

$$h^i(P^b, m) = -\frac{\dfrac{\partial \Psi(P^b, m)}{\partial p_i^b}}{\dfrac{\partial \Psi(P^b, m)}{\partial m}} = -\left(\frac{1}{I^*}\frac{\partial I^*}{\partial p_i^b}\right)m$$

Since the factor in parentheses is independent of m, the demand functions exhibit expenditure proportionality and, therefore, the preference ordering is homothetic to the origin.

We have just proved:

Theorem. The cost-of-living index is independent of the base indifference curve if and only if the preference ordering is homothetic to the origin.

This implies:

Theorem. If the preference ordering is homothetic to the origin, then

$$J(P^a, P^b, X^a) \leqslant I(P^a, P^b, s, R) \leqslant J(P^a, P^b, X^b)$$

That is, if the preference ordering is homothetic, then the cost-of-living index lies between its Paasche and Laspeyres bounds. This follows immediately from our previous theorem which implies that the cost-of-living index is independent of the base indifference curve.

These results are important not because we believe that people's indifference maps are homothetic but because we believe they are not. Our theorem, therefore, implies that the cost-of-living index depends on the choice of the base level of expenditure. We now investigate the ways in which the preference ordering determines the relationship between the cost-of-living index and the base level of expenditure.

5.2 Demand Functions Locally Linear in Expenditure

We say that a system of demand functions is locally linear in expenditure if

$$h^i(P, \mu) = \chi_i(P) + \delta_i(P)\mu, \quad i = 1, \ldots, n$$

These demand functions are of substantially more empirical interest than those exhibiting expenditure proportionality. We now examine the form of the cost-of-living index implied by the preference ordering corresponding to these demand functions. W.M. Gorman (1961) has shown that a system of demand functions is locally linear in expenditure if and only if its indirect utility function can be written in the form

$$s = \Psi(P, \mu) = \frac{\mu - f(P)}{g(P)}$$

where $f(P)$ and $g(P)$ are functions homogeneous of degree 1. The implied expenditure function is given by

$$\mu = E(P, s) = f(P) + g(P)s$$

and the cost-of-living index by

$$I^*(P^a, P^b, m, R) = \frac{1}{m}\left[f(P^a) + g(P^a)\left(\frac{m - f(P^b)}{g(P^b)} \right) \right] = \alpha(P^a, P^b) + \frac{1}{m}\beta(P^a, P^b)$$

where

$$\alpha(P^a, P^b) = \frac{g(P^a)}{g(P^b)}$$

$$\beta(P^a, P^b) = f(P^a) - f(P^b)\frac{g(P^a)}{g(P^b)}.$$

That is, if the demand functions are locally linear in expenditure, then the cost-of-living index is linear in the reciprocal of base expenditure. If $f(P) = 0$, then the indifference map is homothetic to the origin, and the index is independent of m. As m approaches ∞, the cost-of-living index approaches a finite limit, and the influence of m becomes negligible. However, both of these assertions must be viewed cautiously since $f(P) = 0$ and $m \to \infty$ are inadmissible cases for certain g's. The quadratic case ($c = 2$) of Section 6.3 provides an illustration of both possibilities.

The converse of our characterization of the cost-of-living index also holds:

Theorem. The cost-of-living index depends linearly on the reciprocal of base expenditure if and only if the demand functions are locally linear in expenditure.

Proof. If $I = \alpha + (\beta/m)$, then the index is implicitly defined by

$$\Psi(P^b, m) = \Psi(P^a, mI) = \Psi(P^a, \alpha m + \beta)$$

Differentiating with respect to p_i^b, and m and recognizing that the demand functions are the negative of the ratios of these derivatives yields

$$h^i(P^b, m) = \frac{\alpha_i}{\alpha}m + \frac{\beta_i}{\alpha}$$

5.3 Cost-of-Living Index Linear in Base Expenditure

Theorem. If the cost-of-living index is linear in base expenditure, $I(P^a, P^b, m, R) = \alpha(P^a, P^b) + \beta(P^a, P^b)m$, then the demand functions are of the *Törnquist* form

$$h^i(P, \mu) = \frac{\alpha_i m + \beta_i m^2}{\alpha + 2\beta m}$$

Proof. The index is implicitly defined by

$$\Psi(P^b, m) = \Psi(P^a, mI) = \Psi(P^a, \alpha m + \beta m^2)$$

It is easily verified that the implied demand functions are of the Törnquist form.

This is an interesting result because Wold and Jureen (1953, p. 3) suggest that demand functions of this form are not unreasonable. These results hold only for a limited range of values of m. The cost-of-living index cannot be linear for all m unless $\beta = 0$, in which case we are back to expenditure proportionality and homothetic indifference maps. If $\beta \neq 0$, the linear cost-of-living index would soon violate either the upper or lower bounds

$$\min \left\{ \frac{p_i^a}{p_i^b} \right\} \leqslant I^*(P^a, P^b, m, R) \leqslant \max \left\{ \frac{p_i^a}{p_i^b} \right\}$$

6. SPECIFIC PREFERENCE ORDERINGS

In this section I examine the cost-of-living-index formulae which correspond to specific preference orderings. In subsection 6.1 I consider those corresponding to demand functions which exhibit expenditure proportionality and are generated by an additive direct utility function. In 6.2 I examine the cost-of-living indexes corresponding to demand functions which are locally linear in expenditure and are generated by an additive direct utility function. In 6.3 I consider the quadratic direct utility function. Irving Fisher's "ideal index," the geometric mean of the Laspeyres and the Paasche, is equal to the cost-of-living index if and only if the direct utility function is a homogeneous quadratic.

6.1 Additive Utility Functions and Expenditure Proportionality[8]

If an individual's utility function is additive and his demand functions exhibit expenditure proportionality, then his utility function belongs to the *Bergson family*

$$U(X) = \sum a_k \log x_k \quad a_i > 0 \quad \sum a_k = 1^9 \tag{6.1.1}$$

$$U(X) = -\sum a_k x_k^c \quad a_i > 0 \quad c < 0 \tag{6.1.2}$$

$$U(X) = \sum a_k x_k^c \quad a_i > 0 \quad 0 < c < 1 \tag{6.1.3}$$

$$U(X) = \min \left\{ \frac{x_k}{a_k} \right\} \quad a_i > 0 \tag{6.1.4}$$

The demand functions corresponding to (6.1.1) are of the form

$$h^i(P, \mu) = \frac{a_i \mu}{p_i} \tag{6.1.5}$$

while those corresponding to (6.1.2) and (6.1.3) are of the form

$$h^i(P, \mu) = \frac{\left(\dfrac{p_i}{a_i} \right)^{1/(c-1)} \mu}{\sum p_k \left(\dfrac{p_k}{a_k} \right)^{1/(c-1)}} \tag{6.1.6}$$

The demand functions corresponding to the fixed coefficient case (6.1.4) are

$$h^i(P, \mu) = \frac{a_i \mu}{\sum a_k p_k} \tag{6.1.7}$$

The indifference maps of these utility functions are identical with the isoquant maps of the constant elasticity of substitution (CES) production functions.

Since the demand functions exhibit expenditure proportionality, the corresponding indirect utility functions are of the form

$$\Psi(P, \mu) = \frac{\mu}{g(P)} \tag{6.1.8}$$

where $g(P)$ is homogeneous of degree 1. For the Cobb–Douglas case, (6.1.1),

$$g(P) = \prod p_k^{a_k} \tag{6.1.9}$$

In the CES case, (6.1.2) and (6.1.3),

$$g(P) = [\sum a_k^{-(1/(c-1))} p_k^{1/(c-1)}]^{(c-1)/c} \tag{6.1.10}$$

and in the fixed coefficient case (6.1.4)

$$g(P) = \sum a_k p_k \tag{6.1.11}$$

The indirect utility function (6.1.8) implies an expenditure function of the form

$$\mu = E(P, s) = g(P)s \tag{6.1.12}$$

so the cost-of-living index is given by

$$I(P^a, P^b, s, R) = \frac{E(P^a, s, R)}{E(P^b, s, R)} = \frac{g(P^a)}{g(P^b)} \tag{6.1.13}$$

As shown in section 5, expenditure proportionality is a necessary and sufficient condition for independence of the base indifference curve.

Two cases deserve special mention.

Theorem. The cost-of-living index is a geometric mean of the price relatives with weight independent of s

$$I(P^a, P^b, s, R) = \prod \left(\frac{p_k^a}{p_k^b} \right)^{a_k} \tag{6.1.14}$$

if and only if the utility function is of the Cobb–Douglas form (6.1.1).

Proof. It is easy to verify that if the utility function is of the form (6.1.1), then the cost-of-living index is given by (6.1.14), and the weights $(a_1, \ldots, a_n)$ are the budget shares: $a_i = p_i h^i(P, \mu)/\mu$. To prove the converse, write

$$\Psi(P^b, m) = \Psi\left[P^a, m\prod\left(\frac{p_k^a}{p_k^b}\right)^{a_k} \right]$$

differentiate with respect to p_i^b and m, and verify that the implied demand functions are given by $h^i(P^b, m) = a_i m/p_i^b$.

One way in which the Cobb–Douglas case is special is that the cost-of-living index is a function of the price relatives p_i^a/p_i^b. The class of preference orderings with cost-of-living indexes of this type is a generalization of the Cobb–Douglas class.

Theorem. If the cost-of-living index is a function of price relatives,

$$I(P^a, P^b, s, R) = \hat{I}\left(\frac{P^a}{P^b}, s, R\right)$$

then the index is a geometric mean

$$I(P^a, P^b, s, R) = \prod\left(\frac{p_k^a}{p_k^b}\right)^{a_k(s)}$$

and the underlying preference ordering is a generalized Cobb–Douglas whose indirect utility function, $\Psi(P, \mu)$, is defined implicitly by

$$\sum \beta^k(s) \log p_k - \sum \beta^k(s) \log \mu = 1$$

where $a^i(s)$ is defined by $a^i(s) = \beta^i(s)/\sum \beta^k(s)$.[10]

It is sometimes thought that constructing a cost-of-living index is a matter of finding an appropriate way to combine the price relatives. This theorem shows that such a view is incorrect and that, except in the generalized Cobb–Douglas case, the comparison and reference prices do not enter the cost-of-living index in ratio form. Furthermore, the only admissible cost-of-living index based on price relatives is their geometric mean.

Proof. If the indirect utility function $\Psi(P, \mu)$ is implicitly defined by

$$\sum \beta^k(s) \log p_k - \log \mu \sum \beta^k(s) = 1$$

we solve for $\log \mu$ as a function of s:

$$\log \mu = \frac{\sum \beta^k(s) \log p_k - 1}{\sum \beta^k(s)}$$

The logarithm of the cost-of-living index is given by

$$\log I(P^a, P^b, s, R) = \log \frac{\mu^a}{\mu^b} = \log \mu^a - \log \mu^b = \frac{\sum \beta^k(s) \log p_k^a - \sum \beta^k(s) \log p_k^b}{\sum \beta^k(s)}$$

Let $a^i(s) = \beta^i(s) / \sum \beta^k(s)$. Then

$$\log I(P^a, P^b, s, R) = \sum a^k(s) \log \frac{p_k^a}{p_k^b} = \log \prod \left(\frac{p_k^a}{p_k^b} \right)^{a^k(s)}$$

so

$$I(P^a, P^b, s, R) = \prod \left(\frac{p_k^a}{p_k^b} \right)^{a^k(s)}$$

The demand functions corresponding to this utility function are given by $h^i(P, \mu) = a^i(s)\mu/p_i$. This can be verified by differentiating

$$\sum \beta^k(s) \log p_k - \log \mu \sum \beta^k(s) = 1$$

with respect to p_i and μ solving for $\partial \Psi / \partial p_i$ and $\partial \Psi / \partial \mu$.

We now show that this is the only preference ordering to yield a cost-of-living index which depends on price relatives. If

$$I(P^a, P^b, s, R) = \hat{I}\left(\frac{P^a}{P^b}, s, R \right)$$

then

$$\frac{E(p_1^a, \ldots, \lambda p_i^a, \ldots, p_n^a, s)}{E(p_1^b, \ldots, \lambda p_i^b, \ldots, p_n^b, s)} = I(P^a, P^b, s, R)$$

Differentiating with respect to λ and setting $\lambda = 1$ yields

$$p_i^a \frac{\partial E(P^a, s)}{\partial p_i^a} = I(P^a, P^b, s, R) p_i^b \frac{\partial E(P^b, s)}{\partial p_i^b}$$

so

$$\frac{f^i(P^a, s) p_i^a}{f^i(P^b, s) p_i^b} = I(P^a, P^b, s, R) = \frac{E(P^a, s)}{E(P^b, s)}$$

or, equivalently,

$$\frac{f^i(P^a, s) p_i^a}{E(P^a, s)} = \frac{f^i(P^b, s) p_i^b}{E(P^b, s)}$$

That is, along an indifference curve the expenditure weight of each good is independent of prices: we denote the expenditure weight of good i by $a^i(s)$.

But any system of demand functions of this form can be generated by the generalized Cobb–Douglas.

We showed in section 4 that if the demand functions are generated by a homogeneous fixed coefficient utility function, then the Laspeyres and Paasche indexes coincide with each other, are independent of the base indifference curve, and coincide with the cost-of-living index. For completeness we restate that result here:

Theorem. If the direct utility function is of the homogeneous fixed coefficient form (6.1.4), then the cost-of-living index $I(P^a, P^b, s, R)$ coincides with the Laspeyres and Paasche indexes:

$$I(P^a, P^b, s, R) = \frac{\sum a_k p_k^a}{\sum a_k p_k^b} = \frac{\sum h^k(P, \mu) p_k^a}{\sum h^k(P, \mu) p_k^b} = J(P^a, P^b, X^b) = J(P^a, P^b, X^a)$$

(6.1.15)

Since the Laspeyres index can be written as

$$J(P^a, P^b, X^b) = \sum w_k^b \left(\frac{p_k^a}{p_k^b} \right)$$

it might be thought that the homogeneous fixed coefficient case is one in which the cost-of-living index depends on price relatives. But this is not the case because the weights themselves depend on reference prices and not on the price relatives:

$$w_k^b = \frac{p_k^b h^k(P^b, \mu^b)}{\mu^b} = \frac{a_i p_i^b}{\sum a_k p_k^b}$$

6.2. Additive Utility Functions and Linear Engel Curves

In this section I examine the cost-of-living index corresponding to demand functions which are locally linear in income and which are generated by additive direct utility functions. In Pollak (1971) I showed that the utility functions

$$U(X) = \sum a_k \log(x_k - b_k) \qquad a_i > 0, (x_i - b_i) > 0, \sum a_k = 1 \qquad (6.2.1)$$

$$U(X) = -\sum a_k (x_k - b_k)^c \qquad c < 0, (x_i - b_i) > 0 \qquad (6.2.2)$$

$$U(X) = \sum a_k (x_k - b_k)^c \qquad 0 < c < 1, a_i > 0, (x_i - b_i) > 0 \qquad (6.2.3)$$

$$U(X) = -\sum a_k (b_k - x_k)^c \qquad c > 1, a_i > 0, (b_i - x_i) > 0 \qquad (6.2.4)$$

$$U(X) = -\sum a_k^{(b_k - x_k)/a_k} \qquad a_i > 0 \qquad (6.2.5)$$

$$U(X) = \min \left\{ \frac{x_k - b_k}{a_k} \right\} \qquad a_i > 0 \qquad\qquad (6.2.6)$$

The utility functions considered in subsection 6.1 are special cases of (6.2.1), (6.2.2), (6.2.3), and (6.2.6), which correspond to these functions when all of the b's are 0.

The demand functions corresponding to (6.2.1) are of the form

$$h^i(P, \mu) = b_i - \frac{a_i}{p_i} \sum b_k p_k + \frac{a_i}{p_i} \mu \qquad\qquad (6.2.7)$$

This is the well-known Klein–Rubin (1947) linear expenditure system. The utility function (6.2.1) is a translated Cobb–Douglas. Similarly, (6.2.2), (6.2.3) and (6.2.6) are translations of the CES and fixed coefficient cases considered in subsection 6.1. The demand functions corresponding to (6.2.2), (6.2.3), and (6.2.4) are given by

$$h^i(P, \mu) = b_i - \gamma_i(P) \sum b_k p_k + \gamma_i(P) \mu \qquad\qquad (6.2.8)$$

where

$$\gamma_i(P) = \frac{\left(\dfrac{p_i}{a_i} \right)^{1/(c-1)}}{\sum p_k \left(\dfrac{p_k}{a_k} \right)^{1/(c-1)}}$$

The utility function corresponding to $c > 1$, (6.2.4), is not a generalization of an admissible CES case, but it includes the familiar additive quadratic ($c = 2$). The demand functions corresponding to (6.2.5) are given by

$$h^i(P, \mu) = b_i - \frac{a_i \sum p_k b_k}{\sum p_k a_k} + \frac{a_i \mu}{\sum p_k a_k} - a_i \log p_i + \frac{a_i \sum p_k a_k \log p_k}{\sum p_k a_k} \qquad (6.2.9)$$

The income-consumption curves are parallel straight lines. The demand functions corresponding to the translated fixed coefficient case, (6.2.6), are given by

$$h^i(P, \mu) = b_i - \left[\frac{a_i}{\sum a_k p_k} \right] b_k p_k + \left[\frac{a_i}{\sum a_k p_k} \right] \mu \qquad\qquad (6.2.10)$$

Since the demand functions are locally linear in expenditure, the indirect utility functions are of the form

$$\Psi(P, \mu) = \frac{\mu}{g(P)} - \frac{f(P)}{g(P)} \qquad\qquad (6.2.11)$$

where $f(P)$ and $g(P)$ are homogeneous of degree 1. For the linear expenditure system, (6.2.1),

$$g(P) = \prod p_k^{a_k} \tag{6.2.12}$$

and

$$f(P) = \sum b_k p_k \tag{6.2.13}$$

In the three CES-like cases, (6.2.2), (6.2.3), and (6.2.4),

$$g(P) = \left[\sum a_k^{-1/(c-1)} p_k^{1/(c-1)} \right]^{(c-1)/c} \tag{6.2.14}$$

and $f(P)$ is given by (6.2.13). In the case of parallel income-consumption curves, (6.2.5),

$$g(P) = \sum a_k p_k \tag{6.2.15}$$

$$f(P) = \left(\sum a_k p_k \right)\left(\log \sum a_k p_k \right) + \sum b_k p_k - \sum a_k p_k \log p_k \tag{6.2.16}$$

Finally, in the translated fixed coefficient case, (6.2.6), $f(P)$ is given by (6.2.13) and $g(P)$ by (6.2.15).

Solving the indirect utility function, (6.2.11), for μ, we find that the expenditure function is of the form

$$\mu = E(P, s) = f(P) + g(P)s \tag{6.2.17}$$

Hence, the cost-of-living index is of the form

$$I(P^a, P^b, s, R) = \frac{f(P^a) + g(P^a)s}{f(P^b) + g(P^b)s} \tag{6.2.18}$$

It is often more useful to specify the base indifference curve in terms of base income m and to write the cost-of-living index in the form

$$I^*(P^a, P^b, m, R) = \alpha(P^a, P^b) + \frac{1}{m}\beta(P^a, P^b) \tag{6.2.19}$$

where

$$\alpha(P^a, P^b) = \frac{g(P^a)}{g(P^b)} \tag{6.2.20a}$$

$$\beta(P^a, P^b) = f(P^a) - f(P^b)\frac{g(P^a)}{g(P^b)} \tag{6.2.20b}$$

Two cases are of special interest.

Theorem. The cost-of-living index corresponding to the linear expenditure system, (6.2.1), is of the form

$$I(P^a, P^b, s, R) = \frac{\sum b_k p_k^a + s\prod(p_k^a)^{a_k}}{\sum b_k p_k^b + s\prod(p_k^b)^{a_k}} \tag{6.2.21}$$

This result was the conclusion of the article by Klein and Rubin (1947) in which they introduced the linear expenditure system. Interestingly enough, they entitled that paper "A Constant-Utility Index of the Cost of Living."

Theorem. If the direct utility function is of the translated fixed coefficient form (6.2.6), then the cost-of-living index $I(P^a, P^b, s^b, R)$ is equal to its Laspeyres upper bound $J(P^a, P^b, X^b)$; the cost-of-living index $I(P^a, P^b, s^a, R)$ is equal to its Paasche lower bound $J(P^a, P^b, X^a)$.

6.3. Quadratic Direct Utility Function

The quadratic utility function is best treated in matrix form. Let B denote an $n \times 1$ vector and A and $n \times n$ matrix. The direct quadratic utility function is given by

$$U(X) = X'B - \tfrac{1}{2}X'AX \tag{6.3.1}$$

where X is an $n \times 1$ vector of commodities and primes denote transpose. We do not explicitly specify the regularity conditions for this utility function but restrict ourselves to a region of the commodity space in which it is well behaved. We also ignore the problems posed by goods that are not consumed; we work in a region of the price-expenditure space in which the set of goods consumed remains unchanged. As Wegge (1968) shows, this is not a trivial restriction in the case of the direct quadratic.

It is easy to verify that the demand functions corresponding to (6.3.1) are of the form

$$X = A^{-1}B + A^{-1}P\left[\frac{\mu - P'A^{-1}B}{P'A^{-1}P}\right] \tag{6.3.2}$$

where the expression in brackets is a scalar. Thus, the implied demand functions are locally linear in expenditure. The indirect utility function is given by

$$-\frac{1}{2}\frac{(\mu - P'A^{-1}B)^2}{P'A^{-1}P}$$

If $P'A^{-1}P$ is positive within the admissible region of the price-expenditure space, we rewrite the indirect utility function in its *Gorman form*:

$$\Psi(P, \mu) = \frac{\mu - P'A^{-1}B}{\sqrt{P'A^{-1}P}} \tag{6.3.3a}$$

If $P'A^{-1}P$ is negative, then

$$\Psi(P, \mu) = \frac{\mu - P'A^{-1}B}{\sqrt{-P'A^{-1}P}} \qquad (6.3.3b)$$

The corresponding expenditure function is given by

$$\mu = P'A^{-1}B + s\sqrt{\pm P'A^{-1}P}$$

and the cost-of-living index by

$$I(P^a, P^b, s, R) = \frac{P^{a'}A^{-1}B + s\sqrt{\pm P^{a'}A^{-1}P^a}}{P^{b'}A^{-1}B + s\sqrt{\pm P^{b'}A^{-1}P^b}} \qquad (6.3.4)$$

If $B = 0$, the direct utility function is a *homogeneous quadratic*, and the cost-of-living index is independent of the base indifference curve:

$$I(P^a, P^b, s, R) = \sqrt{\frac{P^{a'}A^{-1}P^a}{P^{b'}A^{-1}P^b}} \qquad (6.3.5)$$

The homogeneous quadratic is of particular importance because it corresponds to Irving Fisher's Ideal Index, the geometric mean of a Laspeyres and a Paasche:

$$[J(P^a, P^b, H(P^b, \mu^b; R))J(P^a, P^b, H(P^a, \mu^a; R))]^{\frac{1}{2}}$$

Furthermore, the homogeneous quadratic is the only preference ordering for which this is true:

Theorem. The cost-of-living index coincides with Fisher's Ideal Index

$$I^*(P^a, P^b, m, R) = [J(P^a, P^b, H(P^b, \mu^b; R))J(P^a, P^b, H(P^a, \mu^a; R))]^{\frac{1}{2}}$$

if and only if the preference ordering is a homogeneous quadratic.[11]

Proof. If the direct utility function is homogeneous quadratic, then the Laspeyres and Paasche indexes are given by

$$J[P^a, P^b, H(P^b, \mu^b; R)] = \frac{P^{a'}A^{-1}P^b}{P^{b'}A^{-1}P^b}$$

$$J[P^a, P^b, H(P^a, \mu^a; R)] = \frac{P^{a'}A^{-1}P^a}{P^{b'}A^{-1}P^a}$$

Since $P^{a'}A^{-1}P^b = P^{b'}A^{-1}P^a$, the ideal index is (6.3.5).

If the cost-of-living index coincides with the Ideal Index, then the Laspeyres index is independent of μ^b, and hence the demand functions exhibit expenditure proportionality. We write the indirect utility function in its Gorman form, $\Psi(P,\mu) = \mu/\phi(P)$, where $\phi(P)$ is a function homogeneous of degree 1. The demand functions are given by $h^i(P,\mu) = \phi_i(P)\mu/\phi(P)$. The cost-of-living index I is implicitly defined by

$$\Psi(P^b, m) = \Psi(P^a, mI)$$

so

$$\frac{\phi(P^a)}{\phi(P^b)} = I.$$

The product of the Laspeyres and Paasche indexes can be written as

$$\frac{\sum h^k(P^b,\mu^b)p_k^a}{\sum h^k(P^b,\mu^b)p_k^b} \frac{\sum h^k(P^a,\mu^a)p_k^a}{\sum h^k(P^a,\mu^a)p_k^b} = \frac{\sum \phi_k(P^b)p_k^a}{\sum \phi_k(P^b)p_k^b} \frac{\sum \phi_k(P^a)p_k^a}{\sum \phi_k(P^a)p_k^b}$$

$$= \frac{\sum \phi_k(P^b)p_k^a}{\phi(P^b)} \frac{\phi(P^a)}{\sum \phi_k(P^a)p_k^b}$$

If the cost-of-living index is equal to the ideal index, then

$$\left(\frac{\phi(P^a)}{\phi(P^b)}\right)^2 = \frac{\sum \phi_k(P^b)p_k^a}{\phi(P^b)} \frac{\phi(P^a)}{\sum \phi_k(P^a)p_k^b}$$

or, equivalently,

$$\phi(P^a)\sum \phi_k(P^a)p_k^b = \phi(P^b)\sum \phi_k(P^b)p_k^a$$

Differentiating with respect to p_i^a yields

$$\phi_i(P^a)\sum \phi_k(P^a)p_k^b + \phi(P^a)\sum \phi_{ki}(P^a)p_k^b = \phi(P^b)\phi_i(P^b)$$

Differentiating this with respect to p_j^b yields

$$\phi_i(P^a)\phi_j(P^a) + \phi(P^a)\phi_{ji}(P^a) = \phi_j(P^b)\phi_i(P^b) + \phi(P^b)\phi_{ij}(P^b)$$

Since the right-hand side and the left-hand side are equal regardless of the values of P^a and P^b, both must be independent of P and hence constant:

$$\phi_i(P)\phi_j(P) + \phi(P)\phi_{ji}(P) = c_{ij}$$

Multiplying by p_j and summing over j yields

$$\phi_i(P)\phi(P) = \sum_j p_j c_{ij}$$

since the homogeneity of ϕ implies

$$\sum_j p_j \phi_{ji}(P) = 0$$

Multiplying by p_i and summing over i yields

$$[\phi(P)]^2 = \sum_i \sum_j p_i p_j c_{ij}$$

so

$$\phi(P) = \pm \sum_i \sum_j p_i p_j c_{ij}$$

which is the homogeneous quadratic.

We remark that if $c_{ij} = a_i a_j$, then

$$\phi(P) = \sum_k a_k p_k$$

and that

$$\Psi(P, \mu) = \frac{\mu}{\sum_k a_k p_k}$$

is the indirect utility function corresponding to the homogeneous fixed coefficient utility function. It should be no surprise that the homogeneous fixed coefficient case appears here, for this is the case in which the cost-of-living index coincides with both the Laspeyres and the Paasche indexes, and, hence, it must coincide with their geometric mean.

7. PREFERENCE FIELD QUANTITY INDEX

As we have seen, the cost-of-living index provides a precise answer to a narrow and specific question. If one wishes to compare expenditures required to attain a particular base indifference curve at two sets of prices, then, by definition, the cost-of-living index is the appropriate index. But price indexes are often used to deflate an index of total expenditure to obtain an index of quantity or "real consumption." With less logic but the same purpose they are used to deflate indexes of money income to obtain indexes of real income or money wages to obtain real wages. Although the last two cases are clouded by problems involving saving and the labor–leisure choice, the purpose of these indexes is to measure "quantity."[12] In this section we show how a quantity index can be constructed by a procedure analogous to that used to construct the cost-of-living index. We call such an index a *preference field quantity index* to distinguish it from other types of quantity indexes and to suggest its relation to the *preference field price index* or cost-of-living index of section 2. Before constructing the preference field quantity index, we give a careful summary of the logic which lies behind the preference field price index. In section 8 we examine the conditions under which the preference field quantity index coincides with the quantity index obtained by using the cost-of-living index to deflate an index of expenditure.

7.1. The Preference Field Price Index

Given a preference ordering R and a base indifference curve s we defined the cost-of-living index by

$$I(P^a, P^b, s, R) = \frac{c_a}{c_b} \qquad (7.1.1)$$

where c_a and c_b are implicitly defined by

$$s = \Psi(P^a, c_a; R)$$
$$s = \Psi(P^b, c_b; R)$$

In theoretical work involving indirect utility functions, it is standard practice to work with *normalized prices*. We define y_i, the normalized price of the ith good, by $y_i = p_i/\mu$ and let Y denote the corresponding vector. The ordinary demand functions $h^i(P, \mu; R)$ can be written as $g^i(Y; R)$ since they are homogeneous of degree 0 in all prices and expenditure:

$$g^i(Y; R) = h^i(Y, 1; R) = h^i\left(\frac{p_1}{\mu}, \ldots, \frac{p_n}{\mu}, 1; R\right) = h^i(P, \mu; R)$$

Similarly, the indirect utility function $\Psi(P, \mu; R)$ can be written as $\phi(Y; R)$ since it, too, is homogeneous of degree 0 in all prices and expenditure:

$$\phi(Y; R) = \Psi(Y, 1; R) = \Psi\left(\frac{p_1}{\mu}, \ldots, \frac{p_n}{\mu}, 1; R\right) = \Psi(P, \mu; R)^{13}$$

The ordinary demand functions are related to the normalized indirect utility function by

$$g^i(Y) = h^i(Y, 1) = \frac{\phi_i(Y)}{\sum y_k \phi_k(Y)}$$

Using this new notation, the cost-of-living index is given by (7.1.1) where c_a and c_b are implicitly defined by

$$s = \phi\left(\frac{1}{c_a} P^a; R\right)$$

$$s = \phi\left(\frac{1}{c_b} P^b; R\right)$$

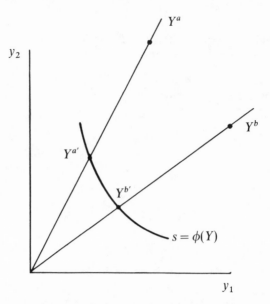

Figure 1

We can give a straightforward interpretation of the cost-of-living index in terms of the indifference curves corresponding to the indirect utility function $\phi(Y)$. We remind the reader that in Figure 1 utility *increases* as you move *toward* the origin. We begin with the base preference ordering (represented by the indifference map) and, from the map, the base indifference curve, which we denote by s. We let $Y^a = P^a$ and $Y^b = P^b$ denote the comparison and reference prices, respectively. In general, neither the reference nor the comparison prices will lie on the base indifference curve. We let $Y^{a'}$ denote the point at which the ray from the origin through Y^a intersects the base indifference curve. Similarly, $Y^{b'}$ denotes the intersection of the base indifference curve with the ray from the origin through Y^b.

It is instructive to decompose the construction of the cost-of-living index comparing Y^a with Y^b using the base indifference curve s into three separate parts: a comparison of Y^a with $Y^{a'}$, a comparison of $Y^{a'}$ with $Y^{b'}$, and a comparison of $Y^{b'}$ with Y^b. First, we compare Y^a with $Y^{a'}$. That is, suppose the comparison prices Y^a and the reference prices (for our present purpose, $Y^{a'}$) lie on the same ray: $Y^a = c_a Y^{a'}$. Then the cost-of-living index $I(Y^a, Y^{a'}, s, R)$ is equal to c_a, a result which is intuitively obvious and natural. Formal justification is provided by

$$s = \phi\left(\frac{1}{c_a} Y^a; R\right) = \phi(Y^{a'}; R)$$

If, for example, $Y^a = 4Y^{a'}$, and $Y^{a'}$ is on the base indifference curve, then $I(Y^a, Y^{a'}, s, R) = 4$.

We now compare $Y^{a'}$ with $Y^{b'}$. That is, suppose the comparison prices are $Y^{a'}$ and the reference prices $Y^{b'}$. Since, by construction, both $Y^{a'}$ and $Y^{b'}$ lie on the base indifference curve, the value of the index is $1 : I(Y^{a'}, Y^{b'}, s, R) = 1$.

Finally, we compare $Y^{b'}$ with Y^b. In this case the comparison prices $Y^{b'}$ and the reference prices Y^b lie on the same ray: $Y^b = c_b Y^{b'}$. Hence, the cost-of-living index $I(Y^{b'}, Y^b, s, R)$ is equal to $1/c_b$, as common sense requires. For example, if $Y^b = 3Y^{b'}$, then $I(Y^{b'}, Y^b, s, R) = \frac{1}{3}$.

We must now combine these three results to obtain the cost-of-living index we originally sought: $I(Y^a, Y^b, s, R)$. It is at this stage that our argument loses some of its intuitive appeal. It is perfectly clear how we ought to compare two price situations which lie on a common ray or two price situations which lie on the base indifference curve, but it is less clear how we ought to proceed in other cases. Formally, we can proceed by introducing a formal rule which enables us to combine indexes with a common base indifference curve:

$$I(Y^a, Y^c, s, R) = I(Y^a, Y^b, s, R)I(Y^b, Y^c, s, R)$$

We saw in section 2 that cost-of-living indexes can be combined in this way. But the intuitive justification for this step is not a completely comfortable one. To understand the way in which this multiplication rule operates, suppose that the reference prices lie on the base indifference curve but not on the same ray as the comparison prices. The index is then equal to the ratio of the comparison prices to the point where the comparison ray intersects the base indifference curve. In effect, we construct the index as if the reference prices were at this intersection. Our rationale for this is that the reference prices and the intersection lie on the base indifference curve, and we regard points on the base indifference curve as "equivalent."

We now take account of the fact that the reference prices Y^b need not lie on the base indifference curve. We do this by making use of $P^{b'}$, the point at which the reference ray intersects the base indifference curve. As we saw, if $Y^b = c_b Y^{b'}$, then $I(Y^{b'}, Y^b, s, R) = 1/c_b$. Furthermore, if the comparison prices lie anywhere on the base indifference curve, the value of the index would still be $1/c_b$. If neither the comparison nor the reference prices lie on the base indifference curve, we construct the index by reducing both reference and comparison prices to the base indifference curve and making use of the "equivalence" of all price situations on the base indifference curve. Thus, in our example, the value of the index would be

$$I(Y^a, Y^b, s, R) = I(Y^a, Y^{a'}, s, R)I(Y^{a'}, Y^{b'}, s, R)I(Y^{b'}, Y^b, s, R) = 4 \times 1 \times \tfrac{1}{3} = \tfrac{4}{3}$$

The procedure for constructing a cost-of-living index based on a particular indifference curve s can be summarized in three simple axioms:

If $s = \phi(Y^a; R)$ and $s = \phi(Y^b; R)$,   then $I(Y^a, Y^b, s, R) = 1$ (A1)

That is, if the comparison and the reference prices both lie on the base indifference curve, then the value of the index is 1.

$$\text{If } \quad s = \phi(Y^b; R) \quad \text{and} \quad Y^a = \lambda Y^b, \quad \text{then } I(Y^a, Y^b, s, R) = \lambda \qquad \text{(A2)}$$

In words, if the reference prices lie on the base indifference curve and the comparison prices lie on the same ray as the reference prices, then the value of the index is the factor of proportionality relating the comparison to the reference prices:

$$I(Y^a, Y^b, s, R)I(Y^b, Y^c, s, R) = I(Y^a, Y^c, s, R) \qquad \text{(A3)}$$

If two cost-of-living indexes are based on the same base indifference curve, and the reference prices in the first are the same as the comparison prices in the second, then the product of these two indexes is the cost-of-living index whose comparison prices are those of the first and whose reference prices are those of the second. Irving Fisher (1922, p. 270) called this the *circular* property.

This axiomatic treatment of the procedure for constructing the cost-of-living index makes it clear that the base indifference map plays no role and that the base curve does all the work. It is sometimes useful to discard the original indifference map and work only with the base indifference curve. Sometimes, however, it is useful to go a step further and think of the index as being constructed from a pseudoindifference map which is defined as the radial or homothetic blowup of the base indifference curve. Unless the original indifference map was homothetic to the origin, the pseudomap does not coincide with the original map. One advantage of introducing the pseudomap is that because it is homothetic to the origin, the cost-of-living index is independent of which pseudoindifference curve is treated as the base. In particular, without loss of generality, we may use the curve on which the reference prices lie as the base curve. On the pseudomap (but not on the original map unless it was homothetic), if the reference prices and the comparison prices lie on the same curve, then the value of the index is 1. Notice, however, that if the reference and comparison prices lie on the same indifference curve on the original map, and their common curve is not the base curve, then the value of the index need not be 1.

7.2. Preference Field Quantity Indexes

We now use the same formal procedure to define a preference field quantity index as we used to define a preference field price index or cost-of-living index. That is, we define the preference field quantity index $Q(X^a, X^b, s, R)$ by

$$Q(X^a, X^b, s, R) = \frac{\theta_a}{\theta_b}$$

where θ_a and θ_b are defined by

$$s = U\left(\frac{1}{\theta_a} X^a\right)$$

and

$$s = U\left(\frac{1}{\theta_b} X^b\right)$$

The verbal and graphical interpretation of the preference field quantity index is essentially the same as that of the preference field price index. We begin by choosing a base preference ordering and from it a base indifference curve. In general, neither the comparison quantities X^a nor the reference quantities X^b lie on the base indifference curve. Instead of comparing X^a directly with X^b, we compare X^a with a collection of goods $X^{a'}$ which lies on s and which is proportional to X^a. Similarly, we compare X^b with a collection $X^{b'}$ which lies on s and which is proportional to X^b. Graphically, the preference field quantity index can be represented by a diagram, Figure 2, identical to that used to illustrate the construction of the cost-of-living index.

Since the preference field quantity index is less familiar than the cost-of-living index, it is useful to examine the meaning of this index. Formally, the axioms satisfied by this index are identical with those satisfied by the

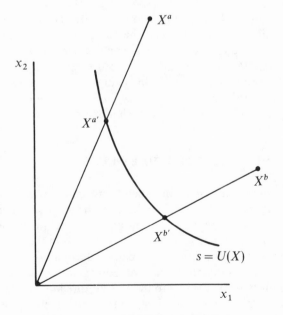

Figure 2

preference field price index:

$$\text{If} \quad s = U(X^a) \quad \text{and} \quad s = U(X^b) \quad \text{then} \quad Q(X^a, X^b, s, R) = 1 \qquad (A1)$$

$$\text{If} \quad s = U(X^b) \quad \text{and} \quad X^a = \lambda X^b \quad \text{then} \quad Q(X^a, X^b, s, R) = \lambda \qquad (A2)$$

$$Q(X^a, X^b, s, R)Q(X^b, X^c, s, R) = Q(X^a, X^c, s, R) \qquad (A3)$$

That is, (A1) if both the comparison and reference quantities lie on the base indifference curve, then the value of the index is 1. (A2) If the reference quantities lie on the base indifference curve, and the comparison quantities and the reference quantities lie on a common ray, then the value of the index is the ratio of the comparison to the reference quantities. (A3) If two indexes have the same base, and the reference quantities of the first are equal to the comparison quantities of the second, then the product of the two indexes is an index whose comparison quantities are equal to those of the first and whose reference quantities are equal to those of the second. These three axioms uniquely determine the preference field quantity index corresponding to any base indifference curve.

As with the preference field price index, the construction of the index depends only on the base indifference curve but not on the underlying preference ordering or indifference map. It is useful to consider the index in relation to a pseudoindifference map constructed as the homothetic blowup of the base indifference curve. On the pseudoindifference map the index is independent of the choice of the pseudoindifference curve used as the base. Thus, we can choose the curve corresponding to the reference quantities with no loss of generality. If the comparison and reference quantities lie on the same pseudoindifference curve, then the value of the index is 1. But if the comparison and reference quantities lie on the same indifference curve on the original map, the value of the index need not be unity unless they both lie on the base indifference curve. This is important because it underscores the fact that the preference field quantity index does not compare the levels of utility corresponding to the reference and comparison quantities.

8. PRICE, QUANTITY, AND EXPENDITURE INDEXES

Since expenditure is a scalar, an expenditure index $M(\mu_a, \mu_b)$ is naturally defined by $M(\mu_a, \mu_b) = \mu_a/\mu_b$. Such an index is independent of preferences. In this section we examine the relationships among price, quantity, and expenditure indexes. In particular, we are interested in the conditions under which the expenditure index $M(\mu^a, \mu^b)$ can be decomposed into the product of a price index and a quantity index, or, equivalently, the conditions under which the quantity index is equal to the expenditure index deflated by a price index, or, equivalently, the conditions under which the price index is equal to the expenditure index deflated by a quantity index. The answers to these questions depend on the types of price and quantity indexes which are admissible.

One approach is to require the price index to be a cost-of-living index and to define the quantity index by

$$Q(P^a, P^b, \mu^a, \mu^b, s, R) = \frac{M(\mu^a, \mu^b)}{I(P^a, P^b, s, R)}$$

Alternatively, if we insist that the quantity index be a preference field index, we can define the price index by

$$I(X^a, X^b, \mu^a, \mu^b, s, R) = \frac{M(\mu^a, \mu^b)}{Q(X^a, X^b, s, R)}$$

The drawback of this approach is that the derived indexes do not satisfy the axioms discussed in section 7 unless the base preference ordering is homothetic. Furthermore, it is easy to verify that

$$Q(P^a, P^b, \mu^a, \mu^b, s, R)Q(P^b, P^c, \mu^b, \mu^c, s, R) = Q(P^a, P^c, \mu^a, \mu^c, s, R)$$

so that A3, the least intuitively appealing of our axioms, is always satisfied by a quantity index defined in this way. Hence, failure of the quantity index to satisfy our axioms implies a violation of either A1, which requires that if both the comparison and reference quantities lie on the base indifference curve, then the value of the index is 1; or A2, which requires that if the reference quantities lie on the base indifference curve and both the comparision and reference quantities lie on a common ray, then the index is the ratio of the comparison to the reference quantities. Both of these axioms have such strong intuitive appeal that a quantity index which violates them has little conceptual appeal. We show in this section that the preference field quantity index is equal to the expenditure index deflated by the cost-of-living index if and only if preference ordering is homothetic to the origin. This implies that unless the preference ordering is homothetic, $Q(P^a, P^b, \mu^a, \mu^b, s, R)$ violates either A1 or A2.

We now require both the price and the quantity indexes to be preference field indexes and determine the class of preference orderings for which their product is equal to the expenditure index.

Theorem. $M(\mu^a, \mu^b) = I(P^a, P^b, s, R)Q[H(P^a, \mu^a; R), H(P^b, \mu^b; R), s, R]$, for all P^a, P^b, μ^a, μ^b, if and only if the preference ordering is homothetic to the origin.

The statement of the theorem requires that the result hold for only one base indifference curve, s, but the conclusion implies that if it holds for one base curve, then the preference ordering is such that it holds for every base curve.

Proof. If the preference ordering is homothetic to the origin, and the demand functions were generated by this preference ordering, we can write the direct utility functions $U(X)$ as a function homogeneous of degree 1; the indirect utility function $\Psi(P, \mu) = U[H(P, \mu)] = U[H(P, 1)]\mu$ can be written as $\mu/\phi(P)$ where $\phi(P)$ is homogeneous of degree 1, $\phi(P) = 1/U[H(P, 1)]$.

The cost-of-living index is given by

$$I(P^a, P^b, s, R) = \frac{\phi(P^a)}{\phi(P^b)}$$

The preference field quantity index is given by

$$Q(X^a, X^b, s, R) = \frac{\theta_a}{\theta_b} = \frac{U(X^a)}{U(X^b)}$$

since

$$s = U\left(\frac{1}{\theta_a} X^a\right) = \frac{1}{\theta_a} U(X^a)$$

and

$$s = U\left(\frac{1}{\theta_b} X^b\right) = \frac{1}{\theta_b} U(X^b)$$

But $U(X^a) = \mu^a/\phi(P^a)$ and $U(X^b) = \mu^b/\phi(P^b)$, so the product of the preference field price and quantity indexes is μ^a/μ^b.

We prove the second part of the theorem by showing that if the expenditure index is equal to the product of the preference field price and quantity indexes, then the demand functions exhibit expenditure proportionality. We first observe that the quantity index must be homogeneous of degree 1 in μ^a since μ^a appears only in $M(\mu^a, \mu^b)$ and in $H(P^a, \mu^a)$. Let P^a be any price vector; set P^b equal to P^a. Choose μ^b so that $\Psi(P^b, \mu^b) = s$. Then $X^b = H(P^b, \mu^b)$ lies on the base indifference curve. If we set μ^a equal to μ^b, then $X^a = X^b$ and $Q(X^a, X^b, s, R) = 1$. Suppose $\mu^a = \lambda\mu^b$. Since the quantity index is homogeneous of degree 1 in λ, its value is λ. This means that X^a lies on the pseudoindifference curve which is a radial blowup of the base indifference curve by the scale factor λ. But X^a must lie in the feasible set defined by P^a, μ^a. This feasible set is a radial blowup of the feasible set defined by P^b, μ^b. If the indifference curves are strictly convex, X^b is the only point on the base indifference curve in the feasible set of P^b, μ^b. Hence, λX^b is the only point on the radial blowup of the base indifference curve which lies in that feasible set of P^a, μ^a. Hence, $X^a = \lambda X^b$ and the demand functions exhibit expenditure proportionality.

It might be argued that this theorem is not surprising since we have not allowed the base indifference curve to vary with μ^a or μ^b. If the base indifference curve were always chosen so that $s = \Psi(P^b, \mu^b)$, perhaps some nonhomothetic preference ordering would suffice. We now show that this is not the case.

Theorem. $M(\mu^a, \mu^b) = I[P^a, P^b, \Psi(P^b, \mu^b; R), R]Q[H(P^a, \mu^a; R), H(P^b, \mu^b; R), \Psi(P^b, \mu^b; R), R]$, for all P^a, P^b, μ^a, μ^b if and only if the preference ordering is homothetic to the origin.

That is, allowing the base of index to vary with μ^b does not permit any generalization of our theorem; clearly, allowing it to vary with μ^a would not.

Proof. The proof of the previous theorem showed that if the indifference map is homothetic, both the price and quantity indexes are independent of the base indifference curve, and their product is equal to the expenditure index.

To prove that only homothetic preference ordering will work, we first observe that the quantity index is homogeneous of degree 1 in μ^a. We proceed as in the proof of the previous theorem except that we are free to choose any initial value for μ^b.

It might still be objected (by analogy with the fact that the product of a Laspeyres price index and a Paasche quantity index is equal to the expenditure index) that we should not require the same base indifference curve to serve for both indexes. We now show that basing the price index on the reference situation and the quantity index on the comparison situation does not permit any generalization of our result.

Theorem. $M(\mu^a, \mu^b) = I[P^a, P^b, \Psi(P^b, \mu^b; R), R]Q[H(P^a, \mu^a; R), H(P^b, \mu^b; R), \Psi(P^a, \mu^a; R), R]$ for all P^a, P^b, μ^a, μ^b if and only if the preference ordering is homothetic to the origin.

Proof. We have already seen that if the indifference map is homothetic, the required result holds.

To prove that only a homothetic preference ordering will work, we show that the demand functions exhibit expenditure proportionality. Instead of focusing on the comparison quantities, $H(P^a, \mu^a)$, we focus on the reference quantities, $H(P^b, \mu^b)$. This is simpler because μ^a appears twice in the quantity index while μ^b appears only once. Let P^b be any price vector, and set P^a equal to P^b. Choose μ^a arbitrarily to fix the base indifference curve of the quantity index. Since $P^a = P^b$, the cost-of-living index is 1, and hence the quantity index is equal to μ^a/μ^b for all μ^a, μ^b. Hence, it is homogeneous of degree -1 in μ^b. A slight modification of the argument used in our first proof establishes that $X^b = \lambda X^a$, so the demand functions exhibit expenditure proportionality.

9. PRICE INDEXES FOR DEMAND ANALYSIS

Demand theory tells us that the demand for a good is a function of its own price, the prices of all other goods, and total expenditure. Without additional assumptions, the theory says very little about the form of the demand functions. To estimate demand functions, specific assumptions must be made about their functional form. It is sometimes assumed that the demand for each good is a function of its own price and expenditure where these variables have been deflated by an appropriate price index. That is

$$h^i(P,\mu) = g^i\left[\frac{p_i}{T(P)}, \frac{\mu}{T(P)}\right] \tag{9.1}$$

where the price index $T(P)$ is assumed to be homogeneous of degree 1. The same index is used to deflate both price and expenditure and appears in every demand equation. This means that p_i appears twice in the demand function for the ith good: in its own right as a price variable and again as an argument of the index function T. If the demand functions are of this form, the prices of "other goods" enter the demand functions only through the index function.

In Pollak (1972) I defined *generalized additive separability* as follows: A system of demand functions exhibits generalized additive separability if its demand functions are of the form

$$h^i(Y) = \Gamma^i[y_i, R(Y)], \quad i = 1, \ldots, n$$

That is, the demand for each good is a function of its own normalized price and an index function which depends on all normalized prices. The same index function appears in the demand function for every good.

Theorem. A system of demand functions is of the form (9.1) if and only if it exhibits generalized additive separability and the index function $R(Y)$ is homothetic.

Proof. If the demand functions are (9.1), we can define $\bar{g}^i(.,.)$ by

$$\bar{g}^i\left[\frac{p_i}{\mu}, \frac{T(P)}{\mu}\right] = g^i\left[\frac{p_i}{T(P)}, \frac{\mu}{T(P)}\right]$$

since the original argument of g^i can be recovered from those of $\bar{g}^i$. Since the demand functions are homogeneous of degree 0 in P and μ,

$$\bar{g}^i\left[\frac{p_i}{\mu}, \frac{T(P)}{\mu}\right] = \bar{g}^i\left[\frac{\lambda p_i}{\lambda\mu}, \frac{T(\lambda P)}{\lambda\mu}\right] = \bar{g}^i\left[\frac{p_i}{\mu}, \frac{T(\lambda P)/\lambda}{\mu}\right] = \bar{g}^i[y_i, T(Y)]$$

so the demand functions exhibit generalized additive separability where $T(Y)$ is homogeneous of degree 1.

If $h^i(Y) = \Gamma^i[y_i, R(Y)]$, where R is homothetic, we can redefine R and Γ so R is homogeneous of degree 1. Then

$$h^i(P,\mu) = \Gamma^i\left[\frac{p_i}{\mu}, \frac{R(P)}{\mu}\right] = g^i\left[\frac{p_i}{R(P)}, \frac{\mu}{R(P)}\right]$$

since the original arguments of Γ^i can be recovered from those of g^i.

Fourgeaud and Nataf (1959) explicitly characterize the systems of demand functions of the form (9.1) which satisfy the budget constraint and the Slutsky symmetry conditions and hence are theoretically plausible in the sense that they can be derived from a well-behaved preference ordering. Their results are summarized in Pollak (1972, Section IId). There are four principal cases:

$$h^i(Y) = \frac{\Psi^i[\log y_i - \log R(Y)]}{y_i} \tag{9.2}$$

where $\Psi^i(.)$ is a function of a single variable, and R is defined implicitly by

$$\sum \Psi^k[\log y_k - \log R] = 1.$$

$$h^i(Y) = \frac{a_i R(Y) + b_i[1 - R(Y)]}{y_i} \tag{9.3}$$

where $R(Y)$ is homogeneous of degree 1 in Y and

$$R(Y) = T[\sum a_k \log y_k, \sum b_k \log y_k], \quad \sum a_k = \sum b_k = 1.^{14}$$

The other two cases are

$$h^i(Y) = \frac{\delta[T(Y)][\alpha_i \log y_i - \alpha_i \log T(Y) + \beta_i] + \alpha_i}{y_i} \tag{9.4}$$

$$\sum \alpha_k = 1, \quad \sum \beta_k = 0$$

where $\delta(.)$ is a function of a single variable and

$$T(Y) = \prod y_k^{\alpha_k}$$

and

$$h^i(Y) = \frac{\delta[T(Y)][\beta_i - \alpha_i y_i^c T(Y)^{-c}] + \beta_i}{y_i}, \quad \sum \beta_k = 1 \tag{9.5}$$

where $\delta(.)$ is a function of a single variable and

$$T(Y) = [\sum \alpha_k y_k^c]^{1/c}$$

The first case, (9.2), exhibits expenditure proportionality and hence is not very interesting for empirical demand analysis. In (9.3) the demand functions are locally linear in expenditure; the index function is a function of two Cobb–Douglas functions. In (9.4) and (9.5) the index functions are Cobb–Douglas and CES, respectively.

Thus, the price indexes which appear in the demand functions depend in a specific way on the parameters of the preference ordering. There is no presumption that these price indexes coincide with the cost-of-living index; indeed, it is not entirely clear what the assertion that $T(P)$ coincides with the cost-of-living index $I(P^a, P^b, s, R)$ would mean. To indicate that the prices in the demand functions are variables, we rewrite (9.1) as

$$h^i(P^t, \mu^t) = g^i \left[\frac{p_i^t}{T(P^t)}, \frac{\mu^t}{T(P^t)} \right] \tag{9.1'}$$

We may interpret P^t as the price vector of period t although this is not essential. The cost-of-living index $I(P^t, P^b, s, R)$ is defined by

$$I(P^t, P^b, s, R) = \frac{E(P^t, s, R)}{E(P^b, s, R)}$$

Two difficulties are immediately apparent: the first is that the cost-of-living index depends on the reference prices P^b as well as on P^t while the demand functions depend only on the comparison prices P^t. Since the reference prices (and also the base indifference curve) are held constant, the cost-of-living index is proportional to $E(P^t, s, R)$; the constant factor of proportionality is $1/E(P^b, s, R)$, and it can be absorbed into the parameters of the demand functions. Hence, we interpret the assertion that the cost-of-living index coincides with $T(P)$ to mean that

$$h^i(P^t, \mu^t) = g^i \left[\frac{p_i^t}{E(P^t, s)}, \frac{\mu^t}{E(P^t, s)} \right]$$

The fact that the cost-of-living index depends on the choice of the base indifference curve (unless the demand functions exhibit expenditure proportionality) is a more serious problem. In particular, in the absence of expenditure proportionality the assertion that the cost-of-living index coincides with $T(P)$ must be interpreted to mean that there exists a base indifference curve s^* such that $T(P)$ is proportional to $E(P, s^*, R)$ where the factor of proportionality can be absorbed into $T(P)$.

The linear expenditure system

$$h^i(P, \mu) = b_i - \frac{a_i}{p_i} \sum b_k p_k + \frac{a_i}{p_i} \mu$$

provides a good illustration. These demand functions can be written as

$$h^i(P, \mu) = b_i - \frac{a_i}{\left(\dfrac{p_i}{\sum b_k p_k} \right)} + a_i \frac{\left(\dfrac{\mu}{\sum b_k p_k} \right)}{\left(\dfrac{p_i}{\sum b_k p_k} \right)} \tag{9.6}$$

which belongs to the Fourgeaud–Nataf class. In fact, the linear expenditure system is a special case of (9.5) where $\delta(T) = -T$ and $c = 1$. The cost-of-living index corresponding to the linear expenditure system is given by (6.2.21). For $s = 0$ this becomes

$$I(P^t, P^b, 0, R) = \frac{\sum b_k p_k^t}{\sum b_k p_k^b}$$

which is the appropriate price index for demand analysis in this case.

In general, however, the cost-of-living index does not coincide with $T(P)$. For example, the indirect utility function

$$\Psi(P, \mu) = -\frac{1}{\mu} \prod p_k^{a_k} + \sum (a_k - b_k) \log p_k, \quad \sum a_k = \sum b_k = 1$$

is a special case of (9.4). The demand functions are given by

$$h^i(P, \mu) = \frac{a_i}{p_i} - \frac{(a_i - b_i)\mu^2}{p_i \prod p_k^{a_k}} = \frac{a_i\left(\dfrac{\mu}{T}\right)}{\left(\dfrac{p_i}{T}\right)} - \frac{(a_i - b_i)\left(\dfrac{\mu}{T}\right)^2}{\left(\dfrac{p_i}{T}\right)}$$

where $T(P) = \prod p_k^{a_k}$. The expenditure function corresponding to this indirect utility function is

$$\mu = \frac{-\prod p_k^{a_k}}{s - \sum (a_k - b_k) \log p_k}$$

and there is no value of s (independent of prices) for which $T(P)$ is proportional to $E(P, s, R)$.

This is not too surprising. On reflection, there was no reason to expect $T(P)$ to coincide with the cost-of-living index. Different price indexes are needed for different purposes, and the cost-of-living index should not be expected to play a role in demand analysis. Furthermore, even in those cases in which $T(P)$ and the cost-of-living index coincide, this relationship is of no use in empirical demand analysis. The trouble is that we do not start out knowing the cost-of-living index. The cost-of-living index cannot be calculated until the unknown parameters of the demand system have been estimated, and the fact that the unknown price index $T(P)$ is proportional to the unknown expenditure function $E(P, s^*, R)$ does nothing to simplify the estimation problem.

Of course, if we know the cost-of-living index, the situation is very different. In that case, regardless of whether the demand functions involve price indexes, it is possible to calculate the demand functions directly from the cost-of-living index. The cost-of-living index $I^*(P^t, P^b, m, R)$ contains all the information about preferences, and it is fairly straightforward to retrieve this information and find the implied demand functions. To do this we write

$$E[P^t, \Psi(P^b, m)] = mI^*(P^t, P^b, m, R)$$

Differentiating with respect to p_i^t yields

$$f^i[P^t, \Psi(P^b, m)] = \frac{\partial E[P^t, \Psi(P^b, m)]}{\partial p_i^t} = m \frac{\partial I^*(P^t, P^b, m, R)}{\partial p_i^t}.$$

The ordinary demand functions $h^i(P^t, \mu^t, R)$ can be calculated by finding the value of m, m^t, for which

$$\mu^t = E[P^t, \Psi(P^b, m^t)] = m^t I^*(P^t, P^b, m^t, R)$$

Then

$$h^i(P^t, \mu^t) = f^i[P^t, \Psi(P^b, m^t)]$$

If we begin knowing only the cost-of-living index $I(P^t, P^b, s, R)$, then we cannot retrieve the ordinary demand functions. However, even in terms of the fundamental question which the cost-of-living index is designed to answer, it is not enough to know only $I(P^t, P^b, s, R)$. The difficulty is that unless we also know the indirect utility function $\Psi(P, \mu)$, or have other equivalent information, we have no way to interpret the numerical value of s. We cannot associate it with a particular collection of goods and services or with a particular level of expenditure at a particular set of prices. Hence, if we know $I(P^t, P^b, s, R)$ and have enough information to interpret it meaningfully as a cost-of-living index, we can calculate the implied demand functions.

To summarize: It is useful to consider systems of demand functions which involve price indexes, but the price indexes which are relevant for demand analysis are unlikely to coincide with the cost-of-living index. Even if they coincide, knowing this is of no help in empirical demand analysis because the cost-of-living index cannot be computed until the unknown parameters of the system of demand equations have been estimated. The cost-of-living index formula $I^*(P^t, P^b, m, R)$ contains enough information about preferences to enable us to calculate the demand functions. So, if the formula for the cost-of-living index is known, then the demand functions can be calculated from it, regardless of whether the demand functions involve price indexes.

We now turn to more practical questions about the use of price indexes in empirical demand analysis. Assuming that the demand functions depend on price indexes, (9.1), when will the index $T(P)$ be a linear function of prices? We have already seen that the linear expenditure system is of this form; we now characterize the entire class.

Theorem. If the demand functions are of the Fourgeaud–Nataf form (9.1)

$$h^i(P, \mu) = g^i\left[\frac{p_i}{T(P)}, \frac{\mu}{T(P)}\right], \quad T(\lambda P) = \lambda T(P)$$

and if the index function $T(P)$ is linear in prices

$$T(P) = \sum w_k p_k$$

then, except for degenerate cases in which less than three w's are non-zero, the demand functions fall into two classes:

$$h^i(P,\mu) = \frac{\beta_i \mu}{p_i} + \frac{(1 - \sum \beta_k)\alpha_i \mu}{\sum \alpha_k p_k} \tag{9.7}$$

and

$$h^i(P,\mu) = \frac{\beta_i \mu}{p_i} + \delta\left[\frac{\sum \alpha_k p_k}{\mu}\right]\left[\frac{\beta_i \mu}{p_i} - \frac{\alpha_i}{\sum \alpha_k p_k}\right] \tag{9.8}$$

where $\delta(.)$ is a function of a single variable.

Proof. We sketch the proof in four parts. (1) First, we show that (9.7) is the only nondegenerate admissible case of (9.2). Differentiating

$$\sum \Psi^k[\log y_k - \log \sum w_k y_k] = 1$$

with respect to y_i, we find

$$\frac{\Psi^{i'}}{y_i w_i} = \frac{\Psi^{j'}}{y_j w_j}$$

Differentiating with respect to y_s yields

$$\frac{\Psi^{i''}}{\Psi^{i'}} = \frac{\Psi^{j''}}{\Psi^{j'}} = c$$

where c is a constant. It is easy to show that $c = 0$ corresponds to a degenerate case. If $c \neq 0$, then

$$\Psi^i(z_i) = \beta_i + \alpha_i e^{cz_i}$$

and the demand functions are given by (9.7). (2) There are no nondegenerate cases corresponding to (9.3). To show this we differentiate

$$\sum w_k y_k = T[\sum a_k \log y_k, \sum b_k \log y_k], \quad \sum a_k = \sum b_k = 1$$

with respect to y_i

$$c_i y_i = a_i T_1 + b_i T_2 \quad i = 1, \ldots, n$$

and observe that

$$\sum c_k y_k = T_1 + T_2 = T$$

If two of the equations

$$c_i y_i = a_i T_1 + b_i T_2$$

are independent, we can solve for T_1 and T_2 in terms of the two corresponding y's. Hence, T depends only on those two y's, so this is a degenerate case. If all of the equations are linearly dependent, and some $c_i \neq 0$, we can take $c_1 \neq 0$ with no loss of generality. Then

$$a_i = \lambda a, \quad b_i = \lambda b, \quad c_i y_i = \lambda c_1 y_1$$

The last equation implies $\lambda = 0$, and hence $c_i = 0$, $i = 2, \ldots, n$. So $T(Y) = c_1 y_1$. (3) The only admissible case of (9.4) is a degenerate one in which only one α is nonzero. (4) The nondegenerate admissible cases of (9.5) are those in which $c = 1$, which is (9.8).

We now consider two other price indexes which might be used to deflate p_i and μ in (9.1'): the Laspeyres and Paasche. Deflating by the Laspeyres index implies

$$T(P^t) = \frac{\sum h^k(P^b, \mu^b) p_k^t}{\mu^b}$$

Since P^b and μ^b are constants, this is equivalent to requiring $T(P^t)$ to be a linear function of prices where the weights are proportional to reference period consumption.

This could happen in two ways. First, it might be that the demand functions are such that in every price-expenditure situation the quantities demanded are proportional to the α's. That is,

$$\alpha_i = \lambda(P, \mu) h^i(P, \mu) \quad i = 1, \ldots, n$$

Multiplying by p_i and summing over all goods, we find

$$\lambda(P, \mu) = \frac{\mu}{\sum \alpha_k p_k}$$

so the demand functions are of the homogeneous fixed coefficient form

$$h^i(P, \mu) = \frac{\alpha_i \mu}{\sum \alpha_k p_k}$$

This proves that it is only in the homogeneous fixed coefficient case that the reference period consumption pattern is proportional to the α's for all price-expenditure situations. Second, even if every price-expenditure situation does not imply quantities demanded which are proportional to the α's, there are likely to be some price-expenditure situations in which proportionality holds. If, by a fortunate coincidence, the reference price-expenditure situation were one which implied proportionality, then deflation of price and expenditure by the Laspeyres index would be appropriate. There is little to say about the likelihood of this coincidence occurring, but even if it did occur, it is not clear how one would recognize it.

Deflating by the Paasche index is equivalent to setting

$$T(P^t) = \frac{\lambda(P^b)\mu^t}{\sum h^k(P^t, \mu^t)p_k^b}$$

since we require only proportionality. The factor of proportionality $\lambda(P^b)$ must be independent of both P^t and μ^t. As in the Laspeyres case, this may hold as an identity for all possible reference prices, or if it holds only for some reference prices, it may by coincidence hold for the particular situation we have observed. If it holds for all reference prices, then

$$T(P^t)\sum h^k(P^t, \mu^t)p_k^b = \lambda(P^b)\mu^t$$

is an identity in P^b. Differentiating with respect to p_i^b yields

$$T(P^t)h^i(P^t, \mu^t) = \lambda_i(P^b)\mu^t$$

This implies that $\lambda_i(P^b)$ is a constant, say α_i, and so

$$h^i(P^t, \mu^t) = \frac{\alpha_i \mu^t}{T(P^t)}$$

Multiplying by p_i and summing over all goods, we find

$$T(P^t) = \sum \alpha_k p_k^t$$

which implies that the demand functions are those of the homogeneous fixed coefficient case.

We summarize these results formally:

Theorem. If the demand functions are of the Fourgeaud–Nataf form (9.1)

$$h^i(P, \mu) = g^i\left[\frac{p_i}{T(P)}, \frac{\mu}{T(P)}\right], \quad T(\lambda P) = \lambda T(P)$$

and if the index function $T(P)$ is proportional to either the Laspeyres or the Paasche index for all reference prices, then the direct utility function is of the homogeneous fixed coefficient form

$$U(X) = \min \left\{ \frac{x_i}{a_i} \right\}$$

and the demand functions are of the form

$$h^i(P, \mu) = \frac{a_i \mu}{\sum a_k p_k}$$

This means that neither the Laspeyres nor the Paasche index has any special status in demand analysis. In particular, there is no presumption that deflating price and expenditure by the Laspeyres index is better than deflating by a weighted average of prices whose weights were chosen with the aid of a table of random digits. By the same token, there is no presumption that deflation of U.S. food prices and expenditure by a Laspeyres index based on U.S. consumption patterns is better, from a standpoint of demand analysis, than deflating by one whose weights reflect the consumption pattern of Outer Mongolia. The only way to find the appropriate weights is to estimate them along with the other unknown parameters.

NOTES

This research was supported in part by the Bureau of Labor Statistics and the National Science Foundation. I am grateful to Irving B. Kravis and Karl Shell for helpful discussions, but neither they, the University of Pennsylvania, the Bureau of Labor Statistics, nor the National Science Foundation should be held responsible for the views expressed.

1. (added, 1982). For excellent recent surveys of the literature, see Diewert (1981, 1983). A number of topics not treated here are discussed in my subsequent papers on cost-of-living indexes: Pollak, (1975a, 1975b, 1978, 1980, 1981, 1983), and Pollak and Wales (1979).

2. (added, 1982). In the original version, μ was called "income"; somewhat inconsistently, I have retained such traditional phrases as *income elasticity* and *income-consumption* curve.

3. (added, 1982). It is often, although not always, more convenient to denote a particular indifference curve by specifying a commodity vector X which lies on the indifference curve.

4. (added, 1982). In the original 1971 version of this paper the expenditure function $E(P, s)$ was called the *cost function* and denoted by $C(P, s)$. The new terminology is especially convenient in the household production context where the term *cost function* is used in a different sense. See Pollak (1978). It is often convenient to write the expenditure function as $E(P, X)$, where X identifies the base indifference curve.

5. (added, 1982). I now believe long-run pseudopreferences are inappropriate for welfare comparisons. See Pollak (1976).

6. (added, 1982). In fact, these results do not depend on preferences satisfying the usual regularity conditions.

7. (added, 1982). The procedure she describes in the published version of her paper (McElroy, 1975) is more general than this sentence suggests.

8. Some of the material in 6.1 and 6.2 is taken from Pollak (1971).

9. The requirement $\sum a_k = 1$ is a normalization rule and involves no loss of generality.

10. (added, 1982). This "generalized Cobb–Douglas" is a different form from Diewert's (1974, p. 116).

11. However, as Afriat (1972) points out, there are problems with regularity conditions in the homogeneous quadratic case.

12. "Real wages" are sometimes used as a measure of quantity, but they are also used in empirical analysis of the supply or demand for labor. The appropriateness of using an index of real wages obtained in this way for empirical analysis is not explicitly discussed in this paper although the use of price indexes to deflate prices and expenditure in demand analysis is discussed in section 9. The conclusion there is that such deflation is inappropriate, and it seems clear that deflation of money wages is no better.

13. In section 6 we used $\phi(P)$ to denote a function homogeneous of degree 1; in this section ϕ is not assumed to be homogeneous.

14. There are further restrictions of the function T which we can safely ignore.

REFERENCES

Afriat, S. N., "Theory of International Comparison of Real Income and Prices," in D. J. Daly, ed., *International Comparisons of Prices and Output.* New York: National Bureau of Economic Research, Columbia University Press, 1972.

Fisher, Irving, *The Making of Index Numbers.* Cambridge, Massachusetts: Houghton Mifflin Co., 1922.

Fisher, F. M., and K. Shell, "Taste and Quality Change in the Pure Theory of the True Cost-of-Living Index," in J. N. Wolfe, ed., *Value, Capital and Growth: Papers in Honour of Sir John Hicks.* Edinburgh: University of Edinburgh Press, 1968.

Fourgeaud, C., and A. Nataf, "Consommation en Prix et Revenu Reels et Theorie des Choix," *Econometrica,* Vol. 27, No. 3 (July 1959), pp. 329–354.

Gorman, W. M., "On a Class of Preference Fields," *Metroeconomica,* Vol. 13 (August 1961), pp. 53–56.

Klein, L. R., and H. Rubin, "A Constant-Utility Index of the Cost of Living," *Review of Economic Studies,* Vol. XV (2), No. 38 (1947–48), pp. 84–87.

Malmquist, S., "Index Numbers and Indifference Surfaces," *Trabajos de Estadistica* (1953), 4, pp. 209–242.

McElroy, Marjorie, "A 'Kinked' Linear Expenditure System: An Application to Rural South Vietnamese Households," mimeograph, 1969.

Pollak, Robert A., "Additive Utility Functions and Linear Engel Curves," *Review of Economic Studies,* Vol. 38, No. 4 (October 1971), pp. 401–414.

———, "Habit Formation and Dynamic Demand Functions," *Journal of Political Economy,* Vol. 78, No. 4 (July–August 1970), pp. 745–763.

———, "Generalized Separability," *Econometrica,* Vol. 40, No. 3 (May 1972), pp. 431–453.

Samuelson, Paul A., *Foundations of Economic Analysis.* Cambridge, Massachusetts: Harvard University Press, 1947.

Wegge, L. L., "The Demand Curves from a Quadratic Utility Indicator," *Review of Economic Studies*, Vol. XXXV (2), No. 102 (April 1968), pp. 209–224.

Wold, H. O. A., and L. Jureen, *Demand Analysis*. New York: John Wiley and Sons, 1953.

ADDITIONAL REFERENCES (ADDED, 1982)

Diewert, W. E., "Applications of Duality Theory," in M. Intriligator and D. Kendrick, eds., *Frontiers of Quantitative Economics II*. Amsterdam: North-Holland Publishing Co., 1974, pp. 106–171.

———, "The Economic Theory of Index Numbers: A Survey," in A. Deaton, ed., *Essays in the Theory and Measurement of Consumer Behaviour in Honour of Sir Richard Stone*. London: Cambridge University Press, 1981, pp. 163–208.

———, "The Theory of the Cost-of-Living Index and the Measurement of Welfare Change," *Price Level Measurement: Proceedings from a Conference Sponsored by Statistics Canada*. 1983.

McElroy, Marjorie, "A Spliced CES Expenditure System," *International Economic Review*, Vol. 16, No. 3 (October 1975), pp. 765–780.

Pollak, Robert A., "Subindexes of the Cost-of-Living Index," *International Economic Review*, Vol. 16, No. 1 (February 1975), pp. 135–150. (1975a).

———, "The Intertemporal Cost-of-Living Index," *Annals of Economic and Social Measurement*, Vol. 4, No. 1 (Winter 1975), pp. 179–195. (1975b).

———, "Habit Formation and Long-Run Utility Functions," *Journal of Economic Theory*, Vol. 13, No. 2 (October 1976), pp. 272–297.

———, "Welfare Evaluation and the Cost-of-Living Index in the Household Production Model," *American Economic Review*, Vol. 68, No. 3 (June 1978), pp. 285–299.

———, "Group Cost-of-Living Indexes," *American Economic Review*, Vol. 70, No. 2 (May 1980), pp. 273–278.

———, "The Social Cost-of-Living Index," *Journal of Public Economics*, Vol. 15, No. 3 (June 1981), pp. 311–336.

———, "The Treatment of 'Quality' in the Cost-of-Living Index," *Journal of Public Economics*, Vol. 20, No. 1 (February 1983), pp. 25–53.

Pollak, Robert A., and Terence J. Wales, "Welfare Comparisons and Equivalence Scales," *American Economic Review*, Vol. 69, No. 2 (May 1979), pp. 216–221.

Subindexes in the Cost-of-Living Index

In this paper I discuss the construction of *subindexes* of the cost-of-living index and their relation to the *complete* index. For example, how does one define a cost-of-living-type index for "clothing," "footwear," "men's shoes," or some other category of goods? More technically, suppose the set of all goods is partitioned into m subsets and write the commodity vector as $X = (X_1, \ldots, X_m)$, where X_r denotes the vector of goods in the rth subset.[1] The two principal questions I investigate in this paper are, first, how does one define a cost-of-living-type index for the goods in the rth subset, and, second, assuming that one can define such indexes for each of the m subsets, what is the relationship between the complete index and these m subindexes. I shall develop and attempt to motivate a definition of subindexes, and I shall argue that, except in rare special cases, it is not possible to combine subindexes to obtain the complete index.

There are at least five economically significant situations in which subindexes are of interest. Suppose, first, that the goods are partitioned into "natural" categories such as "food," "clothing," and "housing"; the indexes that correspond to these categories are subindexes. The high level of aggregation is not central to the example; more disaggregated "natural categories" on the level of "footwear," or "men's shoes," or "men's tennis shoes" would serve equally well to make the point. The components of the Consumer Price Index (CPI) are often reported and discussed as if they were approximations to or bounds on subindexes for the categories they represent; to evaluate the legitimacy of this interpretation of the components of the CPI, it is necessary to make explicit the theoretical standing of subindexes.

A one-period cost-of-living index in a multiperiod world is a subindex. If X is an intertemporal consumption vector, $X = (X_1, \ldots, X_T)$, and P the corresponding vector of "futures" prices, $P = (P_1, \ldots, P_T)$, then the complete cost-of-living index reflects the ratio of the wealth required to attain a given indifference curve of the intertemporal utility function in alternative price situations. It is important to emphasize that the p's are futures prices—that is, the prices which must be paid *now* for contracts promising delivery in a future period. A subindex is needed to compare alternative "price" vectors for particular periods, for example, P_t^a and P_t^b, rather than alternative intertemporal price vectors. A discussion of the intertemporal cost-of-living

From *International Economic Review*, Vol. 16, No. 1 (February 1975), pp. 135–150. Copyright © 1975 by the Wharton School of Finance and Commerce, University of Pennsylvania and the Osaka University Institute of Social and Economic Research Association. Reprinted with permission.

index and an application of the theory of subindexes to the construction of one-period indexes in a multiperiod setting can be found in Pollak (1975).

The usual treatment of time and leisure in the cost-of-living index—that is, ignoring them completely—implies that we are dealing with a subindex. This is true whether one views the allocation of time within the traditional framework in which leisure is an argument of the utility function, or whether one adopts Becker's household production function approach (Becker, 1965). In either case, the omission of time from the cost-of-living index must be rationalized by a theory of subindexes. Similarly, environmental variables such as the level of air pollution usually play no role in discussions of the cost-of-living index, and a justification for their omission must be found in a theory of subindexes. Finally, goods provided by governments without user charges—for example, roads and schools—are usually not treated in the cost-of-living index. But because these goods enter the utility function, a theoretical justification for their absence from the index is required; such a justification must come from a theory of subindexes.

This paper is about subindexes. It is not concerned with the proper treatment of leisure, government goods, or the environment in a complete index, but with the conditions under which we can construct a subindex for the remaining goods. The existing literature on the cost-of-living index offers no guidance for constructing subindexes. Furthermore, despite the need for a theory of subindexes to establish a connection between the existing theory of the complete index and applied work, there is virtually no recognition that such a theory is required. To establish the need for a theory of subindexes, I have indicated several areas to which it would be relevant: subindexes for categories of goods; one-period indexes in a multiperiod setting; and indexes that omit leisure, environmental variables, or government goods.

In this paper I define several types of subindexes and investigate their relation to each other and to the complete index. I use the word *subindex* in an informal sense to refer to any index whose scope is narrower than that of the complete cost-of-living index. The *partial cost-of-living index* and the *conditional cost-of-living index* are specific subindexes, which are formally defined below.

In section 1, I discuss the *partial cost-of-living index*. It is defined in the "natural" way on the basis of the category utility functions, but it is defined only when preferences are separable in an appropriate sense. In section 2, I discuss the *conditional cost-of-living index*. The definition of the conditional index places no restriction on preferences, but it holds fixed the levels of consumption of the goods outside the category for which we are constructing the index. When preferences are separable, the conditional index and the partial index coincide. In section 3, I discuss the *generalized conditional index*. I also discuss informally a subindex defined by fixing the prices rather than the quantities of the goods outside the category for which we are constructing the subindex. The results are summarized in section 4.

1. THE PARTIAL COST-OF-LIVING INDEX

We begin with the notion of separability.

Definition. Suppose that the goods are partitioned into two subsets, θ and $\bar{\theta}$; denote the vectors of goods in θ and $\bar{\theta}$ by X_θ and $X_{\bar{\theta}}$, respectively. We say that the goods in θ are *separable* from those in $\bar{\theta}$ if the utility function can be written in the form

$$U(X) = U(X_\theta, X_{\bar{\theta}}) = V[V^\theta(X_\theta), X_{\bar{\theta}}]$$

We call $V^\theta(X_\theta)$ the *category utility function* for category θ and denote the preference ordering corresponding to this category utility function by R^θ.

When we speak of a preference ordering or a utility function as "separable," we refer to this nonsymmetric form of separability rather than the more familiar notion of "weak separability." If the utility function is "weakly separable,"

$$U(X) = V[V^1(X_1), \ldots, V^m(X_m)]$$

then the goods in any category are separable from the remaining goods. But the assumption that the goods in θ are separable from those in $\bar{\theta}$ is less restrictive than weak separability, since separability does not require the goods in $\bar{\theta}$ or its subsets to be separable from those in θ. The earliest papers on separability, Leontief (1947a, 1947b) and Sono (1961), emphasized this nonsymmetric form of separability, but later work such as Strotz (1957) and Goldman and Uzawa (1964) emphasized the symmetric versions. The nonsymmetric version is now undergoing a renaissance as "recursive separability." A good summary and references can be found in Blackorby, Primont, and Russell (1975).

Definition. Suppose that the goods are partitioned into two subsets, θ and $\bar{\theta}$, and that the goods in θ are separable from those in $\bar{\theta}$. The *partial expenditure function* for category θ, $E^\theta(P_\theta, s_\theta)$, is defined by

$$E^\theta(P_\theta, s_\theta) = \min \sum_{k \in \theta} p_k x_k$$

subject to $V^\theta(X_\theta) = s_\theta$ where $V^\theta(X_\theta)$ is the category utility function and s_θ denotes an indifference curve of $V^\theta(X_\theta)$.

That is, the partial expenditure function shows the minimum expenditure required to attain the indifference curve s_θ of the category utility function $V^\theta(X_\theta)$.

We now define the *partial cost-of-living index*.

Definition. Suppose that the goods are partitioned into two subsets, θ and $\bar{\theta}$, and that the goods in θ are separable from those in $\bar{\theta}$. The *partial cost-of-living index* for category θ, $I^{\theta}(P_{\theta}^a, P_{\theta}^b, s_{\theta}, R^{\theta})$, is defined by

$$I^{\theta}(P_{\theta}^a, P_{\theta}^b, s_{\theta}, R^{\theta}) = \frac{E^{\theta}(P_{\theta}^a, s_{\theta})}{E^{\theta}(P_{\theta}^b, s_{\theta})}$$

If the direct utility function is weakly separable, the partial cost-of-living index for the goods in category r, $I^r(P_r^a, P_r^b, s_r, R^r)$, is given by

$$I^r(P_r^a, P_r^b, s_r, R^r) = \frac{E^r(P_r^a, s_r)}{E^r(P_r^b, s_r)}$$

where $E^r(P_r, s_r)$ is the expenditure function corresponding to the category utility function $V^r(X_r)$ and s_r denotes an indifference curve of $V^r(X_r)$.

The partial cost-of-living index for the goods in a particular category, θ, is defined only if the goods in that category are separable from the rest. This requirement is less restrictive than weak separability, since it does not require that the goods in $\bar{\theta}$ or its subsets be separable from those in θ, but it is still highly restrictive.

The partial cost-of-living index differs in concept from the complete index only in that it is based on R^{θ}, the preference ordering corresponding to the category utility function $V^{\theta}(X_{\theta})$, rather than on the complete preference ordering, R. If the complete preference ordering is weakly separable, then we can construct a partial cost-of-living index for each category. In the multiperiod context, if the complete (intertemporal) preference ordering is weakly separable by periods, then we can construct a partial index for each period. Even when intertemporal preferences are not weakly separable by periods, if the current period is separable from the future then we can construct a partial index for the current period.

The basic properties of the complete cost-of-living index follow directly from its definition as the ratio of expenditure functions, and are discussed in Pollak [1971, (11–12)]. Four of the most basic are:

P∗1. $I(P^b, P^a, s, R) = 1/I(P^a, P^b, s, R)$

P∗2. $I(\lambda P^a, P^b, s, R) = \lambda I(P^a, P^b, s, R)$ for all $\lambda \geqslant 0$

P∗3. If $P^{a'} \geqslant P^a$, then $I(P^{a'}, P^b, s, R) \geqslant I(P^a, P^b, s, R)$

P∗4. $\min \dfrac{p_i^a}{p_i^b} \leqslant I(P^a, P^b, s, R) \leqslant \max \dfrac{p_i^a}{p_i^b}$

To show that the partial cost-of-living index exhibits these properties, we observe that the category preference ordering R^{θ} is "well-behaved," that is, complete, reflexive, transitive, monotonic, convex, and continuous. Hence, the partial expenditure function, $E^{\theta}(P_{\theta}, s_{\theta})$ exhibits all the characteristics of an expenditure function corresponding to such a preference ordering. The ratio of these expenditure functions is, therefore, a cost-of-living index satisfying P∗1–P∗4: If the goods in θ are separable from the remaining goods, then the partial cost-of-living index is a subindex satisfying P∗1–P∗4.

We now consider the relationship between the partial indexes and the complete index. Assume that the utility function is weakly separable, so that we have partial indexes for each category. We begin by considering the degenerate case in which each category contains a single good. In this case the partial index for each group is given by the price relative for that good,

$$I^r(P_r^a, P_r^b, s_r, R^r) = p_r^a / p_r^b$$

and is independent of the base indifference curve, s_r. Therefore, when each group contains only a single good, the problem of constructing a complete index from the partial indexes reduces to that of constructing a cost-of-living index from price relatives, p_r^a / p_r^b. This problem is considered in Pollak (1971, section 6.1), where it is shown that the cost-of-living index is a function of price relatives

$$I(P^a, P^b, s, R) = \hat{I}\left(\frac{p_1^a}{p_1^b}, \ldots, \frac{p_n^a}{p_n^b}, s, R\right)$$

if and only if the preference ordering is the generalized Cobb–Douglas form representable by the indirect utility function $\Psi(P, \mu) = s$ implicitly defined by

$$\sum \beta^k(s) \log p_k - \sum \beta^k(s) \log \mu = 1$$

The corresponding cost-of-living index is a geometric mean of the price relatives

$$I(P^a, P^b, s, R) = \prod \left(\frac{p_k^a}{p_k^b}\right)^{a^k(s)}$$

where $a^i(s)$ is defined by

$$a^i(s) = \frac{\beta^i(s)}{\sum \beta^k(s)}$$

Thus, even in the simplest case when each category contains only a single good so that problems arising from aggregation within categories disappear, the complete cost-of-living index cannot be constructed from the partial indexes unless preferences are of a very special form. The impossibility of constructing a cost-of-living index for a general preference ordering from price relatives suggests that the desire to do so is based on a misunderstanding. Since the cost-of-living index is not constructed from price relatives but from reference prices, P^b, and comparison prices, P^a, it should be no surprise that the partial indexes cannot be used to construct the complete index.

If a category contains more than one good and the category utility function is not homothetic, then the relationship between the partial and the complete cost-of-living index is further complicated by the role of the base indifference curves in the partial indexes. The complete cost-of-living index is given by

$$I(P^a, P^b, s, R) = \frac{\sum E^t(P_t^a, s_t^a, R^t)}{\sum E^t(P_t^b, s_t^b, R^t)}$$

where s_t^a and s_t^b denote the *optimal* levels of the category utility functions corresponding to the price-utility situations (P^a, s) and (P^b, s), respectively. That is, $\{s_1^a, \ldots, s_m^a\}$ are the values which minimize

$$\sum E^t(P_t^a, s_t^a, R^t)$$

subject to $U(s_1, \ldots, s_m) = s$. Thus, s_t^a is a function of all prices and s.

It is well known that the Laspeyres index, $J(P^a, P^b, X^b)$, defined by

$$J(P^a, P^b, X^b) = \frac{\sum x_k^b p_k^a}{\sum x_k^b p_k^b}$$

is an upper bound on the cost-of-living index based on the reference period indifference curve, $I(P^a, P^b, s^b, R^b)$:

$$I(P^a, P^b, s^b, R^b) \leqslant J(P^a, P^b, X^b)$$

The Laspeyres index may be expressed as a weighted average of price relatives, where the weights are the expenditure weights of the reference situation:

$$J(P^a, P^b, X^b) = \sum w_k^b \left(\frac{p_k^a}{p_k^b} \right)$$

where

$$w_i^b = \frac{x_i^b p_i^b}{\mu^b}$$

Although the partial indexes cannot be used as building blocks to construct the complete index, they can be used in conjunction with reference period expenditure weights to construct a Laspeyres type index which is an upper bound on the complete index.

Theorem. Suppose the utility function is weakly separable and that at reference prices P^b the individual attains the category indifference curves $\{s_1^b, \ldots, s_m^b\}$ where $U(s_1^b, \ldots, s_m^b) = s^b$. Then

$$I(P^a, P^b, s^b, R^b) \leqslant \sum_{t=1}^{m} w_t^b I^t(P_t^a, P_t^b, s_t^b, R_t^b)$$

where w_r^b is the expenditure weight of the rth category,

$$w_r^b = \frac{E^r(P_r^b, s_r^b)}{\sum E^t(P_t^b, s_t^b)}$$

Proof. Clearly,

$$E(P^b, s^b) = \sum_t E^t(P_t^b, s_t^b)$$

Since the indifference curve s^b can certainly be reached by attaining the category indifference curves $\{s_1^b, \ldots, s_m^b\}$

$$E(P^a, s^b) \leqslant \sum_t E^t(P_t^a, s_t^b)$$

Since the complete index is given by

$$I(P^a, P^b, s^b) = \frac{E(P^a, s^b)}{E(P^b, s^b)}$$

we have

$$I(P^a, P^b, s^b) \leqslant \frac{\sum_r E^r(P_r^a, s_r^b)}{\sum_t E^t(P_t^b, s_t^b)}$$

$$= \frac{\sum_r E^r(P_r^b, s_r^b) \dfrac{E^r(P_r^a, s_r^b)}{E^r(P_r^b, s_r^b)}}{\sum_t E^t(P_t^b, s_t^b)}$$

$$= \sum_r w_r^b I^r(P_r^a, P_r^b, s_r^b). \qquad \text{Q.E.D.}$$

Since the Paasche index cannot be written as an expenditure-weighted average of price relatives, the Paasche lower bound

$$J(P^a, P^b, X^a) \leqslant I(P^a, P^b, s^a, R^a)$$

has no natural analogue in the present context.

For what preference orderings is the complete cost-of-living index equal to the Laspeyres-type weighted average of partial indexes? If the utility function is of the form

$$U(X) = \min_r \{U^r(X_r)\}$$

it is easy to verify that the complete cost-of-living index is equal to its Laspeyres-type upper bound. This utility function allows no substitution between categories, but it does not imply fixed coefficients (or any other restriction) within the category utility functions. It can also be shown that this is the only preference ordering for which the complete index coincides with its Laspeyres-type upper bound. The proof is similar to that used in Pollak (1971, Section 3) to show that the cost-of-living index is equal to the Laspeyres index only in the generalized fixed coefficient case

$$U(X) = \min_i \{g^i(x_i)\}$$

2. THE CONDITIONAL COST-OF-LIVING INDEX

The partial cost-of-living index has two significant limitations: first, it is not defined unless the group of goods for which we are constructing the subindex is separable from the remaining goods; second, even if preferences are weakly separable so that we can construct a partial index for each category, there is no way to combine the partial indexes to obtain the complete index. The second limitation is intrinsic to subindexes, but the first is not. In this section I define the *conditional cost-of-living index*, a subindex which can be constructed for any preference ordering, and examine its relation to the partial index. I begin by introducing a new convention for identifying the base indifference curve.

In section 1, we specified the indifference curve to be attained for the expenditure function and the cost-of-living index by indicating the value to be assumed by the utility function. There is nothing wrong with specifying the base curve in this way, although it is slightly inelegant because it requires us to select a particular utility function to represent the individual's preference ordering. But this method of specifying the base indifference curve unnecessarily complicates the discussion of the relationship between the conditional and the partial indexes, so we now introduce a new convention.

Hereafter, we identify the base indifference curve by means of a "base" commodity bundle, X^0, instead of by the value attained by the utility function. We write the complete expenditure function as $E(P, X^0, R)$ and the complete cost-of-living index as $I(P^a, P^b, X^0, R)$ instead of as $E(P, s, R)$ and $I(P^a, P^b, s, R)$. The notation is slightly sloppy, since the same symbol is used to denote expenditure as a function of the $2n$ variables (P, X^0) and the $n + 1$ variables (P, s), but the meaning is unambiguous. In this new notation the partial expenditure function becomes $E^\theta(P_\theta, X_\theta^0)$ and the partial cost-of-living index $I_\theta(P_\theta^a, P_\theta^b, X_\theta^0, R^\theta)$.

We now define the *conditional expenditure function*.

Definition. Suppose that the goods are partitioned into two subsets, θ and $\bar{\theta}$, and let $X^0 = (X_\theta^0, X_{\bar{\theta}}^0)$ be the base commodity bundle. The *conditional expenditure function* for category θ, $E^\theta(P_\theta, X^0)$, is defined by

$$E^\theta(P_\theta, X^0) = \min \sum_{k \in \theta} p_k x_k$$

subject to $U(X_\theta, X_{\bar{\theta}}) = U(X^0)$ and $X_{\bar{\theta}} = X_{\bar{\theta}}^0$.

That is, the conditional expenditure function shows the expenditure on the goods in θ required to attain the indifference curve of X^0 when the goods in $\bar{\theta}$ are fixed at the levels $X_{\bar{\theta}}^0$. The conditional expenditure function is analogous to a "short run" variable cost function in production theory, where the goods in θ and $\bar{\theta}$ correspond to variable and fixed factors respectively. It is also closely related to the conditional compensated demand functions introduced in Pollak (1969).

Using the conditional expenditure function, we define the conditional cost-of-living index:

Definition. Let $\{\theta, \bar{\theta}\}$ be a partition of the set of all goods. The *conditional cost-of-living index* for category θ, $L^{\theta}(P_{\theta}^a, P_{\theta}^b, X^0, R)$, is given by

$$L^{\theta}(P_{\theta}^a, P_{\theta}^b, X^0, R) = \frac{E^{\theta}(P_{\theta}^a, X^0)}{E^{\theta}(P_{\theta}^b, X^0)}$$

The conditional cost-of-living index $L^{\theta}(P_{\theta}^a, P_{\theta}^b, X^0, R)$ has all the properties of a traditional cost-of-living index. To prove this, we have only to verify that it is the cost-of-living index corresponding to some well-behaved preference ordering. But the conditional index is clearly the cost-of-living index corresponding to the conditional preference ordering over X_{θ} given $X_{\bar{\theta}}$, where the base indifference curve is specified by the requirement that X_{θ} must satisfy

$$U(X_{\theta}, X_{\bar{\theta}}^0) = U(X_{\theta}^0, X_{\bar{\theta}}^0)$$

Theorem. The *conditional cost-of-living index*, $L^{\theta}(P_{\theta}^a, P_{\theta}^b, X^0)$ is independent of $X_{\bar{\theta}}^0$.

$$L^{\theta}(P_{\theta}^a, P_{\theta}^b, X^0) = L^{\theta}(P_{\theta}^a, P_{\theta}^b, X_{\theta}^0)$$

if and only if the goods in θ are separable from those in $\bar{\theta}$.

That is, if preferences are separable, then the conditional index is independent of $X_{\bar{\theta}}^0$ and depends only on X_{θ}^0 and the price vectors P_{θ}^a and P_{θ}^b. Furthermore, the separable case is the only one in which the conditional index is independent of $X_{\bar{\theta}}^0$.

Theorem. If the goods in θ are separable from those in $\bar{\theta}$, then

$$I^{\theta}(P_{\theta}^a, P_{\theta}^b, X_{\theta}^0, R^{\theta}) = L^{\theta}(P_{\theta}^a, P_{\theta}^b, X^0, R)$$

That is, if preferences are separable, then the conditional index coincides with the partial index. This implies that the conditional index is an extension of the partial index to the nonseparable case rather than an essentially different index. Since the partial index is defined only when the goods in θ are separable from those in $\bar{\theta}$, there is no substance to the converse assertion that the partial index and the conditional index coincide only in the separable case.

These two theorems assert the basic relationships between partial and conditional indexes and separability. They confirm the intuitive view that, in the separable case, the partial index is a useful and meaningful way to compare prices of the goods in θ. They also imply serious practical difficulties in the nonseparable case, since, in the absence of separability, the conditional indexes depend on the levels of the goods in $\bar{\theta}$.

Separability is the critical simplifying assumption for the construction of subindexes. It follows from the definition of the partial index that if preferences are separable one can construct a subindex satisfying P∗1–P∗4 without taking any account of the goods outside the category for which the subindex is defined. The analysis of the conditional index shows that there is an important sense in which the separable case is the only one in which goods outside the category can be ignored in constructing a subindex. This statement is overly strong because it presumes that the conditional index is the only valid subindex, an assertion which I have not attempted to formulate rigorously, let alone prove. But if we grant that the conditional index is the most satisfactory subindex, then the theorem implies that separability is the critical simplifying assumption, since it allows us to ignore the goods outside the category for which we are constructing the subindex. Suppose, for example, imports are separable from domestic goods; then the index for imports will be independent of the levels of consumption of domestic goods. Furthermore, the theorem asserts that the separable case is the only one in which the index for imports does not depend on the levels of consumption of domestic goods.

Proof. It is easy to show that if the direct utility function is separable

$$U(X) = V[V^\theta(X_\theta), X_{\bar{\theta}}]$$

then the conditional index is independent of $X_{\bar{\theta}}^0$. To reach the indifference curve of $U(X^0)$ when the goods in $\bar{\theta}$ are fixed at $X_{\bar{\theta}}^0$ is equivalent to reaching the indifference curve of $V^\theta(X_\theta^0)$. Hence, the conditional expenditure function is independent of $X_{\bar{\theta}}^0$, and, therefore, the conditional index is independent of $X_{\bar{\theta}}^0$. It follows immediately that the conditional index coincides with the partial index in the separable case.

To show that the separable case is the only one in which the conditional index is independent of $X_{\bar{\theta}}^0$ is more difficult.[2] We begin by introducing some new notation to distinguish more easily between the goods in θ and those in $\bar{\theta}$. Throughout this proof, we denote the goods in θ by y's and those in $\bar{\theta}$ by z's. Thus, the base indifference curve which was denoted by $(X_\theta^0, X_{\bar{\theta}}^0)$ is now represented by (Y^0, Z^0). The conditional index is now denoted by

$$L(P^a, P^b, Y, Z) = \frac{E(P^a, Y, Z)}{E(P^b, Y, Z)} \tag{1}$$

We have omitted the superscript 0's from the y's and z's and the θ's from P_θ, L^θ, and E^θ.

From the definition of the conditional expenditure function, it is easy to see that the minimum expenditure on the goods in θ required to attain the indifference curve of (Y, Z) at prices P when the goods in $\bar{\theta}$ are fixed at Z is a function of the level of utility to be attained, the levels at which the goods in $\bar{\theta}$ are held fixed, and the prices of the goods in θ. This implies

$$E(P, Y, Z) = D[P, Z, U(Y, Z)] \tag{2}$$

Differentiating (2) with respect to y_i and y_j and forming the ratio yields

$$\frac{\dfrac{\partial U(Y, Z)}{\partial y_i}}{\dfrac{\partial U(Y, Z)}{\partial y_j}} = \frac{\dfrac{\partial E(P, Y, Z)}{\partial y_i}}{\dfrac{\partial E(P, Y, Z)}{\partial y_j}} \tag{3}$$

To show that goods in θ are separable from those in $\bar{\theta}$, it suffices to show that the left hand side of (3) is independent of Z. Our strategy of proof is to show that the right hand side of (3) is independent of the z's. It is convenient to denote derivatives with respect to y_i by E_i and U_i.

If the index L is independent of Z

$$L(P^a, P^b, Y, Z) = L(P^a, P^b, Y)$$

then (1) implies

$$E(P^a, Y, Z) = L(P^a, P^b, Y)E(P^b, Y, Z) \tag{4a}$$

and

$$E(P^b, Y, Z) = L(P^b, P^a, Y)E(P^a, Y, Z) \tag{4b}$$

for all P^a, P^b, Y, Z. Differentiating (4a) with respect to y_i and y_j and forming the ratio, we find

$$\frac{E_i(P^a, Y, Z)}{E_j(P^a, Y, Z)} = \frac{L_i(P^a, P^b, Y)E(P^b, Y, Z) + L(P^a, P^b, Y)E_i(P^b, Y, Z)}{L_j(P^a, P^b, Y)E(P^b, Y, Z) + L(P^a, P^b, Y)E_j(P^b, Y, Z)} \tag{5}$$

Differentiating (4b) with respect to y_i and y_j, we obtain expressions for $E_i(P^b, Y, Z)$ and $E_j(P^b, Y, Z)$, which we substitute into (5). Making use of the identity

$$L(P^a, P^b, Y) \cdot L(P^b, P^a, Y) = 1 \tag{6}$$

(5) becomes

$$\frac{E_i(P^a, Y, Z)}{E_j(P^a, Y, Z)}$$

$$= \frac{L_i(P^a, P^b, Y)E(P^b, Y, Z) + L(P^a, P^b, Y)L_i(P^b, P^a, Y)E(P^a, Y, Z) + E_i(P^a, Y, Z)}{L_j(P^a, P^b, Y)E(P^b, Y, Z) + L(P^a, P^b, Y)L_j(P^b, P^a, Y)E(P^a, Y, Z) + E_j(P^b, Y, Z)} \tag{7}$$

By the law of proportions, (7) implies

$$\frac{E_i(P^a, Y, Z)}{E_j(P^a, Y, Z)}$$

$$= \frac{L_i(P^a, P^b, Y)E(P^b, Y, Z) + L(P^a, P^b, Y)L_i(P^b, P^a, Y)E(P^a, Y, Z)}{L_j(P^a, P^b, Y)E(P^b, Y, Z) + L(P^a, P^b, Y)L_j(P^b, P^a, Y)E(P^a, Y, Z)} \tag{8}$$

Differentiating the identity (6) with respect to y_i and y_j, we obtain expressions for $L(P^a, P^b, Y)L_i(P^b, P^a, Y)$ and $L(P^a, P^b, Y)L_j(P^b, P^a, Y)$, which we substitute into (8). After cancellation, this yields

$$\frac{E_i(P^a, Y, Z)}{E_j(P^a, Y, Z)} = \frac{L_i(P^a, P^b, Y)}{L_j(P^a, P^b, Y)} \tag{9}$$

Hence, the right-hand side of (3) is independent of the z's, and so the goods in θ are separable from those in $\bar{\theta}$.   Q.E.D.

3. OTHER APPROACHES

In this section we consider several other approaches to the construction of subindexes. We begin with a generalization of the conditional index.

Definition. Suppose that the goods are partitioned into two subsets, θ and $\bar{\theta}$, and that the goods in $\bar{\theta}$ are fixed at $X^*_{\bar{\theta}}$. The *generalized conditional expenditure function* for category θ, $E^\theta(P_\theta, X^*_{\bar{\theta}}, X^0)$, is given by

$$E^\theta(P_\theta, X^*_{\bar{\theta}}, X^0) = \min_{k \in \theta} \sum p_k x_k$$

subject to $U(X_\theta, X^*_{\bar{\theta}}) = U(X^0)$ and $X_{\bar{\theta}} = X^*_{\bar{\theta}}$. For brevity, we refer to the generalized conditional expenditure function as the *GC expenditure function*.

The GC expenditure function shows the expenditure on the goods in θ required to attain the indifference curve $U(X) = U(X^0)$ when the goods in $\bar{\theta}$ are fixed at the levels $X^*_{\bar{\theta}}$. Unlike the conditional expenditure function, the GC expenditure function allows us to specify independently the indifference curve to be attained, X^0, and the fixed levels of the goods in $\bar{\theta}$, $X^*_{\bar{\theta}}$. The conditional expenditure function is related to the GC expenditure function by

$$E^\theta(P_\theta, X^0) = E^\theta(P_\theta, X^0_{\bar{\theta}}, X^0)$$

In the definition of the conditional expenditure function, the base commodity bundle X^0 plays a double role: It identifies the base indifference curve, and it also specifies the levels at which the goods in $\bar{\theta}$ are held fixed. In the GC expenditure function, these roles are separated: X^0 identifies the base indifference curve, and $X^*_{\bar{\theta}}$ specifies the levels of the goods in $\bar{\theta}$. Since the

GC expenditure function corresponds to a well-behaved preference ordering —the conditional preference ordering over X_θ given $X_{\bar{\theta}}$—it has all the properties ascribed to an expenditure function by traditional theory.

It is tempting to define a generalized conditional cost of living index,

$$L^\theta(P_\theta^a, P_\theta^b, X_{\bar{\theta}}^a, X_{\bar{\theta}}^b, X^0, R)$$

by

$$L^\theta(P_\theta^a, P_\theta^b, X_{\bar{\theta}}^a, X_{\bar{\theta}}^b, X^0, R) = \frac{E^\theta(P_\theta^a, X_{\bar{\theta}}^a, X^0)}{E^0(P_\theta^b, X_{\bar{\theta}}^b, X^0)}$$

but this is unsatisfactory. The difficulty is that the proposed index reflects not only the change in price from P^b to P^a, but also the change in quantities from $X_{\bar{\theta}}^b$ to $X_{\bar{\theta}}^a$. Thus, if the prices of the goods in θ remain constant, while the quantities of the goods in $\bar{\theta}$ increase, then the proposed index will fall—it takes less expenditure on the goods in θ to attain the indifference curve X^0, since the individual starts out with more of the goods in $\bar{\theta}$. This is not to deny that a cost-of-living index should reflect changes in the quantities of the goods in $\bar{\theta}$; if, for example, the goods in $\bar{\theta}$ are supplied by the government without user charges, then the complete cost-of-living index should reflect increased provision of these public services. But if our objective is to construct a subindex for the private goods which the household purchases on the market, then the subindex should remain constant when the prices of market goods are constant and not change in response to variations in the provision of public services. In more technical terms, the difficulty with the proposed index is that the GC expenditure function $E^\theta(P_\theta, X_{\bar{\theta}}^a, X^0)$ is predicated on the conditional preference ordering corresponding to $X_{\bar{\theta}}^a$, while $E^\theta(P_\theta, X_{\bar{\theta}}^b, X^0)$ is predicated on the conditional ordering corresponding to $X_{\bar{\theta}}^b$. These are distinct preference orderings, and, hence, the ratio of their expenditure functions need not behave as the ratio of expenditure functions from a single preference ordering. Since the two GC expenditure functions do not correspond to the same conditional preference ordering, their ratio need not satisfy $P*1-P*4$.

To avoid this difficulty we define the generalized conditional cost-of-living index in terms of GC expenditure functions which correspond to the same conditional preference ordering.

Definition. Let $\{\theta, \bar{\theta}\}$ be a partition of the set of all commodities. The *generalized conditional cost-of-living index* for category $\theta, L^\theta(P_\theta^a, P_\theta^b, X_{\bar{\theta}}^*, X^0, R)$ is given by

$$L^\theta(P_\theta^a, P_\theta^b, X_{\bar{\theta}}^*, X^0, R) = \frac{E^\theta(P_\theta^a, X_{\bar{\theta}}^*, X^0)}{E^\theta(P_\theta^b, X_{\bar{\theta}}^*, X^0)}$$

We shall refer to $L^\theta(P_\theta^a, P_\theta^b, X_{\bar{\theta}}^*, X^0, R)$ as the *GC cost-of-living index* or the *GC index*.

The GC index is the cost-of-lving index corresponding to the conditional preference ordering over X_θ given $X_{\bar{\theta}}^*$, when the base indifference curve is specified by X^0. Hence, it satisfies P∗1–P∗4. The construction of the GC index for the goods in a subset θ requires us to specify not only R and X^0 but also the levels at which the goods in $\bar{\theta}$ are held fixed. For example, to construct a GC index to compare the prices of imported goods today with their prices a year ago, we must specify the levels at which domestic goods are to be held fixed. Using today's levels for domestic goods may give one answer, while last year's levels give another. Like the choice of a base preference ordering or a base indifference curve, specifying the levels of consumption of the goods outside the category for which we are constructing the index is an intrinsic part of the process of index contruction. The example is instructive because it seems unlikely that imported goods are separable from domestic goods, and a principal motivation for defining conditional and GC indexes was to escape the separability assumption which is inherent in the partial index.

One may regard either the conditional index or the GC index as the primary subindex. The GC index emphasizes the distinction between specifying a base indifference curve and fixing the levels of the goods in $\bar{\theta}$. Even if we consider the conditional index to be the primary one, the GC index clarifies the double role which X^0 plays in the conditional index. The advantage of the conditional index is its simple and direct relation to the partial index.

The conditional and GC indexes are constructed by holding fixed the quantities of goods in certain subsets. One might think that an alternative type of subindex could be constructed by holding fixed the prices of "other goods." We define the "pseudoconditional" expenditure function for category θ,

$$E^\theta(P, X^0) = E^\theta(P_\theta, P_{\bar{\theta}}, X^0)$$

to be the expenditure on the goods in θ associated with the collection of goods which minimizes the expenditure required to attain the indifference curve of X^0 at prices $P = (P_\theta, P_{\bar{\theta}})$. That is, we find the collection of goods which minimizes the expenditure required to attain the indifference curve X^0 at prices P, and we define $E^\theta(P, X^0)$ to be the total expenditure on the goods in that collection belonging to θ. Expenditure minimization takes place over the entire set goods, not just those in θ. Mathematically,

$$E^\theta(P, X^0) = \sum_{k \in \theta} p_k x_k$$

where the x's are chosen to minimize $\sum_{k=1}^n p_k x_k$ subject to $U(X) = U(X^0)$.

We use the pseudoconditional expenditure function to define the *pseudo-conditional (PC) cost-of-living index*, $K^\theta(P^a, P^b, X^0)$:

$$K^\theta(P^a, P^b, X^0) = \frac{E^\theta(P^a, X^0)}{E^\theta(P^b, X^0)}$$

If the goods are partitioned into subsets $\{X_1, \ldots, X_m\}$, then the complete cost-of-living index can be written as

$$I(P^a, P^b, X^0) = \frac{\sum_{t=1}^{m} E^t(P^a, X^0)}{\sum_{t=1}^{m} E^t(P^b, X^0)}$$

It is easy to verify that this implies

$$I(P^a, P^b, X^0) = \sum_{t=1}^{m} W^t(P^b, X^0) K^t(P^a, P^b, X^0)$$

where

$$W^r(P^b, X^0) = \frac{E^r(P^b, X^0)}{\sum_{t=1}^{m} E^t(P^b, X^0)}$$

Thus, there is a simple and direct relationship between the complete index and the PC indexes $\{K^1, \ldots, K^m\}$: the complete index is a weighted average of the PC indexes, where the weights are the category expenditure weights at reference prices.

It looks as if we have found a collection of subindexes which can be combined to form the complete index, contrary to our assertions in section 1 that it could not be done. The difficulty is that the PC indexes are not subindexes; they reflect changes in the prices of goods in $\bar{\theta}$ as well as in θ. For example, if all food prices double and all other prices remain unchanged, the PC index for food will not double unless preferences exhibit fixed coefficients. Without fixed coefficients, expenditure on food would less than double (we are considering compensated changes, since X^0 is fixed), so the food subindex would less than double; expenditure on other goods, say, clothing, would rise, and, hence, the PC index for clothing would rise even though clothing prices had not changed.

Reasoning by analogy with our procedure when we defined the GC index, we might fix the prices of the goods in $\bar{\theta}$ and define the PC index as

$$K^\theta(P_\theta^a, P_\theta^b, P_{\bar{\theta}}, X^0) = \frac{E^\theta(P_\theta^a, P_{\bar{\theta}}, X^0)}{E^\theta(P_\theta^b, P_{\bar{\theta}}, X^0)}$$

But the analogy is false. The new definition destroys the simple relationship between the pseudoindex and the complete index, and our previous example shows that a doubling of food prices will not, in general, cause the food subindex to double.

We can conclude that it is impossible to construct a subindex satisfying P*1–P*4 by holding fixed the prices of the goods outside θ. The analogue of the procedure we used to construct the conditional and GC indexes—holding fixed the quantities of the goods outside the category for which we are constructing the index—when applied to the prices rather than the quantities does not yield a subindex satisfying $P*1$–$P*4$.

4. SUMMARY

In this paper I have examined the theoretical basis for constructing subindexes of the cost-of-living index. The complete index is far more comprehensive in coverage than any price index anyone is likely to compute, so it is the theory of subindexes, not the traditional theory of the complete index, which must provide the theoretical rationale for index-number construction. A theory of subindexes rationalizes the construction of indexes for particular groups of goods such as "food," "meats" or "beef"; for single periods in a multiperiod setting; and for indexes which ignore leisure, the environment, and government goods.

If a group of goods is separable from the rest, then we can use the category utility function in the "natural" way to construct a *partial cost-of-living index*. If the complete utility function is weakly separable, then we can construct partial indexes for each branch or category. One might think that in the weakly separable case these subindexes could be combined to form the complete index, but this is incorrect. The conjecture reflects a basic misconception about cost-of-living indexes. Except in very special cases, the cost-of-living index is not a function of price relatives, but depends on the reference and comparison price vectors. Thus, even when we can construct a subindex with all the properties of a price relative for each category, as we can when each group consists of a single good, we cannot combine these subindexes to form the complete index. The conjecture that the complete index can be constructed from subindexes is based on the mistaken belief that the complete index is built up from price relatives.

The partial index has all the traditional properties of a cost-of-living index, but it is only defined when the group of goods for which we are constructing the subindex is separable from the rest. Even if preferences are not separable, however, we can define the "conditional" and "generalized conditional" indexes. Both correspond to the conditional preference orderings over the goods in the group when "other goods" are held fixed. In the generalized conditional index, the base indifference curve and the fixed levels of the "other goods" are specified separately, by X^0 and $X_{\bar{\theta}}^*$, respectively. In the conditional index, the fixed levels of the other goods are set equal to their levels in the commodity vector used to specify the base indifference curve: $X_{\bar{\theta}}^* = X_{\bar{\theta}}^0$. Thus, $X_{\bar{\theta}}^0$ plays a double role in the conditional index: it specifies the fixed levels of the goods in $\bar{\theta}$, and, in conjunction with X_{θ}^0, it identifies the base indifference curve.

If the goods for which we are constructing the index are separable from the rest, then the conditional index coincides with the partial index. Furthermore, the conditional index is independent of the levels of the goods in $X_\bar{\theta}^0$ if and only if preferences are separable in this sense. Within the framework of conditional indexes, separability provides the only theoretical justification for ignoring "other goods" in constructing subindexes.

NOTES

This research was supported in part by the Bureau of Labor Statistics and the National Science Foundation. I am grateful to Franklin M. Fisher, Kiyoshi Kuga, Stephen A. Ross, Paul A. Samuelson, and Paul J. Taubman for helpful comments, but neither they, the University of Pennsylvania, the Bureau of Labor Statistics nor the National Science Foundation should be held responsible for the views expressed.

1. Although it is often convenient to introduce a double subscript notation for the basic components of X, it is better for our purposes to use single subscripts: $X = (x_1, \ldots, x_n)$.

2. But not as difficult as my original proof made it appear. Kiyoshi Kuga suggested the present proof.

REFERENCES

Becker, Gary S., "A Theory of the Allocation of Time," *Economic Journal*, Vol. 75 (September 1965), pp. 493–517.

Blackorby, Charles, Daniel Primont and R. Robert Russell, "Budgeting, Decentralization, and Aggregation," *Annals of Economic and Social Measurement*; Vol. 4, No. 1 (Winter 1975); pp. 23–44.

Goldman, S. M., and H. Uzawa, "A Note on Separability in Demand Analysis," *Econometrica*, Vol. 32 (July 1964), pp. 387–398.

Leontief, W., "A Note on the Interrelation of Subsets of Independent Variables of a Continuous Function with Continuous First Derivatives," *Bulletin of the American Mathematical Society*, Vol. 53 (1947a), pp. 343–350.

————, "Introduction to a Theory of the Internal Structure of Functional Relationships," *Econometrica*, Vol. 15 (1947b), pp. 361–373.

Pollak, Robert A., "Conditional Demand Functions and Consumption Theory," *Quarterly Journal of Economics*, Vol. 83 (February 1969), pp. 60–78.

————, "The Theory of the Cost-of-Living Index," Research Discussion Paper No. 11, Research Division, Office of Prices and Living Conditions, U.S. Bureau of Labor Statistics, June 1971.

————, "The Intertemporal Cost-of-Living Index," *Annals of Economic and Social Measurement*, Vol. 4, No. 1 (Winter 1975), pp. 179–195.

Sono, M., "The Effect of Price Changes on the Demand and Supply of Separable Goods," *International Economic Review*, Vol. 2. (September 1961), pp. 239–271.

————, Strotz, Robert H., "The Empirical Implications of a Utility Tree," *Econometrica*, Vol. 25 (April 1957), pp. 269–280.

The Intertemporal Cost-of-Living Index

In this paper I extend the theory of the cost-of-living index from its traditional one-period framework to a multiperiod setting. Since we live in a multiperiod world, it might be argued that this is the only appropriate theoretical framework within which to evaluate any calculated index. At the very least, exploring the relationship between the traditional one-period index and the intertemporal model may give us some insight into the proper construction and interpretation of the one-period index in a multiperiod world. This is especially important in the case of those problems which arise in constructing a cost-of-living index which do not make sense in a one-period model—for example, the treatment of interest rates. An intelligible discussion of such problems requires an explicitly intertemporal framework.

This paper is organized as follows. In section 1, I define the complete *intertemporal cost-of-living index*. There are two versions of this index, one based on "futures" prices and the other on "spot" prices and interest rates. The intertemporal cost-of-living index is a straightforward extension of the traditional theory from its familiar one-period setting to an intertemporal one.

In section 2, I discuss the construction of one-period cost-of-living indexes in a multiperiod world. Since the complete intertemporal cost-of-living index compares alternative vectors of future prices (or, equivalently, alternative vectors of spot prices and interest rates), a theoretical rationale for comparing alternative one-period price vectors must be based on a theory of "subindexes." Section 2 summarizes the theory of subindexes developed in Pollak (1975) and applies it to the construction of one-period indexes. If the intertemporal preference ordering is separable by periods, the "partial" cost-of-living index is defined in the "natural" way on the basis of a one-period preference ordering. Without separability, we can only define "conditional" subindexes, which are based on the conditional preference ordering over the goods in a period when the levels of consumption of all goods in all other periods are fixed at predetermined levels.

In section 3, I discuss the implications of habit formation for the construction of the complete intertemporal cost-of-living index and for one-period subindexes. The usual discussion of habit formation begins with a short-run utility function some of whose parameters depend on past consumption. If we specify the consumption levels of all goods in the previous period, we can construct a one-period cost-of-living index on the basis of the preference

From *Annals of Economic and Social Measurement*, Vol. 4, No. 1 (Winter 1975), pp. 179–195.

ordering implied by the specified consumption history. I distinguish between *naive habit formation*, in which an individual does not recognize the impact of his present consumption on his future tastes, and *rational habit formation*, in which he does. Naive habit formation cannot be integrated into an intertemporal allocation model and, therefore, does not lead to a complete intertemporal cost-of-living index. Rational habit formation implies a nonseparable intertemporal utility function which can serve as a base for an intertemporal cost-of-living index. But because the intertemporal preference ordering is not separable by periods, the one-period subindex must be a conditional rather than a partial index.

Section 4 summarizes the results of the previous sections and uses them to discuss the treatment of interest rates in the cost-of-living index.

1. THE INTERTEMPORAL INDEX

A cost-of-living index is the ratio of the expenditures required to attain a particular indifference curve under two price regimes. Let $E(P, s)$ denote the minimum expenditure required to attain the indifference curve s of the preference ordering, R; the cost of living index, $I(P^a, P^b, s, R)$, is defined by

$$I(P^a, P^b, s, R) = \frac{E(P^a, s)}{E(P^b, s)}$$

The notation emphasizes that the index depends not only on the comparison prices, P^a, and the reference prices, P^b, but also on the choice of a base indifference curve, s, from that map.

Strictly speaking, the index depends only on the comparison prices, the reference prices, and the base indifference curve. No other indifference curve from the base preference ordering plays a role in constructing the index. Nevertheless, it is useful and realistic to imagine that the base curve is selected by a two-stage procedure: First, a base map is chosen, and then a curve is selected from that map. Treating the base curve as part of an indifference map focuses attention on the sensitivity of the index to the choice of one base curve rather than another. It is well known that the index is independent of the choice of the base curve if and only if the map is homothetic to the origin; see Pollak (1971) for a discussion of the dependence of the index on the choice of the base curve in nonhomothetic cases.

The traditional cost-of-living index is defined in precisely this way. We let x_i denote the individual's consumption of the ith good; if there are n goods, the corresponding consumption vector is given by $(x_1, \ldots, x_n)$. The individual's preference ordering, R, is defined over these n dimensional consumption vectors, and the reference and comparison price vectors, P^b and P^a, are n dimensional vectors of goods prices.

In the intertemporal context, it is useful to introduce a "double subscript" notation for commodities and prices. We let x_{it} denote consumption of the

ith good in period t, X_t the vector of consumption in period t, $X_t = (x_{1t}, \ldots, x_{nt})$, and X the intertemporal consumption vector, $X = (X_1, \ldots, X_T) = (x_{11}, \ldots, x_{nT})$. *Lifetime consumption paths* are vectors of dimension nT, and R denotes a preference ordering over lifetime consumption paths; I shall assume that R can be represented by an *intertemporal utility function, $U(X)$*.

We now turn to prices. There are two interpretations of "price" in the intertemporal model, one based on "futures prices" and the other on "spot prices and interest rates," or "spot prices" for short. In the futures markets interpretation, $\hat{p}_{it}$ denotes the amount that must be paid now, at the beginning of period 1, for a contract promising to deliver one unit of good i in period t. We let $\hat{P}_t$ and $\hat{P}$ denote the vectors of futures prices corresponding to X_t and X. The total "cost" of the lifetime consumption plan $X = (x_{11}, \ldots, x_{nT})$ is given by

$$\sum_{\tau=1}^{T} \sum_{k=1}^{n} \hat{p}_{k\tau} x_{k\tau}$$

All market transactions are required to take place at the beginning of period 1, and no markets are open thereafter.

The "spot price" interpretation gives a different gloss to the same model. Instead of futures markets, we assume perfect foresight and let p_{it} denote the "spot" price of x_{it}: That is, p_{it} is the amount which must be paid in period t for the delivery of one unit of good i in period t. We also assume perfect capital markets, so that individuals can borrow or lend without limit at the market rate of interest, and we let r_t denote the interest rate connecting period t with period $t + 1$. There is no period 0, but by convention we let $r_0 = 0$. The present value of the lifetime consumption path X is given by

$$\sum_{\tau=1}^{T} \prod_{v=0}^{\tau-1} \left(\frac{1}{1+r_v}\right) \sum_{k=1}^{n} p_{k\tau} x_{k\tau}$$

The formal identity of the perfect foresight model and the futures market model becomes apparent when we define *present value prices, $\hat{p}_{it}$*:

$$\hat{p}_{it} = p_{it} \prod_{v=0}^{t-1} \left(\frac{1}{1+r_v}\right)$$

In terms of present value prices, the present value of the lifetime consumption path is given by

$$\sum_{\tau=1}^{T} \sum_{k=1}^{n} \hat{p}_{k\tau} x_{k\tau}$$

Radner (1970) summarizes both interpretations of the intertemporal allocation model in his review of Arrow–Debreu theory, emphasizing that in the spot as well as in the futures version, "agents have the access to the complete system of prices when choosing their plans." The spot version should not be confused with substantively more complex models involving sequences of markets.

The *futures price intertemporal cost-of-living index*, $\hat{I}(\hat{P}^a, \hat{P}^b, s, R)$, is defined by

$$\hat{I}(\hat{P}^a, \hat{P}^b, s, R) = \frac{E(\hat{P}^a, s)}{E(\hat{P}^b, s)}$$

where $E(\hat{P}, s)$ denotes the expenditure function corresponding to the intertemporal preference ordering R and $\hat{P}^a$ and $\hat{P}^b$ denote comparison and reference vectors of futures prices, respectively. This index, like any cost-of-living index, is the ratio of the expenditure required to attain a particular indifference curve of a particular preference ordering under two price regimes. It differs from the traditional one-period cost-of-living index in that: (a) the preference ordering on which the comparison is based is an intertemporal one which orders lifetime consumption paths; the traditional cost-of-living index is based on a one period preference ordering which orders consumption patterns for a single period and (b) the two price regimes being compared in the intertemporal index are intertemporal price regimes; the traditional cost-of-living index compares alternative price regimes for a single period. From a formal standpoint, the intertemporal index appropriate to a world with four goods and three periods is indistinguishable from a one-period index for a world with 12 goods; hence, all of the theorems of the traditional theory hold for the futures price intertemporal index. From a less formal standpoint, it might appear that the one-period index is relevant only for an individual who knows that he will die before the beginning of the next period, and that the intertemporal index is the appropriate index for anyone who expects to live into the next period. In section 2 I argue that there are analogues of the one-period index which are useful, interesting, and well defined in the intertemporal context under less morbid assumptions.

The *spot price intertemporal cost-of-living index*, $I(P^a, r^a, P^b, r^b, s, R)$, is defined by

$$I(P^a, r^a, P^b, r^b, s, R) = \frac{E(P^a, r^a, s)}{E(P^b, r^b, s)}$$

where $E(P, r, s)$ denotes the minimum value of

$$\sum_{\tau=1}^{T} \prod_{v=0}^{\tau-1} \left(\frac{1}{1 + r_v}\right) \sum_{k=1}^{n} p_{k\tau} x_{k\tau}$$

required to attain the indifference curve s of the intertemporal utility function. The difference between the "spot" and the "futures price" versions of the intertemporal cost-of-living index is one of notation rather than of substance. The "spot" version explicitly identifies the role of interest rates, while their role remains implicit in the "futures price" version.

The effect of a change in an interest rate on the intertemporal cost-of-living index is easy to analyze. Consider an increase in r_t; such an increase will decrease the present value price of every good in every period after period t; hence, an increase in r_t causes the intertemporal index to decline.[1]

It is well known that the Arrow–Debreu theory can be reinterpreted to allow for uncertainty about the environment by treating the x's as *contingent commodities*. (See Radner, 1970, for a summary and references.) Although I shall not elaborate the details here, it is clear that the *contingent commodity* interpretation leads directly to a theory of the cost-of-living index under uncertainty.

2. SUBINDEXES

The traditional theory of the cost-of-living index provides a rationale for constructing complete indexes, that is, for constructing one-period indexes in a one-period world or, what is formally the same thing, for constructing T period indexes in a T period world; but it offers no guidance for constructing one-period indexes in a multiperiod world. We need a theory of "subindexes" of the cost-of-living index to provide a theoretical rationale for comparing alternative one-period price vectors in a multiperiod setting. In this section, I summarize the theory of subindexes developed in Pollak (1975) and apply it to the construction of one-period subindexes.

Although we are interested in applying the theory of subindexes to the construction of one-period indexes in a multiperiod setting, I state the formal definitions in more general terms. In Pollak (1975), I argue that the theory of subindexes is relevant to the construction of indexes for particular groups of goods, such as "clothing," "footwear," or "men's shoes"; to the construction of indexes which ignore the labor–leisure choice and deal only with goods and services; to indexes which ignore the environment, or goods provided by governments; and, of course, to the construction of one-period indexes in a multiperiod setting.

To construct any subindex we must specify the two price regimes to be compared, the base preference ordering, and the base indifference curve. Typically, we begin with the two price vectors we wish to compare, and the problem is to select an appropriate base preference ordering, and, from it, a base indifference curve. If the complete utility function is separable, then it is natural to construct a subindex on the basis of a "specific" utility function. We call a subindex based on a specific or "category" utility function a *partial cost-of-living index*. If we are interested in comparing two vectors of clothing prices, the meaning of this assertion is straightforward; if we want to compare alternative one-period spot price vectors in a multiperiod world, its meaning requires careful interpretation. The most plausible interpretation is the following: we wish to compare two n-dimensional vectors of spot prices, P_*^a and P_*^b; these vectors may correspond to actual spot prices in two periods (for example, this period and the previous period), but they may equally well represent hypothetical vectors of spot prices for the same period generated by alternative public policy measures or by alternative assumptions about the behavior of some exogenous variables such as the weather. The interpretation of the two price regimes as representing hypothetical prices for the same period provides the best starting point for considering one-period subindexes, since some special problems which arise when we compare this period's spot prices with last period's spot prices are absent in hypothetical comparisons.

If the intertemporal utility function is separable by periods, then the one-period utility functions are the "specific" utility functions on which a subindex might be constructed. To focus on the problem of choosing an appropriate one-period preference ordering, consider an individual whose one-period preference orderings vary in a definite and predictable pattern over his life cycle, so that his marginal rate of substitution of baby food for foreign vacations is predictably different depending on whether the calculation is based on his one-period preferences corresponding to age 20, 25, or 50. The construction of a subindex to compare two alternative hypothetical spot price vectors, P_*^b and P_*^a clearly requires the selection of a base one-period preference ordering, just as the construction of the traditional index to compare two price vectors requires the selection of a base preference ordering. The construction of a subindex to compare this period's spot prices with last period's spot prices is essentially the same as the construction of a subindex to compare two hypothetical spot price vectors; there is no presumption in either case that the appropriate one-period preference ordering must be the one corresponding to either this period's or last period's tastes.[2]

We first define the relevant notion of separability.

Definition. Suppose that the goods are partitioned into two subsets, θ and $\bar{\theta}$; denote the vectors of goods in θ and $\bar{\theta}$ by X_θ and $X_{\bar{\theta}}$, respectively.[3] We say that the goods in θ are *separable* from those in $\bar{\theta}$ if the utility function can be written as

$$U(X) = U(X_\theta, X_{\bar{\theta}}) = V[V^\theta(X_\theta), X_{\bar{\theta}}]$$

We call $V^\theta(X_\theta)$ the *category utility function* and denote the corresponding preference ordering by R_θ.

When we speak of a preference ordering or a utility function as *separable*, we refer to this nonsymmetric form of separability rather than the more familiar notion of "weak separability." If the utility function is "weakly separable,"

$$U(X) = V[V^1(X_1), \ldots, V^m(X_m)]$$

then the goods in any category are separable from the remaining goods. But the assumption that the goods in θ are separable from those in $\bar{\theta}$ is less restrictive than weak separability, since separability does not require the goods in $\bar{\theta}$ or its subsets to be separable from those in θ. The earliest papers on separability, Leontief (1947a, 1947b), and Sono (1961) emphasized this nonsymmetric form of separability, but later work such as Strotz (1957) and Goldman and Uzawa (1964) emphasized symmetric versions. The non-symmetric version is now undergoing a renaissance as "recursive separability." A good summary and references can be found in Blackorby, Primont, and Russell (1975).

Definition. Suppose that the goods are partitioned into two subsets, θ and $\bar{\theta}$, and that the goods in θ are separable from those in $\bar{\theta}$. The *partial expenditure function* for category θ, $E^\theta(P_\theta, s_\theta)$, is defined by

$$E^\theta(P_\theta, s_\theta) = \min \sum_{k \in \theta} p_k x_k$$

subject to $V^\theta(X_\theta) = s_\theta$ where $V^\theta(X_\theta)$ is the category utility function and s_θ denotes an indifference curve of $V^\theta(X_\theta)$.

That is, the partial expenditure function shows the minimum expenditure required to attain the indifference curve s_θ of the category utility function $V^\theta(X_\theta)$.

We now define the *partial cost of living index*.

Definition. Suppose that the goods are partitioned into two subsets, θ and $\bar{\theta}$, and that the goods in θ are separable from those in $\bar{\theta}$. The *partial cost of living index* for category θ, $I^\theta(P_\theta^a, P_\theta^b, s_\theta, R^\theta)$, is defined by

$$I^\theta(P_\theta^a, P_\theta^b, s_\theta, R^\theta) = \frac{E^\theta(P_\theta^a, s_\theta)}{E^\theta(P_\theta^b, s_\theta)}$$

The partial cost-of-living index differs from the complete index in that: (a) the preference ordering on which the comparison is based is a category preference ordering rather than the complete preference ordering, and (b) the two price regimes being compared are partial price regimes and, hence, are represented by price vectors of lower dimensionality than the complete price vector. If preferences are separable, then the partial index is a "natural" subindex. Its principal limitation is that it is defined only when preferences are separable.

The subscript θ in the comparison and reference price vectors is somewhat misleading. The base preference ordering is identified by R^θ, and s_θ denotes an indifference curve from that preference ordering. The comparison and reference price vectors, P_θ^a and P_θ^b, must be dimensionally consistent with R. That is, if θ identifies "food" and there are seven goods in the food category, the reference and comparison price vectors must each have seven elements. If P_*^a and P_*^b are any two vectors dimensionally consistent with R, then we can calculate the cost-of-living index $I(P_*^a, P_*^b, s, R)$. We interpret the index by treating P_*^a and P_*^b as if they were alternative vectors of "food" prices. That is, we treat the comparison between P_*^a and P_*^b as one between P_θ^a and P_θ^b where $P_\theta^a = P_*^a$ and $P_\theta^b = P_*^b$. In the "food" context, this is of no importance whatever; even if there happen to be the same number of clothing goods as food goods, no one would form an index to compare a vector of food prices with a vector of clothing prices. But in the intertemporal context, the most natural comparison is between vectors of spot prices corresponding to different periods.[4]

If the intertemporal utility function is weakly separable by periods

$$U(X) = W[V^1(X_1), \ldots, V^T(X_T)]$$

the partial cost-of-living index for period t, $I^t(P_*^a, P_*^b, s_t, R^t)$, is given by

$$I^t(P_*^a, P_*^b, s_t, R^t) = \frac{E^t(P_*^a, s_t)}{E^t(P_*^b, s_t)}$$

where P_*^a and P_*^b are alternative one-period price vectors and $E^t(P_*, s_t)$ is the cost function corresponding to the one-period utility function $V^t(X_t)$ and s_t denotes an indifference curve of $V^t(X_t)$. The partial cost-of-living index for period t is based on the preference ordering for period t, R^t, but it can be used to compare price vectors from any periods. For example, the index $I(P_1^a, P_2^b, s_t, R^t)$ compares spot prices from period 1 with spot prices from period 2 on the basis of the preferences of period t. We can view this as a comparison of two hypothetical vectors of spot prices from period t, P_t^a and P_t^b, where $P_t^a = P_1^a$ and $P_t^b = P_2^b$.

If the intertemporal utility function is weakly separable by periods, we can construct a partial cost-of-living index on the basis of any one of the T one-period utility functions $\{V^1, \ldots, V^T\}$. The choice of an appropriate base preference ordering is not a matter for technical economic analysis, although Fisher and Shell (1968) argue convincingly that the most interesting base preference ordering is likely to be the one reflecting the tastes of the current period.

Thus far we have identified the indifference curve to be attained in the expenditure function and the cost-of-living index by the value of the utility function, s. In discussing the relationship between subindexes, it is more convenient to specify the base indifference curve by means of a "base" commodity bundle, X^0, than by the value of the utility function. We write the expenditure function as $E(P, X^0)$ and the cost-of-living index as $I(P^a, P^b, X^0, R)$ instead of $E(P, s)$ and $I(P^a, P^b, s, R)$. The notation is slightly sloppy, since the same symbol is used to denote expenditure as a function of the $2n$ variables (P, X^0) and the $n + 1$ variables (P, s), but the meaning is unambiguous. In the new notation, the partial expenditure function becomes $E^\theta(P_\theta, X^0)$ and the partial cost-of-living index $I^\theta(P_\theta^a, P_\theta^b, X_\theta^0, R^\theta)$.

We now define the *conditional expenditure function*.

Definition. Suppose that the goods are partitioned into two subsets, θ and $\bar{\theta}$, and let $X^0 = (X^0_\theta, X^0_{\bar{\theta}})$ be the base commodity bundle. The *conditional expenditure function* for category θ, $E^\theta(P_\theta, X^0)$, is given by

$$E^\theta(P_\theta, X^0) = \min_{k \in \theta} \sum p_k x_k$$

subject to $U(X_\theta, X_{\bar{\theta}}) = U(X^0)$ and $X_{\bar{\theta}} = X^0_{\bar{\theta}}$.

That is, the conditional expenditure function shows the expenditure on the goods in θ required to attain the indifference curve of X^0 when the goods in $\bar{\theta}$ are fixed at the levels $X^0_{\bar{\theta}}$. The conditional expenditure function is analogous to a "short-run" variable cost function in production theory, where the goods in θ and $\bar{\theta}$ correspond to variable and fixed inputs, respectively. It is also closely related to the conditional compensated demand functions introduced in Pollak (1969).

Definition. Let $\{\theta, \bar{\theta}\}$ be a partition of the set of all goods. The *conditional cost-of-living index* for category θ, $L^\theta(P^a_\theta, P^b_\theta, X^0, R)$, is given by

$$L^\theta(P^a_\theta, P^b_\theta, X^0, R) = \frac{E^\theta(P^a_\theta, X^0)}{E^\theta(P^b_\theta, X^0)}$$

The conditional cost-of-living index has all the properties of a traditional cost-of-living index. To prove this, we have only to verify that it corresponds to a "well-behaved" preference ordering, namely, the conditional preference ordering over X_θ given $X^0_{\bar{\theta}}$; the base indifference curve is specified by the requirement that X_θ must satisfy $U[X_\theta, X^0_{\bar{\theta}}] = U[X^0_\theta, X^0_{\bar{\theta}}]$.[5]

If the goods in θ are separable from those in $\bar{\theta}$

$$U(X_\theta, X_{\bar{\theta}}) = W[V^\theta(X_\theta), X_{\bar{\theta}}]$$

then the conditional expenditure function for the goods in θ is independent of $X^0_{\bar{\theta}}$. This follows immediately from the definition of the conditional expenditure function as the minimum expenditure on the goods in θ subject to

$$U(X_\theta, X^0_{\bar{\theta}}) = U(X^0_\theta, X^0_{\bar{\theta}})$$

since this constraint becomes

$$V^\theta(X_\theta) = V^\theta(X^0_\theta)$$

and is independent of $X^0_{\bar{\theta}}$. Hence, if the goods in θ are separable from those in $\bar{\theta}$, the conditional cost-of-living index is independent of $X^0_{\bar{\theta}}$.

Conversely, the separable case is the only one in which the conditional cost-of-living index is independent of $X^0_{\bar{\theta}}$. That is, the conditional index is independent of the goods in $\bar{\theta}$ if and only if the goods in θ are separable from those in $\bar{\theta}$. Thus, the separable case is the only one in which the goods in $\bar{\theta}$ drop out and play no role in the conditional cost-of-living index. Furthermore, if the goods in θ are separable from those in $\bar{\theta}$, then the conditional index coincides with the partial index. These results are proved in Pollak (1975).

These theorems summarize the relationships between the partial and conditional indexes. The partial index embodies our intuitive view that in the separable case we can construct meaningful subindexes on the basis of category utility functions. The conditional index is an extension of the partial index to the general case.

In Pollak (1975) I also define the *generalized conditional cost-of-living index*, $L^\theta(P^a_\theta, P^b_\theta, X^*_{\bar{\theta}}, X^0, R)$. This index is based on the conditional preference ordering corresponding to $X^*_{\bar{\theta}}$, which, in the intertemporal context, specifies consumption in "other periods." The base indifference curve is identified by X^0. In the conditional index, X^0 plays a double role: It identifies the base indifference curve and it also specifies the levels at which the goods in $\bar{\theta}$ are held fixed. In the generalized conditional index, these roles are separated. If $X^*_{\bar{\theta}} = X^0_{\bar{\theta}}$, then the generalized conditional index coincides with the conditional index.

Separability is the crucial simplifying condition for the construction of one-period indexes, since it allows us to ignore consumption outside the period for which we are constructing the index. If the period for which we are constructing the index is not separable from the rest, then the conditional index for that period depends on consumption in other periods. In the absence of this type of separability, to construct a subindex for period t we must specify a base consumption vector X^0 which serves a double function: It identifies the conditional preference ordering on which the index is based, and it identifies a base indifference curve. The theory does not dictate the choice of a particular X^0, and guidance must be sought from the problem at hand

3. HABIT FORMATION

In this section I discuss the implications of habit formation for the construction of the complete intertemporal cost-of-living index and for one-period subindexes. The usual discussion of habit formation begins with a short-run utility function some of whose parameters depend on past consumption. Given a specification of the levels of consumption of all goods in the previous period, we can use this preference ordering as a base on which to construct a one-period cost-of-living index. But the dependence of this index on the specified consumption history does present a difficulty unless the problem at hand singles out a particular consumption history as uniquely appropriate. An implication of C. C. von Weizsäcker's analysis of habit formation (von Weizsäcker, 1971) is that one can construct a cost-of-living index without specifying a consumption history by basing it on the *long-run utility function*, that is, the utility function which rationalizes the long-run or steady-state demand functions. I have argued elsewhere (Pollak, 1976) that von Weizsäcker's analysis is incorrect: Except in rare special cases von Weizsäcker's long-run utility function does not exist, and even when it does exist, it has no welfare significance; hence, the "long-run utility function" does not provide a satisfactory framework for constructing a cost-of-living index.[5b]

Virtually all specifications of habit formation assume that the individual does not recognize the impact of his present consumption on his future tastes. This assumption, coupled with the assumption that total expenditure in each period is determined exogenously, substantially simplifies the analysis of demand behavior in each period. But it is difficult to integrate a model of allocation within a single period based on these assumptions into the intertemporal allocation framework. I call a specification of habit formation in which an individual does not recognize that his present consumption has an impact on his future tastes *naive habit formation*. In contrast, *rational habit formation* refers to a specification in which the individual takes full account of the effect of his current consumption on his future preferences. In a model of rational habit formation an individual maximizes an intertemporal utility function, and this utility function can serve as the base preference ordering for a complete intertemporal cost-of-living index. But because current consumption influences future tastes, the intertemporal preference ordering is not separable by periods, so one-period subindexes must be conditional rather than partial indexes. Naive habit formation, because it resists incorporation into a model of intertemporal allocation, does not provide a satisfactory starting point for constructing a complete intertemporal cost-of-living index.

The usual approach to habit formation is to begin with a "short-run" utility function, postulate that some of its parameters depend on past consumption, and examine the resulting system of short-run demand functions. See, for example, Stone (1966) and Pollak (1970). Formally, let $V(X_t; X_{t-1})$ denote a short-run utility function over X_t, given the consumption history X_{t-1}. In period t the individual takes X_{t-1} as given and chooses X_t to maximize $V(X_t; X_{t-1})$ subject to the budget constraint $\sum_{k=1}^{n} p_{kt} x_{kt} = \mu_t$, where μ_t denotes total expenditure. Total expenditure is assumed to be exogenously determined and the focus of the analysis is on the determination of the consumption pattern for a particular period; we denote the short-run demand functions by $X_t = h(P_t, \mu_t, X_{t-1})$. This approach appears somewhat ad hoc when viewed against the models of intertemporal allocation discussed in section 1, but this comparison ignores the essentially empirical orientation of the habit model. The habit model is intended to provide an empirically useful dynamic generalization of the traditional static model of utility maximization, and has been reasonably successful in providing a theoretical foundation for empirical work.

One can certainly base a cost-of-living index on the short-run preference ordering R_* corresponding to the utility function $V(X_t; X_{t-1})$. We first define the expenditure function, $E(P_*, X_*^-, X_*^0)$, as the minimum expenditure required to attain the indifference curve X_*^0 at prices P_* when consumption in the previous period was equal to X_*^-. In this notation, X_*^0 and X_*^- are one-period consumption vectors, and $E(P_*, X_*^-, X_*^0) = \min \sum_{k=1}^n p_{k*} x_{k*}$ subject to $V(X_*; X_*^-) = V(X_*^0; X_*^-)$. We define the cost-of-living index, $I(P_*^a, P_*^b, X_*^-, X_*^0, R_*)$, by

$$I(P_*^a, P_*^b, X_*^-, X_*^0, R_*) = \frac{E(P_*^a, X_*^-, X_*^0)}{E(P_*^b, X_*^-, X_*^0)}$$

The index compares the cost of attaining the indifference curve of X_*^0 in the price situations P_*^a and P_*^b.

Since short-run preferences depend on past consumption, construction of the short-run index requires us to specify the consumption history to identify the base preference ordering. The situation is analogous to the role of consumption in "other periods" in the generalized conditional index. As in that case, specification of an appropriate consumption history must come from the problem being considered.

The short-run demand functions of the habit model imply a system of long-run or steady-state demand functions. Formally, the long-run demand functions are defined as the steady-state solutions to the system of short-run demand functions: $X_* = h(P_*, \mu_*, X_*)$. We denote the long-run demand functions by $X_* = H(P_*, \mu_*)$. C. C. von Weizsäcker (1971) claims that the long-run demand functions of the habit formation model can be rationalized by a utility function, $V(X_*)$, and argues that this utility function is an appropriate indicator of welfare. If von Weizsäcker is correct, then we can use the long-run utility function as a base for the one-period cost-of-living index and avoid the problem of specifying a consumption history. But we can only do this if the long-run utility function exists. In Pollak (1976) I show that von Weizsäcker is incorrect about the existence of the long-run utility function: the long-run demand functions can be rationalized by a utility function only in very special cases. The demonstration is long and tedious, and I shall not attempt to summarize it here. I also argue in Pollak (1976) that even when the long-run utility function exists, it has no welfare significance. That is, the long-run utility function is the same type of construct as a community indifference map which rationalizes market demand functions; if it exists, it is a convenient device for coding all of the information about demand behavior, but this is all. (See Samuelson, 1956). In general, market demand functions cannot be rationalized by a "market utility function." In those special cases when they can be, the utility function must be scrupulously interpreted in terms of positive economics; it has no normative or welfare significance.

The question of the welfare interpretation of the long-run utility function reduces to the following: Suppose that there exists a sequence of consumption bundles which enable an individual to go from an initial consumption situation X_*^0 to a terminal situation $\bar{X}_*$ in a finite number of steps, feeling that he is better off at each step than at the one before. Does this imply that he is better off—in terms of his own preferences—at $\bar{X}_*$ than at X_*^0? To quote from Pollak (1976): "I interpret an individual's willingness to move from X_*^0 to $\bar{X}_*$ in a sequence of small steps when he is unwilling to do so in a single large step as indicative of his failure to understand the habit formation mechanism, and not of the underlying superiority of $\bar{X}_*$." Consider, for example, the process by which a noneater of artichokes develops a taste for artichokes by gradually increasing his consumption of them; consider the same process for cigarettes. This is precisely what von Weizsäcker has in mind when he speaks of long-run preferences, but the interpretation of such sequences in terms of "long-run preferences" is misleading. The relevant notion of preference must surely be an intertemporal one, not one which depends crucially on the individual's failure to understand the dynamics of his own tastes.

One might think that the utility function $V^*(X_*) = V(X_*; X_*)$ would rationalize the steady state demand functions. But even when the long-run demand functions can be rationalized by a utility function, that utility function does not coincide with $V^*(X_*)$. In the habit model, the individual makes a sequence of short-run decisions and always treats his own past consumption as fixed. Maximization of $V^*(X_*)$ implies maximization with respect to both current and past values and hence is not consistent with the habit model.[6]

Since neither the long-run utility function nor an approach based on $V^*(X_*)$ provides a satisfactory cost-of-living index, the construction of a one-period index in the habit model requires the specification of a consumption history, and the resulting index reflects not only the prices being compared, but also the particular consumption history specified.

The habit model of Pollak (1970) is a modification of the static one-period approach of traditional demand theory. Tastes in each period depend on consumption in the previous period, and perhaps also on consumption in the more distant past. However, the model requires that the individual make current consumption decisions in a one-period framework without recognizing that these decisions will affect his future tastes. I say that an individual who fails to take account of the impact of his current consumption on his future tastes exhibits *naive habit formation*.

In the naive habit model of Pollak (1970), total expenditure in each period is taken as given. There are two ways to embed this model in a more general one which explains the determination of total expenditure in each period. The first is to assume that savings decisions reflect some rule of thumb, rather than maximization of an intertemporal utility function. This approach precludes construction of a complete intertemporal cost-of-living index, since such an index is based on an intertemporal utility function. The second way to explain the determination of total expenditure in each period is to integrate naive habit formation into a model of intertemporal allocation. There are several ways to do this, none of them very satisfactory. If we are not concerned with the individual's allocation of expenditure within any period except period 1, then the naive habit model is consistent with an intertemporal utility function of the form

$$U(X) = W[V(X_1; X_0), X_2, \ldots, X_T; X_0]$$

This implies that allocation within period 1 is made without reference to the future; it does not, however, imply that the allocation within period 2 can be made without reference to the future. If we require that allocation in each period be independent of the future, we are led to an intertemporal utility function of the form

$$U(X) = W[V(X_1, X_0), V(X_2, X_0), \ldots, V(X_T, X_0)]$$

This implies that the individual behaves as if his current one-period preferences will persist in all future periods. The persistent preference solution permits the construction of a complete intertemporal cost-of-living index, but the implied index is based on an intertemporal preference ordering which embodies a false and repeatedly falsified assumption about preferences.

The naive habit model is susceptible to two serious criticisms. First, it does not deal with the determination of total expenditure in each period, and it cannot easily be modified to do so in an acceptable way: Neither the rule of thumb nor the persistent preference solution is appealing. Second, the naive model does not even produce a satisfactory account of the allocation of expenditure within a single period. The basic assumption of the naive habit model—an assumption carried over from traditional demand theory—is that total expenditure can be allocated among the goods available in each period without considering the future. But an individual whose current tastes depend on his past consumption might be expected to realize that his future tastes will depend on his current consumption; and once he realizes this, his choice of a current consumption pattern will take account of its impact on his future tastes. The hallmark of naive habit formation is that the individual does not allow for the impact of his current consumption on his future tastes.

We now consider a version of habit formation in which the individual takes full account of the impact of current consumption on future preferences.[7] Consider the weakly separable intertemporal utility function

$$U(X) = W[V(X_1), \ldots, V(X_T)]$$

Now replace each of the one-period utility functions by a *short-run utility function* which depends on both current consumption and consumption in the previous period. This yields

$$U(X) = W[V(X_1, X_0), V(X_2, X_1), \ldots, V(X_T, X_{T-1})]$$

This intertemporal utility function is the basis for the model of *rational* habit formation. Since the new utility function is not separable by periods, it is not correct to call $V(X_t, X_{t-1})$ a *one-period utility function* except in a metaphoric sense. From the standpoint of empirical analysis of the allocation of expenditure within each period, rational habit formation provides a much less tractable model than naive habit formation. Because the intertemporal utility function is not separable, the allocation of expenditure within each period cannot be understood without reference to behavior in future periods. We can define an intertemporal cost-of-living index on the basis of the intertemporal utility function; but since the intertemporal preference ordering is not separable by periods, the appropriate subindex is the conditional rather than the partial cost-of-living index.[8]

4. SUMMARY AND IMPLICATIONS

In this section I summarize the discussion of the last three sections and develop its implications for the treatment of interest rates.

There are two ways in which the theory of the cost-of-living index can be extended from its traditional one-period framework to yield a complete index in a multiperiod setting. The first relies on futures prices and yields an index which has all the properties of the traditional cost-of-living index, differing from it only in that it is based on the intertemporal preference ordering, and the prices it compares are futures prices. The second assumes perfect foresight and perfect capital markets, and uses spot prices and interest rates to construct the complete intertemporal index; the resulting index is formally identical to one based on futures prices with "present-value prices" playing their role. These intertemporal cost-of-living indexes provide a theoretically satisfying solution to the problem of constructing a complete cost-of-living index in a multiperiod framework.

The trouble with these intertemporal cost-of-living indexes is a practical one. Futures markets do not exist for most commodities, expectations are not held with certainty, and capital markets are not perfect. The gap between theory and practice appears greater for the complete intertemporal index than for the usual one-period index. The difficulties which stand in the way of constructing the complete intertemporal index provide one motivation for focusing on subindexes which compare alternative one-period spot price vectors. Such subindexes would be of interest even if we could construct the complete intertemporal index, and since we cannot, they are the best we can hope to do. In Pollak (1975) I develop a theory of subindexes. If preferences are separable, I define the "partial" cost-of-living index in the "natural" way on the basis of the category utility function. If preferences are not separable, I define the "conditional" index. The conditional index is based on the conditional preference ordering; the consumption of other goods is held fixed at predetermined levels. I show that, when the group of goods for which we are constructing the subindex is separable from the rest, then the conditional index is independent of the predetermined levels of the remaining goods and coincides with the partial index. Furthermore, this is the only case in which the conditional index is independent of the other goods.

The theory of subindexes applies directly to the construction of one-period indexes in a multiperiod world. If the period whose preferences we are using as the base for constructing the subindex is separable from the rest, then the partial index is the "natural" one-period index. If it is not, we must turn to the conditional index. To specify the base preference ordering for the conditional index we must specify the level of consumption of every good in every other period. This specification must come from the particular problem which the index is intended to resolve, not from abstract theoretical arguments.

If the intertemporal utility function is weakly separable by periods

$$U(X) = W[V^1(X_1), \ldots, V^T(X_T)]$$

we can base a comparison of one-period price vectors on any of the T one-period preference orderings $\{V^1, \ldots, V^T\}$. Again, the problem at hand must dictate the choice of a particular base preference ordering, and, once it has been selected, the choice of a base indifference curve.

Habit formation presents a new set of conceptual difficulties. Because it was introduced into demand analysis as a dynamic generalization of the one-period static models of traditional demand theory—the usual approach is to begin with a short-run utility function and assume that some of its parameters depend on past consumption—habit formation is difficult to integrate into a model of intertemporal allocation. It is straightforward to construct a one-period cost-of-living index in this model by specifying consumption levels for all goods in the previous period and basing the index on the short-run preference ordering implied by that consumption history. The problem at hand must determine the choice of an appropriate consumption history on which to base the index, and it is incorrect to view the process of selecting a particular consumption history as one which imparts an element of arbitrariness to the index.

Since the habit model leads to long-run or steady-state demand behavior which is independent of past consumption, it might be thought that we could circumvent the problem of specifying a consumption history by following C. C. von Weizsäcker's procedure and basing the cost-of-living index on the utility function which rationalizes the long-run demand functions. This is incorrect. First, except in certain special cases, the long-run demand functions cannot be rationalized by a long-run utility function. Second, even when such a utility function exists, it has no welfare significance. There is no justification for using the long-run utility function as a base for a cost-of-living index.

To construct a complete intertemporal cost-of-living index in a habit formation model it is first necessary to integrate habit formation into an intertemporal allocation model. This requires us to distinguish between naive and rational habit formation. An individual who fails to take account of the impact of his current consumption on his future tastes exhibits naive habit formation; it does not seem to be possible to integrate naive habit formation into a multiperiod model in a way which yields a plausible intertemporal cost-of-living index. This is unfortunate since most habit models considered in demand analysis are of this type.

An individual who recognizes the impact of his current consumption on his future tastes exhibits *rational habit formation*. Since every consumption decision always allows for its impact on "future tastes," rational habit formation can and must be treated in a multiperiod model, and the complete intertemporal cost-of-living index is defined in a straightforward way. Since the intertemporal utility function implied by rational habit formation is not separable, the appropriate one-period subindex is the conditional rather than the partial index.

The implications of this analysis for the treatment of interest rates are straightforward. We first consider their treatment in the complete intertemporal index, and then in one-period subindexes.

We defined two complete intertemporal cost-of-living indexes in section 1, the "futures" index, $\hat{I}(\hat{P}^a, \hat{P}^b, s, R)$, which does not explicitly depend on interest rates, and the "spot" index, $I(P^a, r^a, P^b, r^b, s, R)$, which does. As we saw in section 1, an increase in any interest rate will cause the spot index to decline. If we regard futures prices as functions of spot prices and interest rates, that is, as present value prices, then the futures index will reflect changes in interest rates through the implied changes in present-value prices. If, on the other hand, we regard futures prices themselves as fundamental, then the question of the role of interest rates seems ill-posed, since the question presupposes that it is appropriate to treat interest rates as independent variables.

It might be thought that interest rates would also affect the complete intertemporal index through their effects on the prices of the services of consumer durables. For definiteness, we discuss this problem in terms of the spot index, but essentially the same analysis applies to the futures index. If some of the x's represent the services of consumer durables, then the corresponding p's are the spot prices of these services (that is, the one-period rentals), and there is no difficulty treating a change in interest rates, whether or not it is acompanied by changes in these rental prices (it need not be, if there are offsetting changes elsewhere, say, in factor prices). Changes in spot prices caused by changes in interest rates have the same effect on the index as the same changes in spot prices caused by changes in raw materials prices; the fact that the underlying change was in interest rates does not imply that special treatment is called for. Since we do not usually observe rental prices for the services of consumer durables, we must compute implicit rentals for them from observable prices and interest rates. In the absence of transactions costs and various other "frictions," it is possible to calculate an implicit price for the services of a consumer durable in period t using its purchase price in period t, its expected second-hand price in $t + 1$, and the interest rate, r_t. If we use this procedure, then changes in interest rates will cause changes in the implicit prices of the services of consumer durables. But it is useful to keep separate the direct effects of changes in interest rates and the indirect effects which operate through the implicit prices of the services of consumer durables, just as it is useful to keep separate the direct effect of higher gasoline prices and the indirect effects which operate through higher explicit prices of goods shipped by truck.

Since the purpose of a one-period subindex is to focus on a particular period and to isolate it from intertemporal complications, one would not expect such a subindex to involve the interest rate directly, but only indirectly, through its effect on the implicit prices of the services of consumer durables.

An examination of the definition of the conditional index bears out this expectation. To construct a conditional subindex for period t, we hold fixed the levels of consumption of all goods in all other periods and calculate the ratio of the expenditures on the goods in period t required to attain a particular indifference curve. These expenditures depend on the vectors of spot prices being compared, but are independent of interest rates and of prices in other periods. Hence, interest rates play no direct role in one-period subindexes, but when prices of the services of consumer durables are not observable, interest rates play an indirect role through their effect on the implicit rentals of the services of consumer durables.

NOTES

This research was supported in part by the U.S. Bureau of Labor Statistics and the National Science Foundation. I am grateful to Franklin M. Fisher, Steven M. Goldman and Jack E. Triplett for some very helpful comments, but neither they, the University of Pennsylvania, the Bureau of Labor Statistics, nor the National Science Foundation should be held responsible for the views expressed. Revised October 1974.

1. This does not imply that every individual is better off with higher interest rates. The cost-of-living index measures the effect of changes in prices and interest rates on the present cost of attaining a particular indifference curve, but it ignores their effects on an individual's net worth.

2. The situation is similar in international price comparisons, where there is no presumption that the appropriate preference ordering on which to base a comparison of Japanese and French prices must be either Japanese or French tastes; indeed, if the U.S. government is trying to set cost-of-living differentials for its diplomats in Paris and Tokyo, it would be appropriate to base the comparison on U.S. tastes.

3. Hereafter "goods" or "commodities" will be used interchangeably to refer to the arguments of the complete utility function; the intertemporal model involves nT "goods."

4. It would violate no formal rule of analysis to use the partial index to compare vectors of futures prices corresponding to different periods, but the spot price interpretation seems to be a more "natural" one for one-period subindexes.

5. By a "well-behaved" preference ordering we mean one which can be represented by a continuous utility function which is quasi-concave and nondecreasing in its arguments.

5b. In a very interesting paper, Peter J. Hammond (1974) investigates the existence of a *long-run preference relation* without requiring the relation to be an ordering.

6. Furthermore, the utility function $V^*(X_*)$ depends not only on the conditional preference ordering over X_t given X_*^-, but also on the cardinal properties of the short-run utility function $V(X_t; X_{t-1})$ used to represent that conditional preference ordering. For example, the short-run utility functions $V(X_t; X_{t-1})$ and $V(X_t; X_{t-1}) + \phi(X_{t-1})$ represent the same conditional preference ordering over X_t given X_{t-1}; but the utility functions $V(X_*; X_*)$ and $V(X_*; X_*) + \phi(X_*)$ imply different preference orderings over X_*.

7. See Lluch (1974) for a treatment of consumption patterns and saving behavior in a model of rational habit formation.

8. I am grateful to Steven M. Goldman for helpful comments on this and related issues. See Goldman (1975) for an analysis of when it is possible to construct a conditional cost-of-living index which depends only on past levels of consumption.

REFERENCES

Blackorby, C., D. Primont, and R. R. Russell, "Budgeting, Decentralization, and Aggregation," *Annals of Economic and Social Measurement*, Vol. 4, No. 1 (Winter 1975), pp. 23–44.

Fisher, F. M., and K. Shell, "Taste and Quality Change in the Pure Theory of the True Cost-of-Living Index," in J. N. Wolfe, ed., *Value, Capital, and Growth: Papers in Honour of Sir John Hicks*, Edinburgh: University of Edinburgh Press, 1968.

Goldman, S. M., "Comment," *Annals of Economic and Social Measurement*, Vol. 4, No. 1 (Winter 1975), pp. 197–198.

Goldman, S. M., and H. Uzawa, "A Note on Separability in Demand Analysis," *Econometrica*, Vol. 32, No. 3 (July 1964), pp. 387–398.

Hammond, Peter J., "Endogenous Tastes and Stable Long-Run Choice," 1974, mimeograph. Published in *Journal of Economic Theory*, Vol. 13, No. 2 (October 1976), pp. 329–340.

Leontief, W., "A Note on the Interrelation of Subsets of Independent Variables of a Continuous Function with Continuous First Derivatives," *Bulletin of the American Mathematical Society*, Vol. 53, No. 4 (April 1947). pp. 343–350. (1947a).

———, "Introduction to a Theory of the Internal Structure of Functional Relationships," *Econometrica*, Vol. 15, No. 4 (October 1947), pp. 361–373. (1947b).

Lluch, C., "Expenditure, Savings, and Habit Formation," *International Economic Review*, Vol. 15, No. 3 (October 1974), pp. 786–797.

Pollak, R. A., "Conditional Demand Functions and Consumption Theory," *Quarterly Journal of Economics*, Vol. 83, No. 1 (February 1969), pp. 60–78.

———, "Habit Formation and Dynamic Demand Functions," *Journal of Political Economy*, Vol. 78, No. 4 (July/August 1970), pp. 745–763.

———, "The Theory of the Cost-of-Living Index," Research Discussion Paper No. 11, Research Division, Office of Prices and Living Conditions, U.S. Bureau of Labor Statistics, June 1971.

———, "Subindexes of the Cost-of-Living Index," Research Discussion Paper No.15, Research Division, Office of Prices and Living Conditions, U.S. Bureau of Labor Statistics, June 1973, *International Economic Review*, Vol. 16, No. 1 (February 1975), pp. 135–150.

———, "Habit Formation and Long-Run Utility Functions," 1973, mimeograph. Published in *Journal of Economic Theory*, Vol. 13, No. 2 (October 1976), pp. 272–297.

Radner, R., "Problems in the Theory of Markets Under Uncertainty," *American Economic Review*, Vol. 60, No. 2 (May 1970), pp. 454–460.

Samuelson, P. A., "Social Indifference Curves," *Quarterly Journal of Economics*, Vol. 70, No. 1 (February 1956), pp. 1–22.

Sono, M., "The Effect of Price Changes on the Demand and Supply of Separable Goods," *International Economic Review*, Vol. 2, No. 3 (September 1961), pp. 239–271.

Stone, R., "The Changing Pattern of Consumption," in *Mathematics in the Social Sciences and Other Essays*, Cambridge, Massachusetts: M.I.T. Press, 1966.

Strotz, R. H., "The Empirical Implications of a Utility Tree," *Econometrica*, Vol. 25, No. 2 (April 1957), pp. 269–280.

von Weizsäcker, C. C., "Notes on Endogenous Change of Tastes," *Journal of Economic Theory*, Vol. 3, No. 4 (December 1971), pp. 345–372.

Welfare Evaluation and the Cost-of-Living Index in the Household Production Model

The household production model provides a new framework for the theory of the household, and most applications have focused on its implications for market and nonmarket behavior. In this paper I examine the consequences of the "new home economics" for welfare analysis, and in particular for the cost-of-living index.

In the household production framework market "goods" are combined with time to produce "commodities." These commodities, rather than the market goods, are the arguments of the household's preference ordering; the demand for goods and time is a "derived demand," since goods are not desired for their own sake, but only as inputs into the production of commodities.[1] This paper is an analysis of the implications of the household production model for welfare evaluation, not a critique of the model. Hence, it accepts the fundamental distinction between goods and commodities, and assumes that commodities as well as goods are observable and measurable.[2] The distinction between technology and tastes follows unambiguously from that between goods and commodities.

In orthodox demand theory the household's preference ordering is defined over the "goods space," and welfare analysis is based on those preferences. The cost-of-living index is defined as the ratio of the minimum expenditures required to attain a particular indifference curve of this preference ordering under two price regimes. In the household production model the preference ordering over the commodity space provides a corresponding basis for welfare evaluation. One way to extend the notion of the cost-of-living index to the new framework is to define it as the ratio of the minimum expenditures required to attain a particular indifference curve of this preference ordering under alternative price-technology regimes. This approach recognizes that the objects of the household's preference are commodities rather than goods and that both goods prices and the household's technology impose constraints on its choices; the resulting index, the *variable technology cost-of-living index*, reflects changes in both the technical and market constraints facing the household.

For some purposes we are interested in separating the welfare impact of price changes from that of changes in the household's technology. For example, to measure the effectiveness of monetary and fiscal policy we want

From *The American Economic Review*, Vol. 68, No. 3 (June 1978), pp. 285–299. Reprinted with permission.

a "price index" which reflects prices paid by the consumers but is independent of changes in household technology. On the other hand, if we use a household production framework to analyze the harm done by air pollution or the benefits of an outdoor recreation or child health project, we would want a measure which was independent of whatever price changes happen to have occurred. In all of these cases, we are concerned with "subindexes" which reflect some but not all of the variables which affect the household's welfare. Since measuring the welfare effect of price changes is the traditional concern of cost-of-living index theory, I shall emphasize the *constant technology cost-of-living index*, an index which reflects only the effects of price changes, rather than the *constant price cost-of-living indexes* which reflect only technological and environmental changes. The *constant technology index* is defined as the ratio of the minimum expenditures required to attain a particular indifference curve under two price regimes when the household's technology is held fixed. This index, unlike the variable technology index, exhibits all of the properties familiar from traditional cost-of-living index theory.

Complete information about preferences is usually not available, and the development of indexes which can be calculated with less information and are bounds on exact indexes is a major part of traditional index number theory. In the household production framework, complete information about preferences and technology is unlikely to be available, so there is a similar need for indexes which are bounds on exact indexes. I shall define a number of Laspeyres-type indexes in the household production framework and examine their relations to various exact indexes. I show that the *goods Laspeyres index*–defined in the obvious way—is an upper bound on the constant technology cost-of-living index. I define the *commodity Laspeyres index* in terms of the cost functions implied by the household's technology as the ratio of the cost of producing the reference commodity bundle under the comparison price-technology regime to its cost under the reference price-technology regime. This index is an upper bound on the variable technology cost-of-living index. If we not only know the household's technology but also have additional information about tastes—in particular, if an income-consumption curve in the commodity space is known—then the shadow prices of commodities can be used to construct an index which is a better bound on the variable technology cost-of-living index than that provided by the commodity Laspeyres index.

The literature on welfare evaluation in the household production framework is sparse. John Muellbauer (1974) provides one of the few explicit discussions of the cost-of-living index in the household production model as a foundation for his analysis of quality and hedonic indexes. The other major treatment is that of Franklin Fisher and Karl Shell (1968). The scope of their paper is somewhat broader than is indicated by its title—"Taste and Quality Change in the Pure Theory of the True Cost-of-Living Index"—since they sometimes use the phrase *quality change* to refer to changes in the household's technology.[3] Muellbauer adopts this unfortunate terminology which serves to confuse two important but logically distinct problems. In Pollak (1975b) I suggest that quality and quality change should be thought of in terms of "variety choice," and discuss several formulations emphasizing "characteristics." The frequent identification of quality change with technical change may reflect the fact that both affect the welfare of households by altering the constraints which they face, yet neither is best thought of as a change in the price of a market good.[4] This paper originated in my dissatisfaction with the treatment of quality and quality change, specifically with attempts to justify it in terms of the household production framework. Although the analysis which follows originated as a prolegomenon to the discussion of quality and hedonic indexes, it applies to the entire range of phenomena which can be treated in the household production framework.

The organization of the paper is as follows: Section 1 summarizes the traditional theory of the cost-of-living index. Section 2 introduces the household production model and analyzes the variable and constant technology indexes. Section 3 considers the *goods cost-of-living index* and section 4 discusses bounds on the various exact indexes. Section 5 extends the discussion of bounds by showing that commodity shadow prices may sometimes be used to obtain better bounds than those established in section 4. Section 6 is a brief summary.

1. TRADITIONAL THEORY

In this section I summarize the traditional theory of the cost-of-living index in its conventional setting: a model in which the goods the household purchases on the market are consumed directly rather than used as inputs in the production of commodities. Special attention is paid to the treatment of taste change, since it is instructive to contrast its treatment with that of technical progress in the household production framework.

We denote the goods vector by X, the household's preference ordering by R, and the corresponding utility function by $V(X)$.[5] The cost-of-living index is the ratio of the expenditures required to attain a particular indifference curve under two price regimes. We denote the cost-of-living index by

$$I(P^a, P^b, X^o, R) = \frac{E(P^a, X^o, R)}{E(P^b, X^o, R)}$$

where $E(P, X^o, R)$ is the *expenditure function*, that is, the minimum expenditure required to attain the indifference curve of the goods vector X^o, from the preference ordering R in price situation P.[6] The notation emphasizes that the index depends not only on the "comparison prices" P^a, and the "reference prices" P^b, but also on the choice of a base indifference map or preference ordering R, and the specification of a base indifference curve from that map.

The treatment of taste change in the cost-of-living index is often misunderstood, although careful expositions are presented in Fisher and Shell (1968), and Pollak (1971). The cost-of-living index does not purport to measure or compare utilities or satisfaction actually attained in different periods or situations. Instead it compares two sets of constraints.[7] To do this it considers a particular preference ordering (R) and an indifference curve (X^o) from that ordering and asks: What is the ratio of the minimum expenditure required to attain the indifference curve X^o of the preference ordering R in price situation P^a to that required in price situation P^b? If preferences are the same in both situations, it may seem "natural" to use the common preference ordering as the base for the cost-of-living index, although the theory does not require it.[8] If preferences are different, then the need to choose a base preference ordering cannot be ignored.

The Laspeyres index, $J(P^a, P^b, X^b)$, is defined by

$$J(P^a, P^b, X^b) = \frac{\sum x_k^b p_k^a}{\sum x_k^b p_k^b}$$

where X^b denotes the collection of goods bought in the reference situation.[9] It is well-known that the Laspeyres index is an upper bound on the cost-of-living index based on the reference period tastes R^b, evaluated at the reference period indifference curve X^b: $I(P^a, P^b, X^b, R^b)$.[10]

2. VARIABLE AND CONSTANT TECHNOLOGY INDEXES

In this section I introduce the problem of welfare evaluation in the household production framework and define the variable and constant technology cost-of-living indexes.

According to the household production view, the household purchases goods on the market and combines them with time in a household production process to produce commodities. These commodities, rather than the goods, are the arguments of the household's preference ordering; market goods and time are not desired for their own sake, but only as inputs into the production of commodities. I shall ignore the role of time in the household production process, and treat the production of commodities as depending only on market goods.[11] We denote the n market goods by $X = (x_1, \ldots, x_n)$, the m commodities by $Z = (z_1, \ldots, z_m)$, the household's preference ordering over commodity vectors by R and the corresponding utility function by $W(Z)$.[12] The household's technology is represented by a production set T. Thus, the "output–input" vector $(Z, X) \in T$ if and only if the commodity collection Z is producible from the goods collection X. Unless explicitly stated to the contrary, constant returns to scale and/or the absence of joint production are *not* assumed, so there need not be a separate production function for each commodity.

The *cost function* $C(P, Z; T)$ is defined as the minimum cost of producing the commodity bundle Z with the technology T at goods prices P. The notation explicitly recognizes the role of the underlying technology. Formally,

Definition. The *cost function* $C(P, Z; T)$ is defined by

$$C(P, Z; T) = \min \sum_{k=1}^{n} p_k x_k$$

subject to $(Z, X) \in T$.

Corresponding to the preference ordering R and the technology T we define the expenditure function $E(P, Z^o, R, T)$ which shows the minimum expenditure required to attain the indifference curve of Z^o.

Definition. The *expenditure function* $E(P, Z^o, R, T)$ is defined by

$$E(P, Z^o, R, T) = \min C(P, Z; T)$$

subject to ZRZ^o.

If the household's technology remains unchanged, the obvious extension of the cost-of-living index to the household production model defines the index as the ratio of the expenditures required to attain a particular indifference curve under the two price regimes. But if the "comparison technology" T^α differs from the "reference technology" T^β, there are two plausible ways to formulate the index. One allows the index to reflect both changes in technology and changes in goods prices, while the other holds technology fixed and allows the index to reflect only changes in goods prices. Both are interesting and useful, but they answer different questions. If our purpose is to compare the expenditures required to attain a particular standard of living under alternative price-technology regimes, then the variable technology cost-of-living index is appropriate. If we want to compare the prices of consumer goods in two periods, the constant technology cost-of-living index is called for. Our first task is to set out these two indexes in a notation which makes it clear what the alternatives are.

Definition. The *variable technology cost-of-living index* $I(P^a, P^b, Z^o, R, T^\alpha, T^\beta)$ is defined by

$$I(P^a, P^b, Z^o, R, T^\alpha, T^\beta) = \frac{E(P^a, Z^o, R, T^\alpha)}{E(P^b, Z^o, R, T^\beta)}$$

This index is the ratio of the minimum expenditure required to attain the indifference curve of Z^o at prices P^a with technology T^α, to the minimum expenditure required to attain the same indifference curve at prices P^b with technology T^β. Hence,

Theorem 1. Let $Z^{oa\alpha}(Z^{ob\beta})$ denote the minimum cost commodity bundle which attains the indifference curve of Z^o at prices $P^a(P^b)$ and technology $T^\alpha(T^\beta)$. Then

$$I(P^a, P^b, Z^o, R, T^\alpha, T^\beta) = \frac{C(P^a, Z^{oa\alpha}; T^\alpha)}{C(P^b, Z^{ob\beta}; T^\beta)}$$

That is, the variable technology cost-of-living index can be written as the ratio of cost functions, provided they are evaluated at the "proper" points in the commodity space.

The variable technology cost-of-living index is not simply a "price index," for it depends not only on how P^a differs from P^b, but also on how T^α differs from T^β. It is tempting to identify the technology T^α with the price set P^a, and T^β with P^b; for reasons which will become clear below, I have not incorporated these restrictions into the definition of the variable technology index. The technologies associated with P^a and P^b are of special interest and are denoted by T^a and T^b, respectively.

The variable technology cost-of-living index $I(P^a, P^b, Z^o, R, T^a, T^b)$ yields a plausible answer to a version of the "cost-of-living" question in a household production model: it compares the reference constraint—that corresponding to (P^b, T^b)—with the comparison constraint (P^a, T^a) by indicating the ratio of the expenditure needed to allow the household to attain the base indifference curve at prices P^a with technology T^a to that required at prices P^b with technology T^b. Not surprisingly, this index does not satisfy all the theorems of traditional index number theory.[13] For example, if all prices rise by 5 percent, then the index need not rise by 5 percent, and it might even fall; its behavior depends not only on how prices change, but also on the change in technology from T^b to T^a.

The constant technology cost-of-living index is a subindex of a complete cost-of-living index, namely, the variable technology cost-of-living index. In Pollak (1975a) I developed a theory of subindexes of the cost-of-living index; the discussion there is concerned with subindexes for subsets of goods (for example, "clothing", "footwear", "men's shoes"), but the analysis can be applied when any of the variables which appear in the utility function or any of the constraints facing the household are not explicitly taken into account (for example, leisure, environmental variables, or goods provided by the government without user charges). The complete index reflects changes in all of the constraints which the household faces, while subindexes are concerned only with changes in a subset of the constraints—in the present case, with the market constraints but not with those imposed by the household's technology.[14]

The constant technology cost-of-living index is defined in terms of a particular technology (perhaps T^a, perhaps T^b, perhaps some other) and thus is independent of any actual changes in the household's technology. It is the ratio of the minimum expenditure required to attain the indifference curve of Z^o at prices P^a with technology T to that required at prices P^b with the same technology, T. Its most natural application is in comparing the reference constraint (P^b, T^b) with the hypothetical comparison constraint such as (P^a, T^b).

Definition. The *constant technology cost-of-living index* $\bar{I}(P^a, P^b, Z^o, R, T)$ is defined by

$$\bar{I}(P^a, P^b, Z^o, R, T) = I(P^a, P^b, Z^o, R, T, T) = \frac{E(P^a, Z^o, R, T)}{E(P^b, Z^o, R, T)}$$

This index, unlike the variable technology cost-of-living index, satisfies all of the theorems of cost-of-living index theory. The index depends on the choice of a "base technology," in much the same way that the traditional cost-of-living index depends on the choice of a base preference ordering, so it would not be correct to say that the index is independent of technology. It is, however, independent of changes in the technology in the same sense as the traditional index is independent of changes in tastes; indeed, the treatment of technical change in the constant technology cost-of-living index is parallel to that of taste change in the traditional theory.

If the variable technology cost-of-living index is evaluated at a single technology $T^\alpha = T^\beta = T$, then it reduces to the constant technology index and satisfies all of the theorems of traditional cost-of-living index theory. If it is evaluated at a single set of prices $P^a = P^b = P$, then it reduces to the constant price cost-of-living index, an index which measures changes in the household's technology. This index exhibits a number of properties which are desirable in an index of technical change. For example, if the comparison technology is proportional to the reference technology (i.e., for all $\lambda > 0$, $(Z, \lambda X) \in T^\alpha$ if and only if $(Z, X) \in T^\beta$) then the index is equal to the factor of proportionality. The variable technology cost-of-living index can be decomposed into the product of a constant technology index and a constant price index; indeed, the decomposition can be carried out in two distinct ways, one measuring technology holding prices fixed at P^a and measuring prices holding technology fixed at T^β, the other holding prices at P^b and technology at T^α.[15]

3. THE GOODS COST-OF-LIVING INDEX

The household's preferences for commodities and its technology can be used to define a preference ordering in the goods space. In this section I use this "goods preference ordering" as a basis for welfare evaluation and the construction of a cost-of-living index—the *goods cost-of-living index*. Under certain circumstances we may sensibly set out to construct this index, while under others we may construct it inadvertently. In particular, the goods cost-of-living index is precisely the index we obtain if we estimate the goods preference ordering from observed market behavior and use the estimated preference ordering to construct a cost-of-living index, failing to recognize that production is taking place within the household. Hence, the goods cost-of-living index is of substantial interest.

The goods preference ordering R^* is a derived preference ordering, since households require goods only because goods can produce desired collections of commodities; baskets of goods are evaluated in terms of the best collection of commodities they can produce. Formally, $\hat{X} R^* \bar{X}$ if and only if there exists a $\hat{Z}$ such that $(\hat{Z}, \hat{X}) \in T$ and $\hat{Z} R \bar{Z}$ for all $\bar{Z}$ such that $(\bar{Z}, \bar{X}) \in T$. Hence, the goods preference ordering depends on the household's technology as well as its tastes for commodities; if the reference and comparison technologies are different, they may imply different goods preference orderings even though the household's commodity preferences remain unchanged.[16]

The goods cost-of-living index is the index constructed on the basis of the preference ordering $R*$. We first define the *goods expenditure function* and then the *goods cost-of-living index*.

Definition. The *goods expenditure function* $E*(P, X^o, R*, T)$ is defined by

$$E*(P, X^o, R*, T) = \min \sum_{k=1}^{n} x_k p_k$$

subject to $X R* X^o$.

Definition. The *goods cost-of-living index* $\bar{I}*(P^a, P^b, X^o, R*, T)$ is defined by

$$\bar{I}*(P^a, P^b, X^o, R*, T) = \frac{E*(P^a, X^o, R*, T)}{E*(P^b, X^o, R*, T)}$$

It follows from the definition of the goods preference ordering that $E(P, Z^o, R, T) = E*(P, X^o, R*, T)$ where $(Z^o, X^o) \in T$ and $Z^o R Z$ for all Z such that $(Z, X^o) \in T$; that is, Z^o is the highest indifference curve in the commodity space obtainable from the goods vector X^o.[17] Substituting $E(P, Z^o, R, T)$ for $E*(P, X^o, R*, T)$ in the definition of the goods cost-of-living index implies that it is equal to the constant technology cost-of-living index. Formally,

Theorem 2. The goods cost-of-living index is equal to the constant technology cost-of-living index:

$$\bar{I}*(P^a, P^b, X^o, R*, T) = \bar{I}(P^a, P^b, Z^o, R, T)$$

where Z^o corresponds to X^o in the sense that $(Z^o, X^o) \in T$ and $Z^o R Z$ for all Z such that $(Z, X^o) \in T$.

We can also write the variable technology cost-of-living index as the ratio of expenditure functions based on goods utility functions, but such a ratio is *not* a cost-of-living index corresponding to a goods preference ordering, since the expenditure functions in the numerator and denominator correspond to different preference orderings in the goods space.

The goods preference ordering is a useful construct if we realize that household production is going on behind the scenes, and are satisfied with the constant technology cost-of-living index. If, however, we fail to recognize that production is taking place within the household and treat the goods preference ordering as the household's true preferences, then we may be misled by the goods cost-of-living index. The difficulty is that the goods preference ordering reflects all changes—whether in the household's technology or in its commodity preference ordering—as changes in the goods preference ordering. Hence, when the comparison technology is superior to the reference technology, using the goods index instead of the variable technology index overstates the change in the cost of living.[18] The result is a natural one: An improvement in technology reduces the variable technology cost-of-living index; but the goods index is equivalent to a constant technology index, which by definition does not reflect the improvement in technology. Thus, with technical progress the goods index misrepresents the welfare position of the household and the compensation required to enable it to maintain a particular standard of living.[19]

4. BOUNDS ON EXACT INDEXES

Bounds on cost-of-living indexes are important because we usually do not have enough information to construct exact indexes. In this section and the next I discuss upper bounds on exact indexes in the household production framework.[20] Instead of organizing the discussion of bounding indexes in terms of the exact indexes to which they correspond, I have focused on the information needed to construct them.

In the conventional framework, the Laspeyres index is an upper bound on the cost-of-living index.[21] The Laspeyres index exhibits three important characteristics: (i) it is a fixed-weight index defined as the ratio of the costs of base quantities in the reference and comparison situations; (ii) the only information about preferences used to construct it is inferred from the fact that the base quantities were chosen in the reference situation; and (iii) it is an upper bound on the exact cost-of-living index. When we go from the conventional framework to the household production model there are two Laspeyres-type indexes which exhibit these characteristics. One of these, the *goods Laspeyres index*, is the ratio of the costs of a particular collection of market goods; the other, the *commodity Laspeyres index*, is the ratio of the costs of a particular collection of commodities.

Since inadequate information provides the motivation for constructing bounds on exact indexes, it is useful to recognize a spectrum of cases of information availability. At one pole we have full or complete information about the household's tastes and technology, so that we can construct exact indexes.[22] At the other pole, "extreme ignorance," we know only the prices in the reference and comparison situations. In this case, we can conclude that the exact index is bounded above by the largest percentage price increase; furthermore, this is the "best bound" which can be established given the limited information available.[23] Between these poles are a spectrum of intermediate cases. The closest analogue of the traditional Laspeyres case is one in which we know nothing about the household's tastes or technology beyond what we can infer from the goods collection it purchased in the reference situation; that is, we have no information about household production which may or may not be going on behind the scenes. Using only information about the goods collection purchased in the reference situation, I define the goods Laspeyres index.

Definition. The *goods Laspeyres index* $\bar{J}(P^a, P^b, X^b)$ is defined by

$$\bar{J}(P^a, P^b, X^b) = \sum_{k=1}^{n} x_k^b p_k^a \bigg/ \sum_{k=1}^{n} x_k^b p_k^b$$

where X^b is the collection of goods the household purchased when facing prices P^b with technology T^b and income μ^b.

A version of the usual Laspeyres bounding theorem holds and follows directly from the type of argument used to establish the Laspeyres bounding theorem without household production.

Theorem 3. The goods Laspeyres index is an upper bound on the constant technology cost-of-living index:

$$\bar{I}(P^a, P^b, X^b, R^b, T^b) \leqslant \bar{J}(P^a, P^b, X^b)$$

where X^b is the collection of goods which permits the household to attain the indifference curve of X^b with minimum expenditure when facing goods prices P^b with technology T^b.[24]

The requirement that the index is based on the technology of T^b, the technology corresponding to P^b, is crucial to this result. This condition augments but does not replace the traditional Laspeyres stipulation that the cost-of-living index is based on R^b and evaluated at X^b.[25]

Another intermediate position between the polar cases of complete information and extreme ignorance is one in which technology is known but tastes are not.[26] This is an especially attractive assumption because the usefulness of the household production model is substantially enhanced when we can observe both goods and commodities and infer the household's technology from these observations. When our observations are limited to the household's purchases of market goods and we never observe the commodities it produces with them, the household production model is indistinguishable from the conventional theory of household behavior, even if we have enough data on household purchases of market goods to enable us to infer the goods demand functions and the goods preference ordering.[27]

If we know the household's technology, and if we know the commodity collection the household chose in the reference situation, then we can construct the commodity Laspeyres index.

Definition. The *commodity Laspeyres index* $J(P^a, P^b, Z^b, T^\alpha, T^b)$ is defined by

$$J(P^a, P^b, Z^b, T^\alpha, T^b) = \frac{C(P^a, Z^b; T^\alpha)}{C(P^b, Z^b; T^b)}$$

This is a Laspeyres-type index in the sense that it is based on a fixed commodity consumption pattern Z^b; it can be calculated without knowledge of the household's tastes (beyond what can be inferred from the fact that Z^b

was chosen in the reference situation), but it does require knowledge of the technology. The index reflects changes in the minimum cost of producing the fixed commodity bundle Z^b, and knowledge of the household's technology is needed to calculate the cost-minimizing input combinations in different price-technology situations. Like the Laspeyres index, it does not allow for changes in the commodity consumption pattern induced by such changes. The usual Laspeyres argument shows that it is an upper bound on the variable technology cost-of-living index.

Theorem 4. The commodity Laspeyres index is an upper bound on the variable technology cost-of-living index:

$$I(P^a, P^b, Z^b, R^b, T^\alpha, T^b) \leqslant J(P^a, P^b, Z^b, T^\alpha, T^b)$$

where Z^b is the collection of commodities consumed in the price-technology-expenditure situation (P^b, T^b, μ^b).

5. THE ROLE OF IMPLICIT COMMODITY PRICES

Implicit commodity prices play a major role in the household production literature. In this section I examine their usefulness in welfare evaluation and the construction of cost-of-living indexes. I argue that they have no real role to play in the construction of exact indexes, although there are some important special cases (for example, constant returns together with the absence of joint production) in which exact indexes can be written in terms of implicit commodity prices. But implicit commodity prices can play a major role in the construction of bounds. In particular, if the household's technology is known, and if the income-consumption curve in the commodity space corresponding to the comparison price-technology situation is known, then commodity shadow prices can be used to establish a better bound on the variable technology index than that provided by the commodity Laspeyres index.

The implicit or shadow price of a commodity is its marginal cost. Formally,

Definition. The *implicit price* of commodity $r, \pi_r(P, Z; T)$, is defined by[28]

$$\pi_r(P, Z; T) = \frac{\partial C(P, Z; T)}{\partial z_r}$$

In general, implicit commodity prices depend not only on the household's technology and goods prices, but also on the *quantities of all commodities consumed by the household* (see Pollak and Wachter (1975), and W. E. Diewert, (1976, section 7)). Implicit commodity prices are independent of the particular collection of commodities consumed by the household (and thus independent of the household's tastes) if and only if the technology exhibits constant returns to scale and no joint production.[29] In this case we can write the cost function as

$$C(P, Z; T) = \sum_{t=1}^{m} C^t(P, 1; T) z_t$$

where $C^r(P, z_r; T)$ is the cost function associated with the production of commodity r; implicit commodity prices are equal to the unit cost functions, $C^r(P, 1; T)$.

The commodity price cost-of-living index is defined by imagining that the household purchases commodities instead of producing them, and that it is a price taker in the market for commodities. To emphasize the distinction between the implicit commodity prices $\pi(P, Z; T)$, defined as the partial derivatives of the cost function, and the predetermined commodity prices used to define the commodity price cost-of-living index, we denote the latter by $\bar{\pi}$. We begin by defining the commodity price expenditure function.

Definition. The *commodity price expenditure function* $E^{**}(\bar{\pi}, Z^o, R)$ is defined by

$$E^{**}(\bar{\pi}, Z^o, R) = \min \sum_{t=1}^{m} z_t \bar{\pi}_t$$

subject to ZRZ^o.

Definition. The *commodity price cost-of-living index* $I^{**}(\bar{\pi}^A, \bar{\pi}^B, Z^o, R)$ is defined by

$$I^{**}(\bar{\pi}^A, \bar{\pi}^B, Z^o, R) = \frac{E^{**}(\bar{\pi}^A, Z^o, R)}{E^{**}(\bar{\pi}^B, Z^o, R)}$$

The commodity price cost-of-living index is defined without reference to goods prices or the household's technology; it begins with commodity prices, which it takes as given. The resulting index satisfies all of the theorems of traditional cost-of-living index theory, where the prices referred to in the theorems are understood to be the predetermined commodity prices, $\bar{\pi}$.

If the household's technology exhibits constant returns to scale and no joint production, then implicit commodity prices are uniquely determined by goods prices and the household's technology, and the cost function can be written in terms of implicit commodity prices as $C(P, Z; T) = \sum \pi_t(P; T) z_t$.

It is easy to verify that in this case the variable technology cost-of-living index coincides with the commodity price cost-of-living index when commodity prices are evaluated at corresponding price-technology situations. That is, under constant returns to scale and no joint production[30]

$$I^{**}(\bar{\pi}^A, \bar{\pi}^B, Z^o, R) = I(P^a, P^b, Z^o, R, T^\alpha, T^\beta),$$

where $\bar{\pi}^A = \pi(P^a; T^\alpha)$ and $\bar{\pi}^B = \pi(P^b; T^\beta)$.

We now turn to the role of commodity prices in calculating bounding indexes. I first show that it is sometimes possible to write the commodity Laspeyres index in terms of implicit commodity prices, even when the variable technology index cannot be rewritten in this way. This result is of limited interest, however, because it is difficult to imagine circumstances under which we would know commodity shadow prices but not have enough information to construct the commodity Laspeyres index. I then show that if we have some additional information about tastes it may be possible to use implicit commodity prices to construct a better bound on the variable technology index than that provided by the commodity Laspeyres index.

I begin by defining a family of commodity Laspeyres indexes.

Definition. The *commodity price Laspeyres index* $J^{**}(\pi^A, \pi^B, Z^b)$ is defined by

$$J^{**}(\pi^A, \pi^B, Z^b) = \frac{\sum_{t=1}^{m} z_t^b \pi_t^A}{\sum_{t=1}^{m} z_t^b \pi_t^B}$$

I describe this as a family of indexes rather than a single index because its interpretation and usefulness depend on the further specification of the commodity prices: In particular, I do not require $\pi^A(\pi^B)$ to be the commodity prices corresponding to the comparison (reference) price–technology–consumption situation. When Z^b is the collection of commodities which attains the indifference curve of Z^b at minimum cost when evaluated at the commodity prices π^B, then the commodity price Laspeyres index is an upper bound on the commodity price cost-of-living index: $I^{**}(\pi^A, \pi^B, Z^b, R) \leqslant J^{**}(\pi^A, \pi^B, Z^b)$. This follows from the usual Laspeyres argument, but the result is of limited interest because the two indexes treat commodity prices as exogenous.

In certain cases it is possible to rewrite the commodity Laspeyres index in terms of implicit commodity prices. In particular, suppose we have no information about preferences beyond what can be inferred from the commodity bundle chosen in the reference situation, but that the household's reference and comparison technologies are known and the implied cost functions satisfy the differential equation $C(P, Z; T) = \gamma(Z) \sum_t z_t \partial C_t(P, Z; T) / \partial z_t$ where $\gamma(Z)$ is the same for both technologies. Then the commodity price Laspeyres index is equal to the commodity Laspeyres index and, hence, is an upper bound on the variable technology cost-of-living index

$$I(P^a, P^b, Z^b, R^b, T^\alpha, T^b) \leqslant J(P^a, P^b, Z^b, T^\alpha, T^b) = J^{**}(\pi^A, \pi^B, Z^b)$$

where implicit commodity prices are evaluated at $\pi^A = \pi(P^a, Z^b; T^\alpha)$ and $\pi^B = \pi(P^b, Z^b; T^b)$. This result depends on the fact that the $\gamma(Z)$'s cancel when the cost functions in the numerator and denominator are evaluated at the same value of Z. For example, consider any pair of technologies which can be viewed as two-stage processes in which at the first stage market goods are transformed into a single homogeneous output q, according to a constant returns to scale technology, and, at the second stage the homogeneous output is used to produce commodities. Processes of this type imply cost functions of the form $C(P, Z; T) = \psi(P; T)\phi(Z; T)$ where $\psi(P; T)$ is the unit cost function corresponding to the first-stage technology and $q = \phi(Z; T)$ implicitly defines the second stage. If the second-stage processes are identical for the reference and comparison technologies, then $\phi(Z; T^\alpha) = \phi(Z; T^\beta) = \phi(Z)$ and the cost functions are of the required form.[31]

Neither of the bounding indexes just described yields a better bound on the exact indexes than could be obtained without implicit commodity prices; they are merely restatements in terms of commodity shadow prices of results obtained in section 4. I now show that it is sometimes possible to use implicit commodity prices in conjunction with some additional information to obtain better results. In particular, we can improve on the commodity Laspeyres index if, in addition to knowing the household's technology, we also know the income-consumption curve in the commodity space corresponding to the comparison price-technology situation (P^a, T^a). It is assumed that preferences are convex and are the same in both situations.

The bounding argument combines two observations: first, if a commodity collection Z^* lies on a higher indifference curve than Z^b, then giving the household enough income to produce Z^* will at least compensate it for any price or technological changes which have taken place. Second, suppose that preferences are convex and that Z^* is chosen from a feasible set; if Z^b lies on the "pseudobudget set" defined by the hyperplane tangent to the feasible set at Z^*, then Z^* is "implicitly revealed preferred" to Z^b. This is substantially stronger than the obvious revealed preference assertion that if Z^* is chosen from a feasible set, then it is at least as good as any bundle in the feasible set. A stronger conclusion (stronger, at least, when the feasible set is convex) is possible when preferences are convex and the boundary of the feasible set is not a hyperplane. With convex preferences, a "pseudobudget line" tangent to the feasible set at the chosen bundle is also tangent to the indifference curve at this bundle, so the chosen bundle is at least as good as every bundle in the pseudobudget set.[32] In particular, if Z^b lies in the pseudobudget set corresponding to Z^*, then the variable technology cost-of-living index must be less than $C(P^a, Z^*; T^a)/C(P^b, Z^b; T^b)$. Whether or not this is a better bound than that implied by the commodity Laspeyres index depends on the location of Z^* relative to Z^b. However, if the technology is strictly convex and Z^b happens to lie *on* the pseudobudget line corresponding to Z^*, then this will be a better bound than the commodity Laspeyres index.[33,34]

If we know the income-consumption path in the commodity space corresponding to (P^a, T^a), then we can use the above argument systematically to bound the variable technology cost-of-living index. The procedure works by finding a commodity bundle Z^{oa*} on the income-consumption path of (P^a, T^a) such that Z^b lies on the boundary of the pseudobudget set corresponding to that commodity bundle. The commodity Laspeyres index reflects

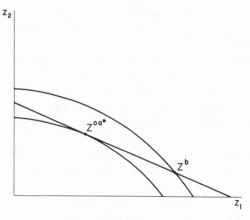

Figure 1

the cost of the feasible set whose boundary passes through Z^b (see Figure 1).

Formally, let Z^{a*} be a point on the income-consumption path corresponding to (P^a, T^a, μ^{a*}). Then there is a shadow price system $\{\pi_t(P^a, Z^{a*}; T^a)\}$ associated with this point, and we define *implicit expenditure*, $\tilde{\mu}(P^a, Z^{a*}; T^a)$ by $\tilde{\mu}(P^a, Z^{a*}; T^a) = \sum z_t^{a*} \pi_t(P^a, Z^{a*}; T^a)$. By the previous argument, Z^{a*} is at least as good as all Z in the pseudobudget set defined by $\sum z_t \pi_t(P^a, Z^{a*}; T^a) \leqslant \tilde{\mu}(P^a, Z^{a*}; T^a)$. Let $S(Z^b)$ denote the set of all Z^{a*} such that $\sum z_t^b \pi_t(P^a, Z^{a*}; T^a) \leqslant \tilde{\mu}(P^a, Z^{a*}; T^a)$. Then $Z^{a*} R Z^b$ for all $Z^{a*} \in S(Z^b)$ and $C(P^a, Z^{oa*}; T^a) \leqslant C(P^a, Z^{a*}; T^a)$ for all $Z^{a*} \in S(Z^b)$. Hence,[35,36]

$$I(P^a, P^b, Z^b, R^b, T^a, T^b) \leqslant \frac{C(P^a, Z^{oa*}; T^a)}{C(P^b, Z^b; T^b)}$$

6. CONCLUSION

The evaluation of welfare and the construction of a cost-of-living index in the household production framework require a careful specification of the alternative situations being compared. The variable technology cost-of-living index measures the total effect on the household of changes in goods prices and changes in its technology; the constant technology index is independent of changes in the household's technology and reflects only changes in goods prices. The first three sections of this paper discussed exact cost-of-living indexes under the assumption that the household's tastes and technology were known. Bounds on exact indexes are important because this complete information is usually not available. When neither the household's tastes nor its technology is known, we can calculate the goods Laspeyres index which is an upper bound on the constant technology index. When the technology is known but tastes are not, we can calculate the commodity Laspeyres index which is an upper bound on the variable technology index. When both the technology and the expansion path corresponding to the comparison price-technology regime are known, we can calculate commodity shadow prices and use them to construct a Laspeyres-type index which provides a better bound on the variable technology index than the commodity Laspeyres index.

Striking similarities exist between the cost-of-living index in the household production framework and two other generalizations of the cost-of-living index from its traditional setting. Both subindexes of the cost-of-living index [see Pollak (1975a) and Blackorby and Russell (1978)] and the "social cost-of-living index" based on a Bergson–Samuelson social welfare function (see Pollak, 1976), like household production indexes, involve two-stage maximization.[37] In the household production framework, one stage corresponds to the household's technology and the other to its tastes; with subindexes, the two stages reflect the household's preferences for goods within each group and for aggregates of goods; and with social cost-of-living indexes, one represents the household's preferences and the other the social preferences expressed by the Bergson–Samuelson social welfare function. In all three, alternative assumptions about the information available for index construction permit the development of a variety of indexes that bound the exact index.

NOTES

University of Pennsylvania. This research was supported in part by the U.S. Bureau of Labor Statistics and the National Science Foundation. I am grateful to Barbara Atrostic, Hugh Davies, W. E. Diewert, Stefano Fenoaltea, Franklin M. Fisher, Robert P. Inman, John Muellbauer, Stephen A. Ross, Paul J. Taubman, Jack E. Triplett, the managing editor, and an anonymous referee. Their helpful comments and suggestions have substantially improved this paper, but I have not always followed their advice and none of them should be held responsible for the views expressed.

1. The locus classicus of the household production literature is Becker (1965). In Kelvin Lancaster's model (1966a, b, 1971) goods possess "characteristics" which are often identified with Becker's commodities and the "technology" is linear. Becker often uses fixed coefficient production functions as an expositional device, but linear technology is not an integral part of his model. For a recent sympathetic statement of the household production approach, see Michael and Becker (1973). For a discussion of some of its limitations, see Pollak and Wachter (1975).

2. The knowledge that production is going on within the household is of no help if our observations are limited to its purchases of market goods. Pollak and Wachter (1975) emphasize that the assumption that commodities are observable and measurable is crucial to exploiting the advantages of the household production model.

3. Fisher and Shell do not explicitly use the household production model, but it is clear from their examples (for example, "refrigerators," "ice cream," "home-refrigerated ice cream") that they sometimes have in mind situations involving household production.

4. In a model of variety choice, quality change may be treated as a change in the price of a market good, provided we treat the prices of unavailable goods as infinite. This formulation is of limited usefulness for empirically oriented work because most

households consume only a small number of the varieties available. In Pollak (1975b) I discuss several "quality models" which avoid this difficulty by relying on characteristics.

5. Assume that the household's preferences are well-behaved in the sense that they can be represented by a continuous utility function which is quasi-concave and nondecreasing in its arguments.

6. I have identified the base indifference curve by specifying a goods vector X^o which lies on it; replacing X^o by any other goods vector on the same indifference curve does not affect the expenditure function or the cost-of-living index. Instead of defining the expenditure function in terms of the weak preference relation R (at least as good as) we could equivalently begin with the utility function $V(X)$ and specify the base indifference curve by requiring $V(X) \geqslant V(X^o)$.

7. For an alternative view based on comparing satisfaction actually attained in each situation and requiring the use of cardinal utility, see Phlips (1974, Chapter 11) and Phlips and Sanz-Ferrer (1975).

8. This may be more transparent in the case of international than intertemporal comparisons. For example, to compare prices in Paris with those in Tokyo, one might use French tastes or Japanese tastes; but if the U.S. government wants to establish appropriate salary differentials for its diplomats, the comparison should presumably be based on U.S. tastes. In intertemporal comparisons, the index may be based on any preference ordering; the choices are not restricted to reference and comparison period tastes.

9. Throughout this paper I discuss the Laspeyres index and leave the Paasche index to the reader.

10. The goods vector X^b plays a very different role in the Laspeyres index than it does in the cost-of-living index. In the cost-of-living index it specifies a particular indifference curve, and the replacement of X^b by another collection of goods on the same indifference curve does not alter the index. In the Laspeyres index it specifies a particular collection of goods, the collection actually bought in the reference situation. The fixed weight index constructed by replacing X^b by another collection of goods on the same indifference curve is not equal to the Laspeyres index and is not an upper bound on the cost-of-living index.

11. I have ignored the role of time to avoid further complicating an already complicated notation. Time can be incorporated into the household production model in a straightforward way if we are willing to treat it as a "market good" whose price is the wage rate. Indeed, the allocation of time was the principal focus of Becker's seminal paper. Pollak and Wachter argue that joint production is likely to be pervasive when time plays a role in household production, and that joint production severely limits the usefulness of implicit "commodity prices" for demand analysis. In section 5, I argue that if the household's technology is known, commodity shadow prices can sometimes be used to obtain a useful bound on the cost-of-living index.

12. The household's preferences over the commodity space are assumed to be well-behaved.

13. See Pollak (1971) for a detailed statement of these theorems.

14. Often we are interested in subindexes for groups of goods or groups of commodities. I discussed the construction of such subindexes in the household production framework in an appendix to an earlier version of this paper which is available on request from the Office of Prices and Living Conditions, U.S. Bureau of Labor Statistics, Washington, D.C. 20212.

15. There are also a number of properties of the variable technology index which do

not depend on restricting prices or technology. For example: $I(P^a, P^b, Z^o, R, \lambda T^\alpha, T^\beta) = \lambda I(P^a, P^b, Z^o, R, T^\alpha, T^\beta)$ and $I(\lambda P^a, P^b, Z^o, R, T^\alpha, T^\beta) = \lambda I(P^a, P^b, Z^o, R, T^\alpha, T^\beta)$.

16. To indicate explicitly the dependence of R^* on R and T, we might write $R^*(R, T)$. The convexity of R^* does not follow from that of R unless we place further restrictions on the technology. In particular, if the production set T is convex, it is easy to show that the convexity of R implies the convexity of R^*. With increasing returns the production set is not convex and it may be so nonconvex as to yield a goods preference ordering which is not convex. For an example, see Pollak and Wachter (1975, p. 262). The referee correctly points out that there exists a convex goods preference ordering which implies a demand correspondence which contains the demand correspondence generated by the example cited, namely, one whose indifference curves are parallel straight lines. We can define the *goods utility function* $V(X; T)$, by $V(X; T) = \max W(Z)$ subject to $(Z, X) \in T$. That is, $V(X; T)$ is the maximum value of the utility function $W(Z)$ which the household can attain from the goods collection X. The goods utility function is useful in discussing the demand functions for goods implied by the household production model, since maximizing it subject to the budget constraint $\sum p_k x_k = \mu$ yields the goods demand functions. If the goods preference ordering is convex, these demand functions exhibit all the properties of conventional demand theory.

17. This equality also holds when Z^o is replaced by any Z on the indifference curve of Z^o, or when X^o is replaced by any X on the indifference curve of X^o.

18. Suppose the household's technology improves so that the expenditure required to attain any particular indifference curve of the commodity preference ordering using the comparison technology is less than the expenditure required using the reference technology. Then $E(P, Z^o, R, T^a) < E(P, Z^o, R, T^b)$. Hence,

$$I(P^a, P^b, Z^o, R, T^a, T^b) = \frac{E(P^a, Z^o, R, T^a)}{E(P^b, Z^o, R, T^b)} < \frac{E(P^a, Z^o, R, T^b)}{E(P^b, Z^o, R, T^b)} = \bar{I}^*(P^a, P^b, X^o, R^*, T^b)$$

where Z^o corresponds to X^o in the sense that $Z^o R Z$ for all Z such that $(Z, X^o) \in T$. Similarly, $I(P^a, P^b, Z^o, R, T^a, T^b) < \bar{I}^*(P^a, P^b, X^o, R^*, T^a)$ where Z^o corresponds to X^o.

19. Fisher and Shell (1968, p. 104) reach essentially the same conclusion in their discussion of "quality change" (read, "technical progress") and "taste change" (focusing on the goods cost-of-living index) without formally introducing the machinery of the household production model.

20. The analysis of lower bounds is left to the reader.

21. A precise statement is given in section 1.

22. If we are only interested in constructing the exact index corresponding to a given Z^o, then we need to know only the indifference curve of Z^o, not the entire indifference map. Similarly, if we are only interested in the index comparing P^a and P^b, we need not know the entire technology or cost function, but only the values of the cost function corresponding to P^a and P^b.

23. See Pollak (1971, section 4) for a discussion of best bounds and the preference orderings to which they correspond in the traditional framework.

24. This bounding theorem does not depend on the convexity of the goods preference ordering.

25. The goods Laspeyres index does not permit us to draw any conclusions about the variable technology cost-of-living index, but if we also know that the comparison technology "dominates" the reference technology—in the sense that any collection of commodities can be produced with the comparison technology using no more

inputs than were required by the reference technology—then the goods cost-of-living index is also an upper bound on the variable technology cost-of-living index.

26. We could also consider the intermediate case in which tastes are known and technology is not, but such a case is less likely and therefore less interesting.

27. See Pollak and Wachter (1975) for a discussion of this point.

28. If the cost function is not differentiable at a particular point, implicit commodity prices are undefined there.

29. A proof can be found in Pollak and Wachter (1975) where it is argued that this is the only case in which implicit commodity prices are useful explanatory variables in demand analysis.

30. The case of constant returns to scale and no joint production is not the only one in which the commodity price cost-of-living index coincides with the variable technology index. Muellbauer (1974) shows that even with joint production, they coincide when the reference and comparison technologies are homogeneous of the same degree. But in this case, the implicit commodity price formulation is no more transparent than the cost function–expenditure function formulation of section 2. Note that to calculate the exact index, implicit commodity prices in the numerator (denominator) must be evaluated at $Z^{oa\alpha}(Z^{ob\beta})$, the least cost commodity basket which attains the indifference curve of Z^o at prices $P^a(P^b)$ with technology $T^\alpha(T^\beta)$. Muellbauer suggests that the commodity shadow price formulation requires less information than the cost-expenditure approach, but I do not find his position persuasive. He assumes that implicit commodity prices of the reference and comparison situations are known or observable, while the household's technology is not. But if we knew the implicit commodity price functions, we could find the associated cost functions and from them the entire technology. Muellbauer assumes that we do not know the implicit commodity price functions, but only the value of these functions at the points $(P^a, Z^a; T^a)$ and $(P^b, Z^b; T^b)$. However, he does little to motivate his assumptions about information. Since implicit commodity prices are not directly observable, they must be calculated using estimates of the parameters of the household's technology. Once a functional form for the technology is specified, its parameters can be estimated from observations on inputs and outputs or on outputs and cost. The parameter estimates can then be used to calculate not only commodity shadow prices at Muellbauer's points, but the implicit commodity prices corresponding to any configuration of goods prices and commodity outputs. Estimating the parameters of the household's technology is a prerequisite to calculating commodity shadow prices.

31. This result is a substantial generalization of a theorem of Muellbauer. Muellbauer's *consistency condition*, (1974, p. 983), which he contends is necessary if the commodity price Laspeyres index is to make sense, is unduly strong, and it is not satisfied by the two-stage technology described above. Unfortunately, this result is only interesting when we know implicit commodity prices but not the household's technology.

32. If the boundary of the feasible set is itself a hyperplane (as it is with constant returns and no joint production), then the pseudobudget set coincides with the feasible set. But if the feasible set is strictly convex, then the pseudobudget set permits us to identify some commodity bundles which were not in the feasible set as being no better than Z^a.

33. Provided Z^* and Z^b are distinct.

34. In the traditional framework without household production the boundary of the feasible set is a hyperplane, and knowing the collection of goods purchased in the comparison price-income situation, or even the entire income-consumption curve, does not enable us to improve on the Laspeyres bound.

35. Muellbauer (1974, pp. 985–86) argues that if the household's preferences are homothetic and identical in the reference and comparison situations, and the household's technology in both periods exhibits constant returns to scale, then the variable technology cost-of-living index is bounded by the commodity price Laspeyres index where $\pi^A = \pi(P^a, Z^a; T^a)$ and $\pi^B = \pi(P^b, Z^b; T^b)$. This result follows from the general procedure just described. Under his assumptions, the income-consumption path corresponding to (P^a, T^a) is a ray from the origin, and hence a single commodity bundle on the path identifies the entire path. With constant returns to scale, implicit commodity prices are constant along such a ray and implicit expenditure at a point on the income-consumption path is equal to the cost of that commodity bundle.

36. If we know the commodity bundle purchased in the comparison situation, (P^a, T^a, μ^a), but not the entire income-consumption curve, we may still be able to establish a better bound on the variable technology cost-of-living index than that provided by the commodity Laspeyres. A prerequisite, however, is that Z^b lie in the pseudobudget set corresponding to Z^a. If this condition is satisfied, we can infer that $C(P^a, Z^a; T^a)/C(P^b, Z^b; T^b) = \mu^a/\mu^b$ is an upper bound on the variable technology index. Of course $C(P^a, Z^a; T^a)$ need not be smaller than $C(P^a, Z^b; T^a)$, so this need not be a better bound than the commodity Laspeyres index. Our general conclusion is that—provided Z^b lies in the pseudobudget set of Z^a—the variable technology index is bounded above by the minimum of μ^a/μ^b and the commodity Laspeyres index. If we also know additional points on the income-consumption curve corresponding to (P^a, T^a), we can use them in the same way to attempt to improve on the commodity Laspeyres index.

37. In Blackorby and Russell (1978) separability of the expenditure function is a prerequisite for defining subindexes. In Pollak (1975a), subindexes are defined without assuming separability, but they are better behaved when the direct utility function is separable.

REFERENCES

Becker, G. S., "A Theory of the Allocation of Time," *Economic Journal*, Vol. 75 (September 1965), pp. 493–517.

Blackorby, C., and R. R. Russell, "Indices and Subindices of the Cost-of-Living and the Standard of Living," *International Economic Review*, Vol. 19 (February 1978), pp. 229–240.

Diewert, W. E., "Walras' Theory of Capital Formation and the Existence of a Temporary Equilibrium," in Gerhard Schwödiauer, ed., *Equilibrium and Disequilibrium in Economics*, Dordrecht, 1976.

Fisher, F. M., and K. Shell, "Taste and Quality Change in the Pure Theory of the True Cost-of-Living Index," in J. N. Wolfe, ed., *Value, Capital and Growth: Papers in Honour of Sir John Hicks*, Edinburgh, 1968, pp. 97–139.

Lancaster, Kelvin J., "A New Approach to Consumer Theory," *Journal of Political Economy*, Vol. 74 (April 1966), pp. 132–57. (1966a).

———, "Change and Innovation in the Technology of Consumption," *American Economic Review*, Vol. 56, (May 1966), pp. 14–23. (1966b).

———, *Consumer Demand: A New Approach*, New York, 1971.

Michael, R. T., and G. S. Becker, "On the New Theory of Consumer Behavior," *Swedish Journal of Economics*, Vol. 75, (December 1973) pp. 378–96.

Muellbauer, John, "Household Production Theory, Quality and 'Hedonic Technique'," *American Economic Review*, Vol. 64, (December 1974), pp. 977–94.

Phlips, Louis, *Applied Consumption Analysis*, Amsterdam, 1974.

―――, and R. Sanz-Ferrer, "A Taste-Dependent True Index of the Cost of Living," *Review of Economics and Statistics*, Vol. 57, (November 1975), pp. 495–501.

Pollak, Robert, A., "The Theory of the Cost-of-Living Index," Research Discussion Paper No. 11, Research Division, Office of Prices and Living Conditions, U.S. Bureau of Labor Statistics, June 1971.

―――, "Subindexes of the Cost-of-Living Index," *International Economic Review*, Vol. 16, (February 1975), pp. 135–50. (1975a)

―――, "The Treatment of 'Quality' in Demand Analysis and the Cost-of-Living Index," Mime, (August 1975), (1975b). Published as "The Treatment of 'Quality' in the Cost-of-Living Index," *Journal of Public Economics*, Vol. 20, No. 1, (February 1983), pp. 25–53.

―――, "The Social Cost-of-Living Index," Discussion Paper No. 378, University of Pennsylvania, (June 1976). Published in *Journal of Public Economics*, Vol. 15, No. 3 (June 1981), pp. 311–336.

―――, and Michael L. Wachter, "The Relevance of the Household Production Function and Its Implications for the Allocation of Time," *Journal of Political Economy*, Vol. 83, (April 1975), pp. 255–77.

Welfare Comparisons and Equivalence Scales

Equivalence scales are used in both demand and welfare analysis. In demand analysis they permit us to pool data from households of different sizes, or, more generally, with different demographic profiles. In welfare analysis, they enable us to compare the well-being of such households, since they purport to answer questions of the form: "What expenditure level would make a family with three children as well off as it would be with two children and $12,000?" Such welfare comparisons are generally thought to provide the rationale for different treatments of different family types in income tax or family allowance schedules, or in income maintenance programs.

In this paper we argue that the equivalence scales required for welfare comparisons are logically distinct from those which arise in demand analysis. The usual practice is to base welfare comparisons on equivalence scales estimated from observed differences in the consumption patterns of households with different numbers of children. This is illegitimate. The expenditure level required to make a three-child family as well off as it would be with two children and $12,000 depends on how the family feels about children. Observed differences in the consumption patterns of two- and three-child families cannot even tell us whether the third child is regarded as a blessing or a curse.

In section 1 we discuss the type of equivalence scale appropriate for demand analysis (conditional equivalence scales) and, in section 2, the type required to make welfare comparisons (unconditional equivalence scales). Conditional equivalence scales can be estimated from observed differences in the consumption patterns of households with different demographic profiles, but construction of unconditional equivalence scales requires more information than is contained in household consumption data. In section 3 we discuss identification of a family's unconditional equivalence scale, and in section 4 we discuss the interpretation of welfare comparisons when families have different tastes. In section 5, the concluding section, we summarize our discussion of welfare comparisons of families with different demographic profiles and question whether such comparisons account for the widespread belief that different treatments of different family types are appropriate.

From *The American Economic Review*, Vol. 69, No. 2 (May 1979), pp. 216–221. Reprinted with permission.

This paper was co-authored by Robert A. Pollak and Terence J. Wales of the University of British Columbia.

1. DEMOGRAPHIC VARIABLES IN DEMAND ANALYSIS:
CONDITIONAL EQUIVALENCE SCALES

In demand analysis, the "objects of choice" are consumption vectors X, and preferences over them depend on an assumed predetermined vector of demographic variables η; we call such a preference ordering "conditional." We denote the conditional preference ordering by $R(\eta)$ and interpret the statement "$X^a R(\eta^*) X^b$" to mean that the family finds X^a at least as good as X^b when its demographic profile is given by η^*. If each family takes its demographic profile as fixed when choosing its consumption pattern, demand analysis need never ask how it would choose between alternatives which differ with respect to the demographic variables; hence, conditional preferences are an appropriate foundation for demand analysis.[1]

In Pollak and Wales (1981), we examine a number of alternative ways to incorporate demographic variables into demand analysis by allowing some of the parameters of a demand system to be functions of demographic variables. These functions, which we call conditional equivalence scales, are usually estimated along with the parameters of the demand system by combining data from households with different demographic profiles. The alternatives to this procedure are (i) to analyze separately data from households with distinct demographic profiles or (ii) to combine data from households with different demographic profiles using conditional equivalence scales estimated from other data or specified a priori. The assumptions that demand functions are independent of demographic variables, or that per capita consumption of each good is a function of per capita total expenditure, are examples of a priori specifications of conditional equivalence scales.

2. DEMOGRAPHIC VARIABLES IN WELFARE ANALYSIS:
UNCONDITIONAL EQUIVALENCE SCALES

In contrast to demand analysis, welfare analysis must compare the well-being of a family in alternative situations which differ with respect to its demographic profile as well as its consumption pattern. For example, we might ask whether a family with given tastes would prefer to have two children and \$12,000 or three children and \$13,000 at a particular set of goods' prices. The traditional approach to welfare comparisons ignores the fact that such comparisons cannot be based on conditional preferences but require a conceptual framework in which preferences are defined over family size as well as goods. In general, welfare analysis requires us to define the objects of choice to include not only the consumption vector, but also the demographic variables, which from the standpoint of conditional preferences are predetermined. We call an ordering over such an augmented set of alternatives an "unconditional preference ordering," and denote it by R: the statement "$(X^a, \eta^a) R (X^b, \eta^b)$" means that the family finds (X^a, η^a) at least as good as

(X^b, η^b). The additional information contained in the unconditional preference ordering is irrelevant for demand analysis, but for welfare comparisons it is indispensable.

Unconditional equivalence scales are index numbers which reflect the ratio of the expenditures required to attain a particular indifference curve under alternative demographic profiles.[2] Corresponding to the unconditional preference ordering R, we define the "unconditional expenditure function," $E[P, \eta, (P^o, \mu^o, \eta^o)]$, whose value is the minimum expenditure required to reach the indifference curve attained in the price-expenditure-demographic situation (P^o, μ^o, η^o), when the household faces prices P with the demographic profile η. The unconditional equivalence scale $I[(P^a, \eta^a), (P^b, \eta^b), (P^o, \mu^o, \eta^o)]$, is defined by

$$I[(P^a, \eta^a), (P^b, \eta^b), (P^o, \mu^o, \eta^o)] = \frac{E[P^a, \eta^a, (P^o, \mu^o, \eta^o)]}{E[P^b, \eta^b, (P^o, \mu^o, \eta^o)]} \tag{1}$$

If we let the base indifference curve correspond to the "reference situation" (P^b, μ^b, η^b), then the denominator is μ^b and the index is equal to $E[P^a, \eta^a, (P^b, \mu^b, \eta^b)]/\mu^b$. In our example, such an index would show the percentage expenditure adjustment which would enable a family with three children to attain the same indifference curve it would attain with two children and $12,000.[3]

We illustrate this with an unconditional preference ordering which is consistent with the familiar linear expenditure system (LES) conditional demand functions. Consider the direct utility function

$$W(X, \eta) = \prod_{k=1}^{n} (x_k - b_k^* - \beta_k \eta)^{a_k} + \phi(\eta); \quad \sum a_k = 1, \quad x_i - b_i^* - \beta_i \eta > 0, \tag{2}$$

where η is the number of children in the family; in some very informal sense the function $\phi(\eta)$ represents the "direct" contribution of children to family utility. Substituting the conditional demand functions into this direct utility function yields a "mixed" indirect utility function whose arguments are P, μ, and η:

$$V(P, \mu, \eta) = (\mu - \sum p_k b_k^* - \eta \sum p_k \beta_k) \prod (p_k)^{-a_k} (a_k)^{a_k} + \phi(\eta) \tag{3}$$

Solving for μ yields the unconditional expenditure function

$$E(P, \mu, \eta, s_o) = \sum p_k b_k^* + \eta \sum p_k \beta_k + [s_o - \phi(\eta)] \prod (p_k)^{a_k} (a_k)^{-a_k} \tag{4}$$

where s_o is the value of the utility function (2) evaluated at any point on the base indifference curve. To find the unconditional equivalence scale evaluated at the base indifference curve corresponding to (P^b, μ^b, η^b), we divide the unconditional expenditure function evaluated at $s_o = V(P^b, \mu^b, \eta^b)$ by μ^b. This yields[4]

$$I[(P^a, \eta^a), (P^b, \eta^b), (P^b, \mu^b, \eta^b)] = \{\sum p_k^a b_k^* + \eta \sum p_k^a \beta_k + [(\mu^b - \sum p_k^b b_k^*$$

$$- \eta^b \sum p_k^b \beta_k) \prod (p_k^b)^{-a_k} (a_k)^{a_k} + \phi(\eta^b) - \phi(\eta^a)] \prod (p_k^a)^{a_k} (a_k)^{-a_k}\}/\mu^b \qquad (5)$$

3. IDENTIFICATION OF UNCONDITIONAL EQUIVALENCE SCALES

Since the unconditional equivalence scale corresponding to $W(X, \eta)$ depends on the function $\phi(\eta)$, we must estimate this function. But if we interpret our data in terms of conditional choices (i.e., choices in which the number of children is taken to be fixed or predetermined) the function $\phi(\eta)$ is not identified.[5] All functions $\phi(\eta)$ imply the same conditional demand functions for goods, so information about how a family would reallocate its expenditure among consumption categories as the number of children varies is not sufficient to identify $\phi(\eta)$.

Of course if $\phi(\eta)$ were assumed to be a constant then it would not appear in (5) and the unconditional equivalence scale corresponding to $W(X, \eta)$ could be identified from conditional choices. This appears to be the assumption generally made, although not explicitly, in the literature on equivalence scales and welfare comparisons. However, this assumption has grossly implausible implications for unconditional preferences and unconditional choices involving family size. In particular, consider a "perfect contraceptive society" — one in which there are no economic costs or preference drawbacks associated with fertility regulation. If $\phi(\eta)$ is a constant and $\sum p_k \beta_k$ is positive, then the family will have no children; if $\phi(\eta)$ is a constant and $\sum p_k \beta_k$ is negative, the family will have as many children as it can. This follows immediately from the fact that when $\phi(\eta)$ is a constant the utility function (3) depends linearly on η.

Another illustration of the counterintuitive results that may occur when we make the transition from household consumption patterns to welfare conclusions by assuming that $\phi(\eta)$ is a constant is provided by the linear expenditure system estimated by Pollak and Wales (1978) using U.K. household budget data. The estimated conditional demand functions exhibit reasonable price and expenditure elasticities, and reasonable consumption responses to changes in family size. The estimated β's, however, are all negative so $\sum p_k \beta_k < 0$. Hence, when $\phi(\eta)$ is assumed to be constant, the unconditional expenditure function decreases with η, and the corresponding unconditional equivalence scale implies that large families need less money than small families to attain any fixed indifference curve.

If unconditional preferences cannot be recovered from conditional demand functions, how can they be discovered? For some demographic variables, information about unconditional preferences is revealed by observable choice behavior. For example, in advanced industrial societies where deliberate choice of completed family size is the rule rather than the exception, an argument can be made for treating the observed consumption–family size configurations as observable unconditional choices, using them to infer unconditional preferences, and using these preferences to make welfare comparisons. Thus, in a perfect contraceptive society, if a family chooses to have three children and $12,000 when it could have had two children and $12,000, then a revealed preference argument implies that the family prefers the alternative it chose.[6] Other demographic variables (say, race) are not susceptible to deliberate control, while still others (say, the sex of a family's first child) may be moving from the uncontrollable to the controllable category. Unconditional preferences for demographic variables might also be obtained by analyzing responses to direct questions about preferences or hypothetical choices, although economists have traditionally been suspicious of this approach.[7]

4. WELFARE COMPARISONS WITH TASTE DIFFERENCES

Taste differences—that is, differences in families' unconditional preferences— substantially complicate welfare comparisons. There are two approaches. The first is to select a particular unconditional preference ordering as the appropriate base for welfare comparisons and proceed as before. The selection is trivial if a particular preference ordering is obviously appropriate as when all families have identical unconditional preferences. It is especially trouble-some when systematic differences in preferences are associated with systematic differences in the demographic variables, as is the case with family size or other demographic variables over which families exercise partial or complete control. For some demographic variables it may be plausible to assume that families with different demographic profiles have the same unconditional preferences, or more precisely, that the distribution of unconditional pre-ferences is independent of the distribution of demographic characteristics. But for demographic variables over which families exercise some deliberate control, this independence assumption is clearly unwarranted.

Suppose, for example, that some families have a strong desire for children while others have a weak desire for children. Then the expenditure required to make a family with three children as well off as it would be with two children and $12,000 depends on which unconditional preference ordering it has. Hence, the unconditional equivalence scale depends on which of the two unconditional preference orderings we select as the base. But neither selection compares the welfare levels of families with different tastes. Instead, they compare two situations (for example, three children, $13,000, vs. two children, $12,000) on the basis of a particular preference ordering—whichever one selected is the appropriate base for the comparison.

The second approach to welfare comparisons requires interpersonal (interfamily) comparisons of happiness or satisfaction. Technically, we need a mapping which associates with each indifference curve from one unconditional indifference map a corresponding curve on the other, so that the corresponding curves represent the same levels of happiness or satisfaction. Only if such a correspondence exists can we compare the welfare of families with different tastes in alternative situations—for example, strong desire for children, three children, $13,000 vs. weak desire for children, two children, $12,000.

5. CONCLUSION

The implications of our analysis of welfare comparisons and equivalence scales should be stated explicitly: 1. Even if all families have identical unconditional preferences, conditional equivalence scales estimated from observed differences in the consumption patterns of families with different demograpic profiles cannot be used to make welfare comparisons; for example, we cannot use such data to determine the amount needed to make families with three children as well off as those with two children and $12,000. Unconditional equivalence scales are required to make welfare comparisons. 2. If tastes vary systematically with demographic characteristics, then the construction of unconditional equivalence scales requires the selection of an appropriate base unconditional preference ordering; theory offers little guidance in making this selection, but there is no selection which permits us to compare the welfare of a family with a strong desire for children with that of one with a weak desire for children. Such comparisons require interpersonal or interfamily comparisons of welfare levels. The question of whether such comparisons are meaningful, and if so, how they can be made, is beyond the scope of this paper.

Our analysis suggests that it is very difficult to make welfare comparisons between families with different demographic profiles. But are comparisons of this sort the principal basis of the widespread belief that it is appropriate to treat different family types differently in income tax or family allowance schedules or in income maintenance programs? We think not. For example, differences in treatment might be justified in terms of effects on the children's present or future welfare, the effects on the children's future productivity, or the effect on the family's fertility.[8] Our analysis implies that differences in treatment cannot easily be justified by an appeal to equity or fairness if this is interpreted in terms of "family preferences" (i.e., the welfare of the adult members of the family). But the arguments one would advance to justify providing children in large families with consumption levels which society somehow establishes to be "socially adequate" are very different from those one would advance for making the adults in large and small families equally well-off. The problem of defining socially adequate consumption levels is a difficult one which has received virtually no attention from economists, in part because of the profession's unfortunate preoccupation with welfare comparisons and equivalence scales.[9]

NOTES

Pollak's research was supported in part by the National Science Foundation, the U.S. Bureau of Labor Statistics, and the National Institutes of Health.

1. By "family preferences" we mean the preferences of the adults in the family; preferences of children are ignored. For a family containing one adult, this notion of family preferences is unambiguous, but for a family containing two adults, there is an aggregation problem unless the adults' preferences happen to coincide. We ignore this and assume that the notion of family preferences is well-defined. Basing welfare comparisons on family preferences means that we can only compare demographic profiles whose adult compositions are identical; thus, we cannot compare the welfare of a family consisting of one adult and two children with that of a family of two adults and two children.

2. This corresponds to John Muellbauer's definition of equivalence scales as "budget deflators which are used to calculate the relative amounts of money two different types of households require in order to reach the same standard of living." However Muellbauer uses what we have called conditional equivalence scales to make welfare comparisons, and his paper provides numerous references to other studies that do so. We contend that such an approach is not valid because unconditional equivalence scales rather than conditional equivalence scales are required for welfare comparisons. Our objection to the use of conditional equivalence scales in welfare analysis does not depend on whether families can or do regulate their fertility.

3. The conventional cost-of-living index holds the demographic profile fixed and compares the expenditure required to attain a particular indifference curve under alternative price regimes. Such an index can be interpreted as a "subindex" of the unconditional equivalence scale which is itself the "complete index." Pollak (1975) develops the theory of subindexes of the cost-of-living index. In this paper we are concerned with complete indexes, or at least with indexes complete enough to include the demographic variables. Subindexes (i.e., conventional cost-of-living indexes) can be constructed separately for each family type, but such indexes do not permit comparisons of families of different types.

4. Notice that the unconditional preference ordering corresponding to the direct utility function $\hat{W}(X, \eta) = \sum a_k \log(x_k - b_k^* - \beta_k \eta) + \phi(\eta)$ is not the same as that corresponding to $W(X, \eta)$, and hence these two unconditional preference orderings yield distinct unconditional equivalence scales. However, both imply the same LES conditional demand functions and, hence, the same conditional equivalence scales.

5. Whether a particular demographic variable should be treated as predetermined or an object of choice is not automatically resolved by the fact that the variable in question is controlled or chosen by the family, and, hence, could legitimately be treated as an object of choice. For purposes of demand analysis, it is useful to treat family size as predetermined and work with conditional demand functions. When we treat such choices as unconditional, estimation of (unconditional) preferences requires us to reconstruct the feasible set from which the choice was made. But estimation of unconditional preferences is a secondary issue for us. We are primarily concerned with drawing the distinction between conditional and unconditional preferences and arguing that the latter are required for welfare comparisons.

6. Multiple births create special problems which we ignore. We interpret the $12,000 as total expenditure on goods and ignore both the labor-leisure choice and the dependence of taxes on demographic variables.

7. For an example of an equivalence scale constructed from responses to a

questionnaire asking individuals what income level corresponds to such verbal evaluations as "good," "sufficient," "bad," etc., see Kapteyn and van Praag (1976).

8. The relevance of these considerations and of welfare comparisons will vary from one policy question to another.

9. There is no reason to think that conditional equivalence scales have any role to play in the determination of socially adequate consumption levels.

REFERENCES

Kapteyn, A. and B. van Praag, "A New Approach to the Construction of Family Equivalence Scales," *European Economic Review*, Vol. 7 (May 1976), pp. 313–335.

Muellbauer, John, "Testing the Barten Model of Household Composition Effects and the Cost of Children," *Economic Journal*, Vol. 87 (September 1977), pp. 460–487.

Pollak, Robert A., "Subindexes in the Cost-of-Living Index," *International Economic Review*, Vol. 16 (February 1975), pp. 135–50.

Pollak, Robert A., and Terence J. Wales, "Estimation of Complete Demand Systems from Household Budget Data: The Linear and Quadratic Expenditure Systems," *American Economic Review*, Vol. 68 (June 1978), pp. 348–359.

———, "Demographic Variables in Demand Analysis," *Econometrica*, Vol. 49, No. 6 (November 1981), pp. 1533–1551.

Group Cost-of-Living Indexes

When households have different consumption patterns, whose cost of living should an actual price index represent? This issue was first raised by J. L. Nicholson and S. J. Prais in the 1950s. Both made essentially the same point: Official price indexes give each household's consumption pattern "an implicit weight proportional to its total expenditures" (see Nicholson 1975, p. 540). Prais (1959) calls such an index "plutocratic," and both Nicholson and Prais suggest an alternative "democratic price index" which gives all households equal weight.

A *group cost-of-living index* is an index that measures the impact of price changes on the welfare of a group or population of households. To define such an index requires an explicit or implicit concept of "the welfare of a group," and hence requires interpersonal comparisons and distributional judgments. Since group indexes such as the Consumer Price Index play an important role in our perception of inflation and the formation of macro-economic policy and are used to escalate wages and Social Security benefits, they have significant effects on government decisions and economic welfare. Despite their intellectual interest and practical importance, however, until recently they have been virtually ignored by index number theorists. The theory of the cost-of-living index (CLI) provides a generally accepted framework for measuring the impact of price changes on the welfare of a particular household. This paper extends the CLI concept to groups and discusses which questions require group indexes and which do not. I begin by introducing some notation and terminology in the context of household CLIs.

A household's CLI is the ratio of the expenditures required to attain a particular base indifference curve in two price situations. Suppose there are n goods and S households, and denote the preference ordering of the rth household by R^r. The base indifference curve can be identified by a goods collection, X^{ro}, which lies on it. The *expenditure function*, $E^r(P, X^{ro}, R^r)$, shows the minimum expenditure required to attain the base indifference curve at prices P. The CLI of the rth household, $I^r(P^a, P^b, X^{ro}, R^r)$, is the ratio of the minimum expenditure required to attain the base indifference curve at prices P^a (comparison prices) to that required at prices P^b (reference prices).

Except in very special cases, the value of the CLI depends on the base indifference curve at which it is evaluated; as successively higher base indifference curves are specified, one would expect the prices of "luxuries" to

From *The American Economic Review*, Vol. 70, No. 2 (May 1980), pp. 273–278. Reprinted with permission.

become more important relative to the prices of "necessities."[1] Hence, it is convenient to regard the CLI as a function of the base indifference curve rather than as a single number corresponding to a particular base. Thus, instead of offering guidance in choosing an appropriate base indifference curve, theory suggests that there is no need to choose.

To construct the exact CLI, an investigator needs to know the household's preferences. Lacking this knowledge, he must fall back on indexes which require less information and which are upper bounds on the exact index. The *Laspeyres index*, $J^r(P^a, P^b, X^{rb})$, is the ratio of the cost of purchasing the reference period consumption basket at comparison prices to its cost at reference prices:

$$J^r(P^a, P^b, X^{rb}) = \frac{\sum_{k=1}^{n} p_k^a x_k^{rb}}{\sum_{k=1}^{n} p_k^b x_k^{rb}}$$

Provided the household's reference period consumption pattern was optimal (according to its own preferences), the Laspeyres index is an upper bound on its cost-of-living index evaluated at the reference period indifference curve: $I^r(P^a, P^b, X^{rb}, R^r) \leqslant J^r(P^a, P^b, X^{rb})$.

To measure the impact of price changes on the welfare of a group of households, I consider two basic group CLIs, the "social CLI" and the "democratic CLI," and several related indexes. Since differences in family size and other demographic characteristics may require special treatment, it is convenient to begin with a group of households with identical demographic profiles. Distributional judgments play a crucial role in constructing an index for such a group, a role most easily seen in the context of Laspeyres-type indexes. Such indexes are ratios of the costs of particular collections of goods at comparison prices to their costs at reference prices. When households have different reference period consumption patterns—reflecting underlying differences in tastes or incomes—some implicit or explicit criterion is required to combine them into a single *social consumption pattern* on which to base the index. Nicholson and Prais, who consider only Laspeyres-type indexes, view the issue as one of weighting the consumption patterns of different households, but distributional judgments also play a crucial role in "exact" group indexes.

The social CLI is a group index based on a Bergson–Samuelson social welfare function, in the same way that a household's CLI is based on its own utility function; the social welfare function provides an explicit criterion for balancing the gains of some households against losses of others. The democratic CLI is not based on any explicit criterion for trading off the welfare of one household against that of another; it is defined as the unweighted average of the CLIs of the covered households (i.e., the households in the group). To construct either of these indexes requires knowledge of household preferences; in addition, the social CLI requires the investigator to specify his Bergson–Samuelson social welfare function.

Since an investigator is unlikely to have enough information to construct either of these exact indexes, he needs indexes which bound them and can be calculated with less information. Bounds on the democratic CLI are relatively easy to construct, but because the social CLI is intimately related to a particular Bergson–Samuelson social welfare function, useful bounds on it can be established only in very special cases.

1. THE SOCIAL CLI[2]

The social CLI is a group index based on a Bergson–Samuelson social welfare function. To construct it, an investigator must know each household's preferences and must express his distributional judgments in the form of a Pareto-inclusive social welfare function. I denote the welfare function by $W(\chi) = \Lambda[U^1(X^1), \ldots, U^S(X^S)]$ (and the corresponding social preference ordering by R) where $\chi = (X^1, \ldots, X^S)$ is the $n \times s$ dimensional *social consumption vector* showing every household's consumption of every good.

The *social expenditure function*, $E(P, \chi^0, R)$, shows the minimum total expenditure required to attain the indifference curve of χ^0 at prices P. The expenditure function represents a "thought experiment" in which expenditure is distributed among households so as to minimize the cost of attaining the specified indifference curve of the social welfare function.[3] The social CLI, $I(P^a, P^b, \chi^0, R)$, is the ratio of the minimum expenditure required to attain an indifference curve of the social welfare function at prices P^a to that required at prices P^b:

$$I(P^a, P^b, \chi^0, R) = \frac{E(P^a, \chi^0, R)}{E(P^b, \chi^0, R)}$$

The information needed to construct the exact social CLI is unlikely to be available. There are, however, two special cases in which the exact social CLI can be constructed with much less information. In a *maximizing society*—one which distributes expenditure among households so as to maximize a social welfare function—the market demand functions contain enough information to construct the exact social CLI corresponding to society's welfare function. The usefulness of this result depends on whether society distributes expenditure among households so as to maximize a social welfare function, and, if it does, on whether the investigator adopts that welfare function as the basis for his social CLI. In an *independent society*—one in which household preferences are such that the market demand functions are independent of the distribution of expenditure among households—it is well-known that the market demand functions can be derived from the preference ordering of a *representative household* and that the corresponding indifference map can be constructed from the market demand functions. In Pollak (1981), I show that in an independent society the social CLI corresponding to any Pareto-inclusive social welfare function is the index corresponding to the preference ordering of the representative household. Hence, disagreement among investigators with different social welfare functions is limited to the selection of an appropriate base indifference curve from the commonly accepted indifference map of the representative household. Because both the maximizing society and the independent society are very special cases, neither provides a general procedure for constructing the exact social CLI.

Lacking the information required to calculate the exact social CLI, an investigator may be able to calculate indexes which are upper bounds on it. However, the assumptions required to place bounds on the social CLI are much less likely to be satisfied than those required to place analogous bounds on a household's CLI. I consider two bounding indexes, the *social Laspeyres index* and the *Scitovsky–Laspeyres index*.

The social Laspeyres index, $J(P^a, P^b, X^b)$, is defined as the ratio of the expenditure required to purchase the reference period social consumption basket, $X^b = \sum X^{sb}$, at comparison prices to its cost at reference prices:

$$J(P^a, P^b, X^b) = \frac{\sum\limits_{k=1}^{n} p_k^a x_k^b}{\sum\limits_{k=1}^{n} p_k^b x_k^b} = \frac{\sum\limits_{s=1}^{S} \sum\limits_{k=1}^{n} p_k^a x_k^{sb}}{\sum\limits_{s=1}^{S} \sum\limits_{k=1}^{n} p_k^b x_k^{sb}}$$

It can be rewritten as a weighted average of household Laspeyres indexes, where the weights are the household's reference period expenditure shares:

$$J(P^a, P^b, X^b) = \sum\limits_{s=1}^{S} \omega^s(P^b, \chi^b) J^s(P^a, P^b, X^{sb})$$

$$\omega^r(P^b, \chi^b) = \frac{\sum\limits_{k=1}^{n} p_k^b x_k^{rb}}{\sum\limits_{s=1}^{S} \sum\limits_{k=1}^{n} p_k^b x_k^{sb}} = \frac{\mu_r^b}{\mu^b}$$

The Scitovsky–Laspeyres index, $J^*(P^a, P^b, \chi^b, R^1, \ldots, R^S)$, is defined as the ratio of the total expenditure required to enable each household to attain its reference period indifference curve at comparison prices to that required at reference prices; it can be rewritten as a weighted average of household CLIs where the weights are again reference period expenditure shares:

$$J^*(P^a, P^b, \chi^b, R^1, \ldots, R^S) = \sum\limits_{s=1}^{S} \omega^s(P^b, \chi^b) I^s(P^a, P^b, X^{sb}, R^s)$$

The social Laspeyres index is an upper bound on the social CLI for an appropriately chosen base indifference curve in the independent society and in the maximizing society, when the investigator adopts society's social welfare function. The Scitovsky–Laspeyres index is an upper bound on the social CLI in a maximizing society when the investigator adopts society's welfare function. However, it is not generally possible to place bounds on the exact social CLI without some assumption which guarantees that the reference period consumption pattern is optimal in terms of the social welfare function on which the index is based. Without such an assumption, we cannot construct indexes which provide bounds on the exact social CLI analogous to the Laspeyres bound on the household's CLI.

2. THE DEMOCRATIC CLI AND THE AXIOMATIC APPROACH

Nicholson and Prais both define the democratic price index, $J^D(P^a, P^b, \chi^b)$, to be a weighted average of "price relatives," where the weight of each item is the mean of its shares in the consumption patterns of the households in the group:

$$J^D(P^a, P^b, \chi^b) = \sum_{k=1}^{n} w_k^D(P^b, \chi^b)\left(\frac{p_k^a}{p_k^b}\right)$$

where

$$w_i^D = \frac{1}{S} \sum_{s=1}^{S} w_i^s(P^b, \chi^b)$$

and

$$w_i^s(P^b, \chi^b) = \frac{p_i^b x_i^{sb}}{\sum_{k=1}^{n} p_k^b x_k^{sb}}$$

The index can be rewritten as an unweighted average of household Laspeyres indexes:

$$J^D(P^a, P^b, \chi^b) = \frac{1}{S} \sum_{s=1}^{S} J^s(P^a, P^b, X^{sb})$$

In contrast, the social Laspeyres index implicitly weights each household's Laspeyres index by its total expenditure. Thus, in the democratic price index, every household counts equally, while in the "plutocratic" social Laspeyres index, every dollar of expenditure counts equally.

The democratic price index, like the social Laspeyres index, is a fixed-weight index and hence fails to take account of the willingness of households to substitute one good for another in response to relative price changes. I define the democratic CLI, $I^D(P^a, P^b, \chi^0)$, to be an unweighted average of household CLIs:

$$I^D(P^a, P^b, \chi^0) = \frac{1}{S} \sum_{s=1}^{S} I^s(P^a, P^b, X^{s0}, R^s)$$

Unlike the democratic price index, the democratic CLI permits some substitution in response to relative price changes; in particular, it permits "within-household" substitution, but unlike the social CLI, it does not permit "between-household" substitution. The democratic CLI is analogous to the Scitovsky–Laspeyres index: Both are fixed-weight indexes which are averages of household CLIs. Just as the social Laspeyres index is an upper bound on the Scitovsky–Laspeyres index, the democratic price index is an upper bound on the democratic CLI: $I^D(P^a, P^b, \chi^b) \leqslant J^D(P^a, P^b, \chi^b)$.[4]

The democratic CLI and the social CLI represent alternative approaches to defining group CLIs. Although the democratic CLI coincides with the social CLI or the Scitovsky–Laspeyres index in certain exceptional cases, it is neither a generalization nor a specialization of these indexes. The democratic CLI is not an approximation to or a bound on some more fundamental index, but is itself a basic index. Although it cannot be interpreted as a CLI corresponding to an underlying social welfare function, the meaning of the democratic CLI is unambiguous: It is an unweighted average of the CLIs of the households in the group, each evaluated at its reference period indifference curve. That is, different households require different percentage increases in their reference period expenditure levels to enable them to maintain their reference period indifference curves under the comparison price regime; the democratic CLI is defined to be the mean of these required percentage adjustments.

The axiomatic approach to price index construction—an outgrowth of the Irving Fisher test tradition—has been largely eclipsed by the modern, preference-based theory of the CLI. As a framework for constructing indexes for particular households, the preference approach is unlikely to be displaced by a revival of the test approach. However, as a framework for constructing group indexes, the axiomatic approach deserves more attention than it has thus far received, since the advantages of the preference approach are greatly attenuated when we turn from household to group indexes.

3. COMPARISONS WITHOUT GROUP INDEXES

Most questions about the distributional effects of price changes can be answered without group indexes. This section discusses which questions require group indexes and which do not.

We can always compare the impact of price changes on the welfare of different households by comparing their (separate) CLIs. Such comparisons do not require balancing one household's interests against another's, and thus can be made without distributional judgements. Group indexes and distributional judgements are necessary only if we require a single summary measure which reflects the impact of price changes on the entire group.

Suppose, for example, we want to compare the impact of price changes on the welfare of households with two children and those with three children.[5] If we know their preferences, we can construct their separate CLIs; however, it is not clear how to compare them, since, except in special cases, the indexes are not single numbers but functions whose values depend on the base indifference curves at which they are evaluated. If we insist on comparing CLI *functions*, there is little to say: Theory offers no guidance for such comparisons. If we reinterpret the problem as one of comparing the *values* of the functions at a particular pair of base indifference curves, then we avoid this difficulty; however, theory offers no guidance for selecting an appropriate pair of base indifference curves. If we specify the base indifference curve for two-child households as that corresponding to an expenditure level of $12,000 at reference prices, and the base for three-child households as that corresponding to $13,000, then a straightforward comparison can be made: however, instead of comparing two-child households and three-child households, we are now comparing $12,000 two-child households and $13,000 three-child households.[6]

Discussions of "whose CLI" have emphasized differences in consumption patterns resulting from income differences and their effect on Laspeyres-type indexes. We can compare the impacts of price changes on rich and poor households with identical tastes by comparing the value of the CLI corresponding to different base indifference curves; the formulation of the question in terms of "rich" and "poor" households implies a particular pair of base indifference curves, or at least a range of appropriate pairs. To formalize this notion, I define the *common* CLI for a group of households with identical tastes, $I^c(P^a, P^b, X^0, R)$, to be the CLI corresponding to their common preference ordering, R. The common CLI coincides with the social CLI if the investigator's social welfare function exhibits "equal concern" for all households—that is, if it treats all households symmetrically. It coincides with the democratic CLI if all households have identical reference period consumption patterns.

When household preference orderings are not known, exact indexes cannot be constructed. However, we can construct Laspeyres indexes from data on the reference period consumption patterns. Robert Michael (1979) reports household-specific Laspeyres indexes for more than 11,000 households and discusses the sources of variations in these indexes.

To summarize: Group CLIs measure the impact of price changes on a group of households, but different group indexes answer different questions, and the selection of a particular index must be determined by its purpose. Since the information required to construct exact indexes is unlikely to be available, we are forced to consider bounds; however, even the construction of bounds presents difficulties for indexes such as the social cost-of-living index, which is based on a Bergson–Samuelson social welfare function. Most questions concerning the distributional impact of price changes can be answered by comparing household CLIs, and do not call for group indexes at all. Group indexes are needed only if we require a summary measure of the welfare impact of price changes on the entire group. In short: distributional comparisons do not require group indexes, but group indexes require distributional judgements.

NOTES

University of Pennsylvania. This research was supported in part by the National Science Foundation, the U.S. Bureau of Labor Statistics, and the National Institutes of Health, none of which are responsible for the views expressed.

1. The value of the cost-of-living index is independent of the base indifference curve at which the index is evaluated if and only if the indifference map is homothetic to the origin, or, equivalently, if and only if all income elasticities are unity.

2. The material summarized in this section is drawn from Pollak (1981).

3. A *constrained social CLI* can be defined if the distribution of expenditure among households must satisfy additional restrictions beyond the requirement that $\sum \mu_s = \mu$.

4. Muellbauer (1974), an interesting unpublished paper, proposes the class of "homogeneous social price indexes," $J^M(P^a, P^b, \chi^b, \beta)$,

$$J^M(P^a, P^b, \chi^b, \beta) = \sum_{s=1}^{S} (\mu_s^b)^{1+\beta} J^s(P^a, P^b, X^{sb}) \sum_{t=1}^{S} (\mu_t^b)^{1+\beta}$$

This class depends on a parameter β, which Muellbauer interprets as a measure of aversion to inequality; when $\beta = -1$, all households receive equal weight (equal "votes" in Muellbauer's terminology) and the index coincides with the democratic price index; when $\beta = 0$, it coincides with the social Laspeyres index. If Muellbauer's parametric weighting procedure is applied to household CLIs instead of household Laspeyres indexes, it yields a class of "homogeneous social CLIs" which permit within-household substitution in response to relative price changes. This class includes the democratic CLI and the Scitovsky–Laspeyres index as special cases. For each β, the price indexes are upper bounds on the corresponding CLIs.

5. This example involves two types of households and taste differences related to demographic characteristics, but it generalizes readily to many household types and any kind of taste difference.

6. This procedure would be somewhat more attractive if we could determine the level of expenditure which would make a household with three children as well off as one with two children and $12,000, since this would enable us to compare the welfare impact of price changes on households at the same "standard of living." I do not believe that it is possible to use household budget data to establish the required correspondence between the indifference curves on one map and those on another, although professional opinion is divided on this question. See Muellbauer (1974) for a defense of the use of "equivalence scales" to make such comparisons, and Pollak and Wales (1979) for an attack on it.

REFERENCES

Michael, R. T., "Variations Across Households in the Rate of Inflation," *Journal of Money, Credit, and Banking*, Vol. 11 (February 1979), pp. 32–46.

Muellbauer, John, "The Political Economy of Price Indices," Disc. Paper No. 22, Birkbeck College (March 1974).

Nicholson, J. L., "Whose Cost of Living?," *Journal of Royal Statistical Society, Series A*, Vol. 138 (1975), pp. 540–542.

Prais, S. J., "Whose Cost of Living?," *Review of Economic Studies*, Vol. 26 (February 1959), pp. 126–134.

Pollak, Robert A., "The Social Cost-of-Living Index," *Journal of Public Economics*, Vol. 15, No. 3 (June 1981), pp. 311–336.

_____, and Terence J. Wales, "Welfare Comparisons and Equivalence Scales," *American Economic Review*, Vol. 69, No. 2 (May 1979), pp. 216–221.

The Social Cost-of-Living Index

Household cost of living indexes reflect household preferences; analogous indexes for groups of households require a corresponding concept of group preferences. In this paper I investigate the *social cost-of-living index*, a group index based on the Bergson–Samuelson social welfare function. I first define the index and examine its properties under the assumption that the investigator constructing it expresses his distributional judgements in an explicit Bergson–Samuelson social welfare function; I then examine the "maximizing society" and the "independent society," two cases in which the index can be constructed from the information contained in the market demand functions. In these two cases a Laspeyres index (i.e., the fixed-weight index based on the reference consumption pattern) is an upper bound on the exact social cost-of-living index. In general, however, the assumptions required to place bounds on the social cost-of-living index are much less likely to be satisfied than those required to place analogous bounds on a household's cost-of-living index.

1. THE SOCIAL COST-OF-LIVING INDEX

In this section I define the social cost-of-living index and examine its properties. I begin by summarizing cost-of-living index theory for a single household.[1]

Suppose there are n goods and S households; denote the consumption pattern of household r by $X^r = (x_1^r, \ldots, x_n^r)$, prices by $P = (p_1, \ldots, p_n)$, the preference ordering of the rth household by R^r, and its direct utility function by $U^r(X^r)$.[2] Assume that there are no consumption externalities, so that each household is concerned only with its own consumption and denote the rth household's ordinary demand functions by $X^r = h^r(P, \mu_r)$, where μ_r is its total expenditure.[3] The indirect utility function, $\Psi^r(P, \mu_r)$, represents the household's preference ordering over price-expenditure situations and shows the maximum utility attainable:

$$\Psi^r(P, \mu_r) = \max U^r(X^r)$$

subject to $\sum p_k x_k^r \leqslant \mu_r$. The indirect utility function can be obtained from the

From *Journal of Public Economics*, Vol. 15, No. 3 (June 1981), pp. 311–336. Copyright © 1981 by North-Holland. Reprinted by permission of Elsevier Sequoia S.A.

direct utility function by substituting the ordinary demand functions for the quantities: $\Psi^r(P, \mu_r) = U^r[h^r(P, \mu_r)]$. The ordinary demand functions can be derived from the indirect utility function using Roy's identity:

$$h^{ri}(P, \mu_r) = -\frac{\partial \Psi^r(P, \mu_r)/\partial p_i}{\partial \Psi^r(P, \mu_r)/\partial \mu_r}$$

A cost-of-living index compares the expenditures required to attain a base indifference curve under two price regimes. There are three ways of identifying base indifference curves: (1) specifying a goods collection, X^{r0}, which lies on the base indifference curve in the commodity space; (2) specifying a price-expenditure situation, (P^0, μ_r^0), which lies on the base indifference curve in the price-expenditure space; and (3) selecting a particular direct or indirect utility function to represent preferences and specifying a value to be attained by that utility function. Sometimes one method of identifying the base indifference curve is more convenient than the others, and in this paper I shall have occasion to use all three.

The "expenditure function" of the rth household $E^r(P, X^{r0}, R^r)$, shows the minimum expenditure required to attain each indifference curve at prices P. Formally

$$E^r(P, X^{r0}, R^r) = \min \sum_{k=1}^{n} p_k x_k^r$$

subject to $X^r R^r X^{r0}$. The indirect utility function and the expenditure function are related by the identity $\Psi^r[P, E^r(P, X^{r0}, R^r)] = U^r(X^{r0})$.

The *cost-of-living index* of the rth household is defined as the ratio of the minimum expenditure required to attain each indifference curve at prices P^a ("comparison prices") to that required at prices P^b ("reference prices"). I denote the cost-of-living index by $I^r(P^a, P^b, X^{r0}, R^r)$:

$$I^r(P^a, P^b, X^{r0}, R^r) = \frac{E^r(P^a, X^{r0}, R^r)}{E^r(P^b, X^{r0}, R^r)}$$

The preference ordering R^r is called the *base preference ordering*; the notation emphasizes the distinction between its selection and the selection of a base indifference curve from it.[4] This represents a slight departure from standard usage which treats both base preferences and the base indifference curve as fixed and regards the index as a function of reference and comparison prices only.[5]

The "Laspeyres index" for the rth household, $J^r(P^a, P^b, X^{rb})$, is the ratio of the cost of purchasing the reference period consumption basket at comparison prices to its cost at reference prices:

$$J^r(P^a, P^b, X^{rb}) = \frac{\sum\limits_{k=1}^{n} p_k^a x_k^{rb}}{\sum\limits_{k=1}^{n} p_k^b x_k^{rb}}$$

The Laspeyres index is an upper bound on the cost-of-living index based on reference preferences evaluated at the reference indifference curve:

$$I^r(P^a, P^b, X^{rb}, R^{rb}) \leqslant J^r(P^a, P^b, X^{rb}).[6]$$

The Laspeyres bounding theorem follows from two observations. First, $E^r(P^b, X^{rb}, R^{rb}) = \sum p_k^b x_k^{rb}$ since $X^{rb} = h^r(P^b, \mu_r^b)$ and the household is assumed to have chosen an optimal consumption pattern in the reference situation given its preferences, the prices it faced, and its total expenditure. Second, $E^r(P^a, X^{rb}, R^{rb}) \leqslant \sum p_k^a x_k^{rb}$ since X^{rb} is a collection of goods which attains the indifference curve of X^{rb}, and hence the minimum expenditure required to attain that indifference curve cannot exceed the cost of X^{rb}. This bounding argument depends crucially on the assumption that the reference consumption pattern is optimal in terms of reference preferences when the household faces the reference constraint. Without it one cannot conclude that the fixed-weight Laspeyres index $J^r(P^a, P^b, X^{rb}, R^{rb})$ is an upper bound on the exact index $I^r(P^a, P^b, X^{rb}, R^{rb})$.[7]

Constructing any type of group cost-of-living index requires weighting one household's welfare against another's. The social cost-of-living index is a particular group index based on a Bergson–Samuelson social welfare function, a preference ordering which ranks social consumption patterns.[8] In this section I assume that the investigator constructing the index is prepared to make explicit distributional judgments which can be summarized by such a function. I denote the investigator's social preference relation by R and the corresponding social welfare function by $W(\chi)$, where $\chi = (X^1, \ldots, X^S)$ is the $n \times S$ dimensional "social consumption vector" showing each household's consumption of every good.[9]

I assume that the investigator's Bergson–Samuelson social preference ordering is "Pareto-inclusive," an assumption which can be satisfied only if he knows each household's preferences. A Pareto-inclusive Bergson–Samuelson social welfare function respects consumer sovereignty by accepting each household's preferences as the definitive standard for evaluating its welfare and by treating an increase in any household's welfare as an increase in social welfare. Any such welfare function can be written in the form $W(\chi) = \Omega[U^1(X^1), \ldots, U^S(X^S)]$. An investigator with a Pareto-inclusive Bergson–Samuelson social welfare function knows each household's preferences, since household preferences can be recovered directly from any such welfare function.[10] Thus, assuming that the investigator can summarize his distributional judgments in a Pareto-inclusive Bergson–Samuelson social welfare function entails not merely his willingness to make ethical judgments of a generally acceptable sort, but also his complete knowledge of household preferences. At least for economists, the informational assumptions are more troubling than the ethical ones, and much of this paper is devoted to examining special cases in which the social cost-of-living index can be constructed with less information.

The *indirect social welfare function* corresponding to $W(\chi)$, $\Lambda(P, \mu_1, \ldots, \mu_S)$, is defined by $\Lambda(P, \mu_1, \ldots, \mu_S) = \Omega[\Psi^1(P, \mu_1), \ldots, \Psi^S(P, \mu_S)]$. Its value is the maximum "social utility" attainable in the price situation P when the distribution of expenditure among households is given by $(\mu_1, \ldots, \mu_S)$. The social expenditure function, $E(P, \chi^0, R)$, is defined as the minimum expenditure required to attain each indifference curve of the social welfare function at prices P. Formally

$$E(P, \chi^0, R) = \min \sum_{s=1}^{S} E^s(P, X^s, R^s)$$

subject to $\chi R \chi^0$.

I define the *social cost-of-living index*, $I(P^a, P^b, \chi^0, R)$, as the ratio of the minimum expenditure required to attain each indifference curve of the social welfare function at prices P^a to that required at prices P^b:

$$I(P^a, P^b, \chi^0, R) = \frac{E(P^a, \chi^0, R)}{E(P^b, \chi^0, R)}$$

As with the household's cost-of-living index, I treat the base indifference curve as an argument of the index.

Lump sum transfers among households underlie the social cost-of-living index. Because it is defined as the ratio of the minimum costs of attaining a given indifference curve of the social welfare function under two price regimes, the social cost-of-living index presupposes that expenditure can be redistributed among households while the total remains fixed. When the class of feasible redistributions is further restricted, additional constraints can be incorporated into the index. I discuss the *constrained social cost-of-living index* in the Appendix.[11]

The aggregate social preference ordering **R**, is a preference ordering over *aggregate commodity vectors*, $X = \sum_{s=1}^{S} X^s$. I now show that the social cost-of-living index is equal to the index based on the aggregate social preferences corresponding to the investigator's disaggregate preferences, R. More precisely, the utility function corresponding to **R**, the *aggregate direct social utility function*, shows the maximum "social utility" obtainable from the aggregate commodity vector X. Formally, $U(X) = \max \Omega[U^1(X^1), \ldots, U^S(X^S)]$, subject to $\sum_{s=1}^{S} X^s \leqslant X$. The corresponding indirect utility function, the *aggregate indirect social welfare function*, $\Psi(P, \mu)$, shows the maximum "social utility" attainable in the price situation P when μ is distributed among households so as to maximize $W(\chi)$. Formally, the aggregate indirect social welfare function is given by $\Psi(P, \mu) = \max \Lambda(P, \mu_1, \ldots, \mu_S)$, subject to $\sum_{s=1}^{S} \mu_s \leqslant \mu.$[12]

The aggregate social expenditure function, $E(P, X^0, \mathbf{R})$, is defined in the obvious way as the minimum expenditure required to attain each indifference curve of the aggregate social welfare function at prices P.[13] The cost-of-living index corresponding to the aggregate social welfare function is given by

$$I(P^a, P^b, X^0, \mathbf{R}) = \frac{E(P^a, X^0, \mathbf{R})}{E(P^b, X^0, \mathbf{R})}$$

Proposition 1. Let $\mathbf{R}$ be the aggregate social preference ordering corresponding to the disaggregate social preference ordering R. The cost-of-living index based on the aggregate social preference ordering $\mathbf{R}$ evaluated at the base indifference curve X^0 is equal to the social cost-of-living index based on R evaluated at the base indifference curve χ^0, where χ^0 is the best disaggregate consumption vector corresponding to X^0 under R:

$$I(P^a, P^b, X^0, \mathbf{R}) = I(P^a, P^b, \chi^0, R)$$

where $\chi^0 R \chi$ for all χ such that $\sum_{s=1}^{S} X^s \leqslant X^0$.

Proof. The proposition follows immediately from the observation that $E(P, X^0, \mathbf{R}) = E(P, \chi^0, R)$, where $\chi^0 R \chi$ for all χ such that $\sum_{s=1}^{S} X^s \leqslant X^0$.

The social cost-of-living index based on the aggregate social preference ordering is the formal analogue of the household cost-of-living index, since both use preference orderings over n-dimensional commodity spaces to compare n-dimensional price vectors. It follows directly that the social cost-of-living index exhibits all of the properties familiar from traditional cost-of-living index theory (e.g., if all prices increase by 5 percent then the index increases by 5 percent).[14]

If the base indifference curve were specified in aggregate terms, a research assistant could construct the social cost-of-living index from the investigator's aggregate social preferences. But if the base indifference curve were specified in disaggregate terms, he could not construct the index without knowing the investigator's disaggregate preferences; he needs this additional knowledge to identify the indifference curve of the aggregate preference ordering corresponding to the disaggregate base indifference curve.[15]

A group cost-of-living index reflects an explicit or implicit valuation of the welfare of different households (Pollak 1980). Such valuations are necessary for comparing price regimes which different households evaluate differently (e.g., rich vs. poor; meat-eaters vs. vegetarians). A principal advantage of the social cost-of-living index is that its reliance on the Bergson–Samuelson social welfare function makes explicit the underlying distributional judgements. For an investigator who knows the preferences of each household and who is willing to express distributional judgements in the form of a Bergson–Samuelson social welfare function, the social cost-of-living index is an appealing group index. In the following sections I explore the maximizing society and the independent society, two special cases in which an investigator who is unable or unwilling to specify his Bergson–Samuelson social welfare function might still construct a social cost-of-living index.

2. THE "MAXIMIZING SOCIETY"

The "maximizing society" approach avoids the stringent information requirements of section 1 by combining two assumptions: (1) that society distributes
expenditure among households to maximize a social welfare function, and
(2) that this welfare function is an appropriate base for the social cost-of-living
index. I show that in a maximizing society the market demand functions
contain enough information to construct this index. An assessment of the
maximizing society approach depends on the empirical validity of the
maximizing society assumption and the ethical appeal of a social cost-of-living
index based on society's preferences.

The social philosopher might refuse to consider seriously, much less adopt,
the maximizing society's welfare function.[16] First, he could argue that it is
logically impossible for a society to have "preferences": Only persons
can have preferences, and the phrase "society's preferences" reflects an
anthropomorphic conception of society.[17] Second, granting that a society
can have some kinds of preferences, the social philosopher could claim that
it is a mistake to speak of a society having "ethical preferences": Only persons
can make moral judgements, and the evaluations of alternative distributions which underlie the social cost-of-living index must represent ethical
evaluations.[18] Third, even assuming that it is not a category mistake to
attribute ethical preferences to a society, the social philosopher could argue
that in practice society's preferences are the outcome of a political process
in which the conflicting views and interests of the members of society are
aggregated; the social preferences which emerge from the political process
reflect the distribution of power in the society. In practice, therefore, society's
preferences are not ethical judgements but political compromises, and are
not an appropriate base for a social cost-of-living index.[19]

The official statistician or statistical agency, unlike the social philosopher,
might embrace the maximizing society's welfare function as the uniquely
appropriate base for the official social cost-of-living index. He might argue
that a society's welfare function reflects its values, as articulated through its
political processes. Thus, while conceding that society's social welfare function
reflects political as well as ethical considerations, the official statistician denies
the social philosopher's claim that the social cost-of-living index must be
based on purely ethical preferences. The official statistician might go on to
argue that if it is not logically possible for a society to have ethical preferences,
then society's social welfare function—the amalgamation of the views
and interests of the members of society produced by society's political
institutions—is the best possible base for the official index.[20]

The official statistician might go on to point out that if he were to seek
the advice of a committee of social philosophers they would not reach a
consensus. This failure might not disturb the social philosophers, but from
the standpoint of the official statistician it argues against convening such a
committee. Furthermore, even if the social philosophers were unanimous in
advocating a particular social welfare function, the case for basing the official

social cost-of-living index on the values or weighting scheme which society itself has adopted would be strong: Democratic political theory has never been comfortable with philosopher-kings.

I begin by establishing the relationship between the maximizing society's market demand functions and its aggregate indirect social welfare function. A full statement requires some additional notation. Let R^* denote the maximizing society's social preference ordering and $W^*(\chi)$ its direct social welfare function. By definition, expenditure is always distributed so as to maximize $W^*(\chi) = \Omega^*[U^1(X^1), \ldots, U^S(X^S)]$, subject to $\sum_{s=1}^{S} \sum_{k=1}^{n} p_k x_k^s \leq \mu$, or, equivalently, so as to maximize $\Lambda^*(P, \mu_1, \ldots, \mu_S)$, subject to $\sum_{s=1}^{S} \mu_s \leq \mu$. Let $\mu_r = \phi^r(P, \mu)$ denote the implied "expenditure distribution functions." The market demand functions, $h(P, \mu)$ are given by

$$h(P, \mu) = \sum_{s=1}^{S} h^s[P, \phi^s(P, \mu)].^{21}$$

Proposition 2. In a maximizing society the market demand functions can be derived from the aggregate indirect social welfare function $\Psi^*(P, \mu)$ using Roy's identity:

$$h^i(P, \mu) = -\frac{\partial \Psi^*(P, \mu)/\partial p_i}{\partial \Psi^*(P, \mu)/\partial \mu}$$

I sketch a proof of this proposition, since it not only establishes the relationship between the aggregate indirect social welfare function and the market demand functions, but also provides an alternative proof of Samuelson's theorem that if expenditure is distributed among households so as to maximize a social welfare function, then the implied market demand functions can be rationalized by a utility function.[22]

Proof.[23] The aggregate indirect social welfare function is given by

$$\Psi(P, \mu) = \Omega\{\Psi^1[P, \phi^1(P, \mu)], \ldots, \Psi^S[P, \phi^S(P, \mu)]\}$$

so

$$-\frac{\partial \Psi/\partial p_i}{\partial \Psi/\partial \mu} = -\frac{\sum\limits_{s=1}^{S} \Omega_s \Psi_i^s + \sum\limits_{s=1}^{S} \Omega_s \Psi_{\mu_s}^s \phi_i^s}{\sum\limits_{s=1}^{S} \Omega_s \Psi_{\mu_s}^s \phi_\mu^s}.^{24}$$

The derivation of the expenditure distribution functions yields first-order conditions $\Omega_r \Psi_{\mu_r}^r = \lambda$. Hence,

$$-\frac{\partial \Psi/\partial p_i}{\partial \Psi/\partial \mu} = -\frac{\sum\limits_{s=1}^{S} \Omega_s \Psi_{\mu_s}^s \Psi_i^s / \Psi_{\mu_s}^s + \lambda \sum\limits_{s=1}^{S} \phi_i^s}{\lambda \sum\limits_{s=1}^{S} \phi_\mu^s}$$

Since the expenditure distribution functions satisfy $\sum_{s=1}^{S} \phi^s(P, \mu) = \mu$, we have $\sum_{s=1}^{S} \phi_i^s(P, \mu) = 0$ and $\sum_{s=1}^{S} \phi_\mu^s(P, \mu) = 1$. Hence,

$$-\frac{\partial\Psi/\partial p_i}{\partial\Psi/\partial\mu} = -\frac{\sum\limits_{s=1}^{S} \lambda\Psi_i^s/\Psi_{\mu s}^s}{\lambda} = \sum_{s=1}^{S} h^{si}(P, \mu)$$

since $h^{si}(P, \mu) = -\Psi_i^s/\Psi_{\mu s}^s$.

Proposition 3. Consider a maximizing society with a disaggregate social preference ordering R^*, and let $\mathbf{R}^M$ be the aggregate preference ordering which rationalizes the market demand functions. The cost-of-living index based on $\mathbf{R}^M$ evaluated at the base indifference curve X^0 is equal to the social cost-of-living index based on R^* evaluated at the base indifference curve χ^0, where χ^0 is the best disaggregate consumption vector corresponding to X^0 under R^*:

$$I(P^a, P^b, X^0, \mathbf{R}^M) = I(P^a, P^b, \chi^0, R^*)$$

where $\chi^0 R\chi$ for all χ such that $\sum X^s \leq X^0$.[25]

Proof. This follows immediately from propositions 1 and 2 and the definition of a maximizing society.

In a maximizing society the disaggregate consumption vector associated with an aggregate consumption vector can be inferred directly from household consumption patterns. However, if an investigator knows only the market demand functions, the base indifference curve must be specified in aggregate terms.

The informational requirements and distributional judgments underlying the maximizing society approach are quite different from those used to define the social cost-of-living index in section 1. There the investigator knew the preferences of each household and used his own Bergson–Samuelson social welfare function to compare price vectors which different households evaluated differently; nothing was assumed about the actual distribution of expenditure. The maximizing society approach requires the investigator to know the market demand functions and to know that they reflect an underlying distribution of expenditure which maximizes a social welfare function. From this he can infer society's aggregate welfare function and construct the corresponding social cost-of-living index.[26] The appeal of the maximizing society approach depends on the empirical validity of the maximizing society assumption and the propriety of basing a social cost-of-living index on society's preferences.[27]

3. THE "INDEPENDENT SOCIETY"

Consider an "independent society," one in which market demand functions are independent of the distribution of expenditure among households.[28] It is well known that in such a society the market demand functions can be derived from a "market preference ordering" which is essentially the preference ordering of a "representative household." In this section I show that in an independent society an investigator's aggregate social preference ordering is independent of his disaggregate preferences and coincides with the market preference ordering. Hence, regardless of an investigator's disaggregate preferences, the market preference ordering is the base of his social cost-of-living index. Thus, the scope for disagreement among investigators with different disaggregate social welfare functions is limited to the selection of an appropriate base indifference curve from a commonly accepted preference ordering, the market preference ordering.[29] With an aggregate specification of the base indifference curve this source of disagreement disappears and every disaggregate social welfare function implies the same social cost-of-living index.

Proposition 4. In an independent society, the market demand functions can be rationalized by a market preference ordering, $\mathbf{R}^M$.

Proof. This follows from the maximizing society results: Select an arbitrary disaggregate social preference ordering, $\bar{R}$, denote the corresponding aggregate social preference ordering by $\bar{\mathbf{R}}$, and distribute expenditure among households in accordance with $\bar{R}$. By proposition 2, the implied market demand functions are rationalized by $\bar{\mathbf{R}}$. But the market demand functions are independent of the distribution of expenditure among households, so the aggregate social preference ordering $\bar{\mathbf{R}}$ rationalizes the market demand functions regardless of how expenditure is distributed among households. Thus, $\bar{\mathbf{R}} = \mathbf{R}^M$.

Proposition 5. In an independent society, all disaggregate social preference orderings imply the same aggregate social preference ordering.

Proof. This follows immediately from proposition 4, provided that the market demand functions cannot be rationalized by more than one preference ordering.[30]

Proposition 6. In an independent society, the base preference ordering for the social cost-of-living index corresponding to every Pareto-inclusive disaggregate social preference ordering is the market preference ordering, $\mathbf{R}^M$.

Proof. This follows directly from the two preceding propositions and proposition 1.

Proposition 7. In an independent society with an aggregate specification of the base indifference curve, every disaggregate social preference ordering implies the same social cost-of-living index.[31]

Proof. Identifying the base indifference curve in aggregate terms eliminates the only possible type of disagreement in the light of proposition 6.

What class of household preferences yields market demand functions independent of the distribution of expenditure among households?[32] If independence is required for all possible allocations (i.e., all allocations of μ for which $\mu_s \geq 0$ for all s and $\sum \mu_s = \mu$ are admissible), then independence implies that each household's demand for every good is proportional to its total expenditure and all households have identical demand functions. This is the case if and only if all households have identical homothetic preferences. If independence is required "locally" rather than "globally" (i.e., if it is only required for allocations satisfying $\underline{\mu}_s \leq \mu_s \leq \bar{\mu}_s$, for all s, and $\sum \mu_s = \mu$), then it implies that each household's demand for every good is a linear function of its total expenditure, and that all households have identical marginal budget shares. This is the case if and only if each household's indirect utility function can be written in the Gorman form

$$\Psi^r(P, \mu_r) = \frac{\mu_r - f^r(P)}{g(P)}$$

where the functions $f^r(P)$ and $g(P)$ are homogeneous of degree one and $g(P)$ is the same for all households.[33] The implied household demand functions are given by

$$h^{ri}(P, \mu_r) = f_i^r(P) - \frac{g_i(P)}{g(P)} f^r(P) + \frac{g_i(P)}{g(P)} \mu_r$$

The market demand functions,

$$h^i(P, \mu) = \sum_{s=1}^{S} f_i^s(P) - \frac{g_i(P)}{g(P)} \sum_{s=1}^{S} f^s(P) + \frac{g_i(P)}{g(P)} \mu$$

are generated by the indirect utility function

$$\Psi(P, \mu) = \left(\mu - \sum_{s=1}^{S} f^s(P) \right) \bigg/ g(P)$$

Identifying the base indifference curve by the value of the indirect utility function, which we denote by σ, the expenditure function is given by $E(P, \sigma) = \sum f^s(P) + g(P)\sigma$ and the social cost-of-living index by

$$I(P^a, P^b, \sigma, \mathbf{R}^M) = \frac{\displaystyle\sum_{s=1}^{S} f^s(P^a) + g(P^a)\sigma}{\displaystyle\sum_{s=1}^{S} f^s(P^b) + g(P^b)\sigma} \ .[34]$$

Gorman's characterization of the class of household preferences generating demand functions independent of the expenditure distribution permits a revealing alternative proof of these results.[35] I begin by restating the general definition of the social expenditure function, identifying the base indifference curve using the values of particular household and social utility functions. Given a disaggregate social welfare function $\Omega(u_1, \ldots, u_S) = \Omega[U^1(X^1), \ldots, U^S(X^S)]$, and corresponding indirect utility functions $u_r = \Psi^r(P, \mu_r)$ and expenditure functions $\mu_r = E^r(P, u_r)$ for each household, the social expenditure function $E(P, \omega)$ is given by

$$E(P, \omega) = \min_{\{u_r\}} \sum_{s=1}^{S} E^s(P, u_s)$$

subject to $\Omega(u_1, \ldots, u_S) = \omega$. Solving the constrained minimization problem yields *utility distribution functions* $u_r = \theta^r(P, \omega)$, so the social expenditure function is given by

$$E(P, \omega) = \sum_{s=1}^{S} E^s[P, \Theta^s(P, \omega)]$$

Consider an independent society and select the Gorman representation of each household's indirect utility function. Then the household expenditure functions are given by $\mu_r = f^r(P) + g(P)u_r$, and the objective function of the constrained minimization problem becomes $\sum f^s(P) + g(P)\sum u_s$. Minimizing this expression subject to $\Omega(u_1, \ldots, u_S) = \omega$ requires minimizing $\sum u_s$ subject to this constraint, and the implied utility distribution functions are clearly independent of prices: $u_r = \theta^r(\omega)$.[36] Substituting these utility distribution functions into the social expenditure function yields

$$E(P, \omega) = \sum f^s(P) + g(P)\sum \Theta^s(\omega)$$

so the corresponding social cost-of-living index is given by

$$I(P^a, P^b, \omega, R) = \frac{\sum f^s(P^a) + g(P^a)\sum \Theta^s(\omega)}{\sum f^s(P^b) + g(P^b)\sum \Theta^s(\omega)}$$

Thus, the disaggregate social preference ordering influences the social cost-of-living index only through its influence on $\sum \Theta^s(\omega)$, which is the base indifference curve in the market cost-of-living index $I(P^a, P^b, \sigma, \mathbf{R}^M)$.

We can use the Gorman forms to motivate the conclusion that, in an independent society, all investigators have identical aggregate preferences (proposition 5). Consider first an investigator's preference between two aggregate price-expenditure situations without assuming an independent society. Once a set of utility functions is selected to represent individual preferences, a set of prices and a level of aggregate expenditure determines a frontier in the utility space $(u_1, \ldots, u_S)$. Each investigator identifies the best point on his frontier according to his disaggregate social welfare function $\Omega(u_1, \ldots, u_S)$, and his ranking of aggregate price-expenditure situations coincides with his ranking of the "best points" corresponding to them. Now consider an independent society and represent individual preferences by their Gorman indirect utility functions. Then the frontier corresponding to any price-expenditure situation is linear with slope -1: $\sum f^s(P) + g(P) \sum u^s = \mu$. Hence, in an independent society, an investigator's preference between two aggregate price-expenditure situations reduces to his preference between two such situations in the utility space. All investigators, regardless of their disaggregate social preferences, prefer the frontier further from the origin, and thus they unanimously prefer the aggregate price-expenditure situation corresponding to this outer frontier. Thus, all investigators have identical aggregate indirect social preferences.

This section's results contradict the usual belief that the market preference ordering is relevant for positive economics but has no welfare significance. In an independent society the market preferences are the base for the social cost-of-living index, an "evaluative statistic" with strong normative connotations.[37] Unfortunately, the empirical validity of the independent society assumption is dubious.[38]

4. UPPER BOUNDS

In this section I define two indexes which require less information than is generally needed to construct the exact social cost-of-living index. One of these, the *social Laspeyres index*, uses only knowledge of society's reference consumption pattern; it is an upper bound on the exact index in maximizing and independent societies.[39] The other index, the *Scitovsky–Laspeyres index*, assumes knowledge of household preferences; it is an upper bound on the exact index in a maximizing society and coincides with it in an independent society.

I define the *social Laspeyres index*, $J(P^a, P^b, X^b)$, as the ratio of the expenditure required to purchase the reference social consumption basket at comparison prices to its cost at reference prices:

$$J(P^a, P^b, X^b) = \frac{\sum\limits_{k=1}^{n} p_k^a x_k^b}{\sum\limits_{k=1}^{n} p_k^b x_k^b} = \frac{\sum\limits_{s=1}^{S} \sum\limits_{k=1}^{n} p_k^a x_k^{sb}}{\sum\limits_{s=1}^{S} \sum\limits_{k=1}^{n} p_k^b x_k^{sb}}. \quad 40$$

Proposition 8. In a maximizing society the social Laspeyres index is an upper bound on the social cost-of-living index based on society's social preference ordering, R^*, and evaluated at the reference indifference curve, χ^b:

$$I(P^a, P^b, X^b, R^*) \leqslant J(P^a, P^b, X^b)$$

Proof. The proof is essentially identical to that of the Laspeyres theorem for a household's cost-of-living index.[41]

The Laspeyres argument, for household or society, hinges on the reference consumption pattern's optimality with respect to the preferences on which the index is based.[42] The assumptions needed to guarantee this severely limit the scope of the result: It requires both a maximizing society and the investigator's willingness to adopt society's social welfare function as the base for his social cost-of-living index.

Proposition 9. In an independent society the social Laspeyres index is an upper bound on the social cost-of-living index based on any social preference ordering evaluated at the aggregate reference indifference curve, X^b:

$$I(P^a, P^b, X^b, \mathbf{R}) \leqslant J(P^a, P^b, X^b)$$

This result depends crucially on identifying the base indifference curve in aggregate terms.

Proof. For any disaggregate social preference ordering, the corresponding aggregate social preference ordering is $\mathbf{R}^M$. Since $\mathbf{R}^M$ rationalizes the market demand functions and $X^b = h(P^b, \mu^b)$, the usual Laspeyres argument applies.

Relatively little information is needed to construct the social Laspeyres index: Only the reference market consumption pattern and prices in both situations are required. The bounds, however, depend not only on this information but also on the assumption that these data are generated by maximizing or independent societies.

I define the *Scitovsky–Laspeyres index*, $J^*(P^a, P^b, \chi^b, R^1, \ldots, R^S)$, as the ratio of the total expenditure required to enable each household to attain its reference indifference curve at comparison prices to that required at reference prices:

$$J^*(P^a, P^b, \chi^b, R^1, \ldots, R^S) = \frac{\displaystyle\sum_{s=1}^{S} E^s(P^a, X^{sb}, R^s)}{\displaystyle\sum_{s=1}^{S} E^s(P^b, X^{sb}, R^s)}$$

I use Scitovsky's name in conjunction with this index to suggest its relation to Scitovsky community indifference contours, the set of commodity vectors X which can be allocated to enable each household to attain a prespecified indifference curve.[43] The Scitovsky–Laspeyres index can be rewritten as a weighted average of household cost-of-living indexes:

$$J^*(P^a, P^b, \chi^b, R^1, \ldots, R^S) = \sum_{s=1}^{S} w^s(P^b, \chi^b) I^s(P^a, P^b, X^{sb}, R^s)$$

where the weights are the household's reference expenditure shares. In the subindex context there is an analogous relationship between the complete index and partial indexes. See Pollak (1975a).

The Scitovsky–Laspeyres index assumes households substitute one good for another to attain their reference indifference curve at minimum cost. It does not, however, assume that society allocates resources among households so as to minimize the expenditure required to attain the base social indifference curve, and it provides no mechanism for balancing some households' gains against others' losses. Thus, the Scitovsky–Laspeyres index stands between the social Laspeyres and the exact index: In response to relative price changes, it takes account of intra-household substitution but not the inter-household substitution which is also allowed for by the exact social cost of living index.

Proposition 10. In a maximizing society the Scitovsky–Laspeyres index is an upper bound on the social cost-of-living index based on society's social preference ordering, R^*, and evaluated at the reference indifference curve, χ^b:

$$I(P^a, P^b, \chi^b, R^*) \leqslant J^*(P^a, P^b, \chi^b, R^1, \ldots, R^S)$$

Proof. The proof is similar to the usual Laspeyres argument: Since expenditure is optimally distributed among households, we have

$$E(P^b, \chi^b, R^*) = \sum_{s=1}^{S} E^s(P^b, X^{sb}, R^s)$$

and, regardless of the form of the social welfare function,

$$E(P^a, \chi^b, R^*) \leqslant \sum_{s=1}^{S} E^s(P^a, X^{sb}, R^s)$$

The Scitovsky–Laspeyres index is a better bound on the exact index than the social Laspeyres index, but more information is needed to construct it. In particular, the investigator must know not only each household's reference consumption pattern, but also its preferences. Because it requires more information about preferences than can be inferred from the reference consumption pattern, the Scitovsky–Laspeyres's information requirements are qualitatively greater than those of the usual Laspeyres index.[44] The Scitovsky–Laspeyres uses no information about the maximizing society's preferences beyond what can be inferred from the optimality of the reference expenditure distribution, so its information requirements are far less than those of the exact social cost-of-living index.

Proposition 11. In an independent society the Scitovsky–Laspeyres index coincides with the exact social cost-of-living index based on any social preference ordering evaluated at the aggregate reference indifference curve:

$$I(P^a, P^b, X^b, \mathbf{R}) = J^*(P^a, P^b, \chi^b, R^1, \ldots, R^S)$$

or, equivalently,

$$I[P^a, P^b, (P^b, \mu^b), \mathbf{R}] = J^*[P^a, P^b, (P^b, \mu^b_1, \ldots, \mu^b_S), R^1, \ldots, R^S]$$

Proof. Identifying the base indifference curve in terms of the price-expenditure situation leads to a straightforward proof based on the Gorman indirect utility function.[45] The Scitovsky–Laspeyres index is given by $[\sum f^s(P^a) + g(P^a)\sum \sigma^{sb}]/\mu^b$, where $\sigma^{rb} = [\mu^{rb} - f^r(P^b)]/g(P^b)$ so $\sum \sigma^{sb} = [\mu^b - \sum f^s(P^b)]/g(P^b)$. Substituting for $\sum \sigma^{sb}$ yields $[\sum f^s(P^a) + g(P^a)\sigma^b]/\mu^b$, where $\sigma^b = [\mu^b - \sum f^s(P^b)]/g(P^b)$, and this is the expression for the exact social cost-of-living index evaluated at (P^b, μ^b).

An alternative argument provides a different insight. Consider a "Leontief" or "fixed coefficient" social welfare function consistent with the reference distribution of expenditure. Since this social welfare function permits no substitution of one household's utility for another's, the implied social cost-of-living index coincides with the Scitovsky–Laspeyres index. But in an independent society, the social cost-of-living index is the same for all disaggregate social preferences, so for all social preferences it coincides with the Scitovsky–Laspeyres index.

This result is less striking than at first appears. A much simpler argument shows that the information required to construct the Scitovsky–Laspeyres index permits construction of the exact index in an independent society. Constructing the Scitovsky–Laspeyres index requires knowledge of household preferences; in an independent society, household preferences permit the construction of household demand functions; in an independent society, household demand functions permit the construction of market demand functions; and, in an independent society, market demand functions identify the market preference ordering. By proposition 6, the market preference ordering is the base for the social cost-of-living index.

Muellbauer (1974) argues that the social Laspeyres index gives undue importance to the consumption patterns of high-expenditure households because it implicitly weights each household's Laspeyres index by its total expenditure. He raises a similar objection to chain (Divisia) indexes, and presumably also would raise it to the Scitovsky–Laspeyres index. Muellbauer shows that if all households have identical preferences exhibiting what he calls *price independent generalized linearity* (PIGL), then the social Laspeyres index can be interpreted as the Laspeyres index of a single household with these preferences; more precisely, there exists a level of expenditure, μ^*, not necessarily the mean, such that at reference prices a household with expenditure μ^* will choose a consumption pattern whose expenditure shares are equal to those of the social Laspeyres index.[46] Assuming that household preferences are identical and belong to the PIGL class, Muellbauer estimates that the expenditure level which would generate the consumption weights used to construct the UK Retail Price Index is around the 71st percentile of the expenditure distribution.[47] This is consistent with his theoretical results, which imply that μ^* could be well above the median.

Muellbauer's main point is essentially nontechnical: If an index is intended to reflect the experience of a "typical" household, then it is inappropriate to weight each household's consumption pattern by its total expenditure. Muellbauer examines several alternative procedures for calculating group indexes, including one in which each household's consumption pattern has equal importance regardless of its expenditure (his "Democratic Price Index").

This section provides a limited rationale for the social Laspeyres index. In an independent or a maximizing society, the weighting used in the social Laspeyres index follows directly from the definition of the social cost-of-living index. In a maximizing society, the social Laspeyres index is an upper bound on the social cost-of-living index based on society's welfare function and evaluated at the reference period indifference curve; weighting each household's Laspeyres index by its expenditure share yields a group index which reflects the valuation of households embodied in society's welfare function. In an independent society with the aggregate specification of the base indifference curve, the index constructed by weighting each household's Laspeyres index by its expenditure share is an upper bound on the exact index. This section's rationale for the social Laspeyres index applies to maximizing and independent societies. Except in very special cases, a fixed-weight index does not bound an exact index unless its weights correspond to an optimal consumption pattern for the preferences on which the exact index is based.

5. CONCLUSION

In this paper I have defined and investigated the social cost-of-living index, a group index which uses the Bergson–Samuelson social welfare function as an explicit criterion for combining the differing evaluations of different households to form a single index. Except in certain special cases, constructing a social cost-of-living index requires the investigator to specify his social welfare function, a requirement with both ethical and informational implications; the informational burden is particularly heavy, implying that the investigator knows each household's preferences.

In certain special cases the market demand functions contain enough information to construct the social cost-of-living index without requiring an explicit social welfare function. In a maximizing society, one which distributes expenditure among households so as to maximize a social welfare function, the market demand functions contain enough information to calculate the exact index corresponding to society's welfare function; but society's welfare function is more attractive to the official statistician than to the social philosopher. In an independent society, one in which market demand functions are independent of the distribution of expenditure among households, all social welfare functions imply the same base preference ordering for the social cost-of-living index, and this preference ordering can be inferred from the market demand functions; thus, the scope for disagreement among investigators with different social welfare functions is limited to selecting an appropriate base indifference curve from this commonly accepted preference ordering.

When an investigator does not have enough information to calculate the exact social cost-of-living index, he can sometimes calculate bounds on it. The social Laspeyres index, the fixed-weight index calculated on the basis of society's reference consumption pattern, is an upper bound on the social cost-of-living index in the maximizing society and the independent society. The Scitovsky–Laspeyres index, an index which holds constant a base indifference curve for each household, is an upper bound on the exact index in the maximizing society and coincides with it in the independent society. Establishing bounds on the exact index depends on assumptions which guarantee that the reference consumption pattern is optimal in terms of the preferences on which the index is based. Hence, the assumptions required to place bounds on the social cost-of-living index are much less likely to be satisfied than those required to place analogous bounds on a household's cost-of-living index.

APPENDIX: THE CONSTRAINED SOCIAL COST-OF-LIVING INDEX

The social cost-of-living index assumes that lump sum transfers permit redistributions of expenditure among households subject only to the requirement that $\sum \mu_s = \mu$. When redistributions must satisfy other restrictions, I define the *constrained social cost-of-living index*. Let $(\mu_1, \ldots, \mu_S, \mu)$ denote the $S + 1$ dimensional vector whose first S components are the expenditures of households 1 through S and whose final component is total expenditure, μ. Let T be the set of feasible vectors in this space, so that $(\mu_1, \ldots, \mu_S, \mu) \in T$ if and only if $(\mu_1, \ldots, \mu_S)$ is an admissible distribution of μ.[48]

I define the *constrained social expenditure function*, $E(P, \chi^0, R, T)$, as the minimum total expenditure (μ) required to attain the indifference curve of χ^0 of the social preference ordering R subject to the distributional constraint represented by T:

$$E(P, \chi^0, R, T) = \min \sum_{s=1}^{S} E^s(P, X^s, R^s)$$

subject to $(X^1, \ldots, X^S) R \chi^0$ and $(\mu_1, \ldots, \mu_S, \mu) \in T$. I define the *constrained social cost-of-living index*, as the ratio of the minimum expenditures required to attain χ^0 subject to the distributional constraint, T:

$$I(P^a, P^b, \chi^0, R, T) = \frac{E(P^a, \chi^0, R, T)}{E(P^b, \chi^0, R, T)}$$

Finally, I define the *constrained social Laspeyres index*, $J(P^a, P^b, \chi^b, T)$, to be the ratio of the minimum total expenditure required to permit each household to purchase the collection of goods it purchased in the reference situation:

$$J(P^a, P^b, \chi^b, T) = \mu^*/\mu^b$$

where μ^* is defined by

$$\mu^* = \min \sum_{s=1}^{S} \mu_s$$

subject to $\mu_r \geqslant \sum_{k=1}^{n} x_k^{rb} p_k^a$ for all r and $(\mu_1, \ldots, \mu_S, \mu^*) \in T$.

In a maximizing society the constrained social Laspeyres index is an upper bound on the constrained social cost-of-living index based on society's social preferences and evaluated at the reference period indifference curve. The constrained social Laspeyres index reflects total expenditure required to compensate each household subject to the distributional constraint; in general, the distributional constraint will require that some households be overcompensated in order to compensate others fully. Calculating the constrained social Laspeyres index does not require knowing household preferences or social preferences, but unlike the social Laspeyres index, calculating it requires knowing each household's reference period consumption pattern. As with the social Laspeyres index, interpreting the constrained social Laspeyres index as an upper bound on the exact index requires that the investigator adopt the maximizing society's welfare function: The reference period expenditure distribution must be optimal in terms of the preferences on which the index is based.[49]

NOTES

This research was supported in part by the United States Bureau of Labor Statistics and the National Science Foundation. I am indebted to anonymous referees for their suggestions, to John Muellbauer for his comments, and to Judith Lachterman for editorial assistance, but the opinions expressed are my own and neither they nor the BLS nor the NSF should be blamed for them.

1. I take households rather than individuals to be the basic units of analysis and assume they have well-behaved preferences. See Samuelson (1956) for the classic statement of the problem of aggregating individual preferences into household preferences.

2. I assume a one-period time horizon, so there can be no saving or dissaving; in a multiperiod framework defining a cost-of-living index is difficult unless there is a complete system of futures markets. See Pollak (1975b).

3. I assume the household preference relations R^r, "at least as good as," are orderings (complete, reflexive, and transitive), and sufficiently well-behaved to justify the calculus arguments employed.

4. If the base indifference curve is identified by specifying a goods vector X^{r0} which lies on it, then replacing X^{r0} by any other goods vector on the same indifference curve does not affect the value of the expenditure function or the cost-of-living index.

5. For a more detailed discussion of the traditional theory of the cost-of-living index and references to the literature, see Pollak (1971), Samuelson and Swamy (1974), or Diewert (1978, sections 12, 13).

6. Defining the cost of living as $E^r(P^a, X^{rb}, R^r)/\sum p_k^b x_k^b$ would require the base indifference curve to be the one attained in the reference situation. Such a definition puts the Paasche index in limbo, since the Paasche index is a lower bound on the cost-of-living index evaluated at the indifference curve attained in the comparison situation.

7. The goods vector X^{rb} plays a very different role in the Laspeyres index from its role in the cost-of-living index. In the cost-of-living index it specifies a particular indifference curve, and the replacement of X^{rb} by another collection of goods on the same indifference curve does not alter the index. In the Laspeyres index it specifies the particular collection of goods actually bought in the reference situation. The fixed-weight index constructed by replacing X^{rb} by another collection of goods on the same indifference curve is not equal to the Laspeyres index and is not an upper bound on the cost-of-living index.

8. See Bergson (1938), Samuelson (1947, ch. VIII), Graaf (1957, ch. 3) and Sen (1970, pp. 33–35). For some recent critical discussion see Kemp and Ng (1976, 1977), Parks (1976), Pollak (1979), and Samuelson (1977).

9. I assume that the social preference relation R ("at least as good as") is an ordering and sufficiently well-behaved to justify the calculus arguments employed. Further properties are discussed below.

10. To recover the preferences of household r, consider two social consumption vectors which differ only in the consumption assigned to household r; then the social preference between these social consumption vectors coincides with R^r, the preferences of household r over the subvectors X^r.

11. There are interesting parallels between the social cost-of-living index, the theory of "subindexes," and the cost-of-living index in the household production model. The theory of subindexes (Pollak, 1975a) defines indexes for categories for goods (e.g. food, clothing, housing), and investigates the relationship between these partial indexes and the household's overall cost-of-living index. If the household's overall preference ordering is separable in these categories, then the complete index is analogous to a social cost-of-living index and each category preference ordering to the preferences of a single household. Since the analogy requires each household to consume different goods, the parallel is really between subindexes and a generalization of the social cost-of-living index which allows geographical price differences. To construct the generalized index, we define an $n \times S$ dimensional price vector by stringing together the price vectors faced by each of the S households, and then define the social cost-of-living index in the obvious way. In the household production model (Pollak, 1978), the household purchases market goods and uses them as inputs to produce commodities, which are the arguments of its preference ordering. In the absence of joint production, the commodity production functions are analogous to the utility functions of individual households, and the commodity utility functions correspond to the Bergson–Samuelson social welfare function.

12. Samuelson (1956, p. 18) calls the indifference curves of $U(X)$ "social welfare contours," while Graaf (1957, pp. 49, 53–54) describes them as "Bergson frontiers."

13. The aggregate social expenditure function, $E(P, X^0, \mathbf{R})$, is related to the aggregate indirect social welfare function by the identity $\Psi[P, E(P, X^0, \mathbf{R})] = U(X^0)$ and can be found by solving $\Psi(P, \mu) = U(X^0)$ for μ.

14. This follows immediately from the fact that the social cost-of-living index is

simply the cost-of-living index corresponding to a particular preference ordering, namely, the investigator's aggregate social preference ordering. Alternatively, we can regard it as the cost-of-living index corresponding to his disaggregate social preference ordering provided we generalize the social cost-of-living index to allow different households to face different prices, as they do when there are geographical price differences.

15. Although the aggregate social welfare function uniquely determines the base indifference map for the social cost-of-living index, it does not contain enough information to determine the optimal distribution of expenditure among households. Thus, the disaggregate social preference ordering contains far more information than the aggregate social preference ordering **R**, but with an aggregate specification of the base indifference curve, this additional information is not needed to construct the social cost-of-living index.

16. The concept of the maximizing society, although not the term, is familiar; see Samuelson (1956). Throughout this section I assume maximization takes place subject to the linear constraint $\sum \mu_s \leqslant \mu$ (i.e., that lump sum transfers are possible).

17. Plott (1976, p. 525) takes this view and points out that Buchanan (1954a, b) originally objected to Arrow's possibility theorem on these grounds.

18. Harsanyi (1955) emphasizes the distinction between an individual's "subjective preferences" and his "ethical peferences." Sen (1977a) discusses the distinction between aggregating "interests" and aggregating "judgments." The transition from "individuals" to "households" is questionable.

19. Pollak (1979) argues that the Bergson–Samuelson social welfare function is usually interpreted as an ethical ranking of social states, not simply an ordering which rationalizes choices in a single profile framework. Gorman (1959, p. 492) writes that "the main ambiguity in the concept of a social welfare function" is whether it represents "an ethic or the effective balance of forces in a community".

20. A referee points out that this assumes that the political process yields preferences (rather than choices) and that these preferences are an ordering (transitive, etc.). He goes on to suggest: "Surely the most straightforward interpretation is that the social investigator who believes in the "maximizing society" is merely one with the private welfare function which tells him that whatever is, is best. This would seem to be a not unrealistic *description* of the welfare function of some official statisticians.... Whether one *ought* to recommend these preferences to social investigators or official statisticians is a different matter." John Muellbauer, in a letter to me, calls the maximizing society approach "Panglossian."

21. I use the phrase *market demand functions* to indicate the aggregate demand behavior of the group of households in which we are interested. It may refer to a particular subset of the households in a "market" or a "society" (e.g., households which include retired persons; urban wage and clerical workers; or farmers) rather than to all households (and nonprofit institutions?) in an economy.

22. Samuelson (1956) explicitly assumes that individual indifference contours and the social welfare function have the usual convexity properties.

23. The proof rests on the assumption that society's welfare function is strictly quasi-concave, an assumption which is usually regarded as more dubious than the corresponding assumption about individual preferences [(see Graaf, 1957, pp. 50–51)]. On the other side, Gorman (1959, p. 494) argues that "whenever it is reasonable to assume that a social welfare function exists at all, it is reasonable to assume that the social indifference curves are convex." If the social welfare function does not have the "usual" curvature properties, then the market demand functions may exhibit the

same type of behavior as the demand functions of an individual whose indifference map has the "wrong" curvature.

It is more straightforward to state the regularity properties of the social welfare function in terms of $W(\chi)$ than $\Omega[U^1, \ldots, U^S]$. The relevant notation of convexity has nothing to do with "measurable utility" or with the convexity of Ω in terms of the u's Instead, it is essentially identical to the convexity of a household's preference ordering under weak separability. This approach avoids treating the social welfare function as an ordinal function of ordinal functions (i.e., household utility functions); instead it treats R as the fundamental preference relation rather than as one built up from more basic household preference relations. The social welfare function is Pareto-inclusive if for every r the conditional preference ordering over the subset of variables X^r is independent of the levels of the remaining variables and coincides with R^r.

24. I have replaced Ψ^* and Ω^* by Ψ and Ω to simplify the notation.

25. If the social welfare function does not have the usual curvature, the social cost-of-living index can still be constructed from the information contained in the market demand relations, but the demand relations may be correspondences rather than functions and may fail to exhibit the usual continuity and convexity properties.

26. Some restrictions must be placed on demand functions or preferences to guarantee the recoverability of a unique preference ordering from demand functions. See Mas-Colell (1977).

27. How can an investigator determine whether the market demand functions reflect a distribution of expenditure among households which maximizes a social welfare function (cf. Samuelson, 1956, p. 17)? If the investigator knows only the market demand functions, a weak test is to check whether they can be rationalized by an aggregate indirect social welfare function. If he also knows household preferences and the distribution of expenditure among households for each price-expenditure situation (i.e., if he knows the expenditure distribution functions, $\phi^r(P, \mu)$), then he can test whether they can be rationalized by a disaggregate social welfare function. An alternative approach is to attempt to infer society's welfare function from the tax and transfer schedules it has adopted. See, for example, Mera (1969).

28. The independent society is familiar from the literature on "community indifference curves" and "representative consumers," although the term itself is new. See Chipman (1965, pp. 689–798) and Muellbauer (1976).

29. I consider only Pareto-inclusive social preferences.

30. See footnote 28.

31. Identifying the base indifference curve in aggregate terms is crucial for this result. I am grateful to an anonymous referee for clarifying this point.

32. Chipman (1970, p. 356, footnote 7) traces the question to Antonelli in 1886; Gorman (1953) provided the answer.

33. Gorman (1961) established the closed-form characterization of the class of demand functions and indirect utility functions implied by the (local) independent society.

34. In an independent society the market demand functions are the same as those generated by a society of S identical "representative households" with preferences R^R corresponding to the indirect utility function.

$$\Psi^R(P, \mu_R) = \left(\mu_R - \frac{1}{S} \sum f^s(P) \right) \Big/ g(P)$$

each with expenditure μ/S. Letting σ_R denote the value of the representative household's indirect utility function, the cost-of-living index is given by

$$I(P^a, P^b, \sigma_R, R^R) = \frac{\dfrac{1}{S}\sum f^s(P^a) + g(P^a)\sigma_R}{\dfrac{1}{S}\sum f^s(P^b) + g(P^b)\sigma_R}$$

Thus, the market cost-of-living index $I(P^a, P^b, \sigma, \mathbf{R}^M)$ is equal to the cost-of-living index of the representative household evaluated at the indifference curve σ/S: $I(P^a, P^b, \sigma/S, R^R)$.

35. I am grateful to an anonymous referee for this argument.

36. Unless household preferences are homothetic, there are limits on the admissible distributions of utility among households, so the assumption of an interior solution is not innocuous. This price independence result for utility distribution functions complements various price independence results for expenditure distribution functions reported in Roberts (1980).

37. Sen (1977b) argues that the theory of collective choice ought to provide theoretical underpinnings for evaluative statistics (e.g., national income, inequality measures), and that the theory should be reformulated to do so. In this paper I use a concept from welfare economics and the theory of collective choice, the Bergson–Samuelson social welfare function, to provide a foundation for an evaluative statistic, the social cost-of-living index.

38. The global version is untenable; the evidence against the local version, although strong, is not conclusive.

39. All results in this section hold for an appropriately selected base indifference curve; I spell this out below. The maximizing society results also assume that the investigator adopts society's social welfare function.

40. It can be rewritten as a weighted average of household Laspeyres indexes:

$$J(P^a, P^b, X^b) = \sum_{s=1}^{S} w^s(P^b, \chi^b) J^s(P^a, P^b, X^{sb})$$

where the weights are the household's reference expenditure shares:

$$w^r(P^b, \chi^b) = \mu_r^b/\mu^b$$

This is analogous to writing the household Laspeyres index as a weighted average of price relatives where the weights are reference expenditure shares.

41. As with the Laspeyres bounding theorem for a single household, the exact index must be evaluated at the indifference curve corresponding to the reference period consumption pattern. This clause should be read into all assertions about Laspeyres bounds on exact indexes. Like all Laspeyres-type results, this does not depend on preferences having the "usual" curvature.

42. For a household, establishing that the Laspeyres index is an upper bound on the exact index depends on basing the index on the household's reference period preferences. If the household's preferences change, both reference and comparison tastes are plausible candidates for the base preference ordering. The Laspeyres index is an upper bound on the index based on reference period preferences evaluated at the reference period indifference curve. Fisher and Shell (1968, pp. 100–101) argue

that with changing preferences, comparison tastes are more likely to be the appropriate base for the index but the choice of an appropriate base preference ordering is a matter of judgment and is not dictated by theoretical considerations. For a discussion of the household cost-of-living index with changing tastes, see Fisher and Shell (1968), Pollak (1975b, 1976), Phlips (1974, ch. 9), and Phlips and Sanz–Ferrer (1975). For a more general analysis of welfare evaluation with changing tastes, see Harsanyi (1953–1954).

It can be argued that changing tastes take us out of the realm of Bergson–Samuelson social welfare functions and into that of Arrow social welfare functions. See Samuelson (1967) and Sen (1970, ch. 3). In Pollak (1979) I argue that the essential difference between the Bergson–Samuelson problem and the Arrow problem is that the former is concerned with ethical evaluations, not that its domain is restricted to a single profile of individual preference orderings. Samuelson (1977) is consistent with this view, although Samuelson (1967) is not. Throughout this paper I assume that household preferences remain unchanged.

43. For Scitovsky social indifference curves, see Scitovsky (1941–1942). Samuelson (1956) and Graaf (1957, ch. 3).

44. The Scitovsky–Laspeyres index bears a striking similarity to the *commodity Laspeyres index* in the household production model (Pollak, 1978). In the household production model market goods are inputs in the production of commodities which are arguments of the household's utility function. The commodity Laspeyres index is the ratio of the cost of producing the reference period commodity bundle at comparison prices to its cost at reference prices; it is an upper bound on the household's cost-of-living index and can be calculated by an investigator who knows the household's technology and its reference consumption pattern, but who does not know the household's preferences.

The commodity Laspeyres index permits technical substitution of one input for another so the household can produce the fixed collection of commodities at minimum cost; it does not, however, permit the household to substitute one commodity for another in consumption, so it cannot choose the commodity consumption pattern which attains the base indifference curve at minimum cost. Similarly, the Scitovsky–Laspeyres index permits each household to substitute one good for another in order to "produce" its fixed level of utility at minimum cost, but it does not permit the substitution of the welfare of one household for that of another to attain the base indifference curve of the social preference ordering at minimum cost.

45. All summations in this proof are over s, $s = 1, \ldots, S$; indexes and limits of summations are omitted.

46. Muellbauer calls such a household "representative," but it is not "representative" in the traditional sense; that is, it does not reproduce society's mean demand pattern when its expenditure is equal to the social mean.

47. To obtain this estimate, Muellbauer uses adult equivalence scales to pool observations for households of different compositions. The normative interpretation of empirically estimated equivalence scales poses a number of important issues. Muellbauer (1977) defends their use; for a critical view, see Pollak and Wales (1979).

48. It is not difficult to generalize the analysis to allow the set of feasible distributions to depend on prices.

49. If the distributional constraint is different in two periods, the situation is much like one of technical change in the household production model (see Pollak, 1978). I assume that the distributional constraint remains fixed.

REFERENCES

Bergson, Abram, "A Reformulation of Certain Aspects of Welfare Economics," *Quarterly Journal of Economics*, Vol. 52 (1938), pp. 310–334.

Buchanan, James M., "Social Choice, Democracy, and Free Markets," *Journal of Political Economy*, Vol. 62, No. 2 (1954a), pp. 114–123.

———, "Individual Choice in Voting and in the Market," *Journal of Political Economy*, Vol. 62, No. 4 (1954b), pp. 334–343.

Chipman, John S., "Survey of the Theory of International Trade: Part 2, The Neo-Classical Theory," *Econometrica*, Vol. 33, No. 4 (1965), pp. 685–760.

———, "External Economies of Scale and Competitive Equilibrium," *Quarterly Journal of Economics*, Vol. 84, No. 3 (1970), pp. 347–385.

Diewert, W. E., "Duality Approaches to Microeconomic Theory," in K. J. Arrow and M. D. Intrilligator, eds., *Handbook of Mathematical Economics*, Amsterdam: North-Holland (1978).

Fisher, Franklin M., and Karl Shell, "Taste and Quality Change in the Pure Theory of the True Cost-of-Living Index," in J. N. Wolfe, ed., *Value, Capital and Growth: Papers in Honour of Sir John Hicks*, University of Edinburgh Press, Edinburgh, (1968), pp. 97–139.

Gorman, W. M., "Community Preference Fields", *Econometrica*, Vol. 21, (1953), pp. 63–80.

———, "Are Social Indifference Curves Convex?" *Quarterly Journal of Economics*, Vol. 73, (1959), pp. 485–496.

———, "On a Class of Preference Fields, "*Metroeconomica*, Vol. 13, (1961), pp. 53–56.

Graaf, J. de V., "Theoretical Welfare Economics," Cambridge University Press, Cambridge, (1957).

Harsanyi, John S., "Welfare Economics of Variable Tastes," *Review of Economic Studies*, Vol. 21 (1953–1954), pp. 204–213.

———, "Cardinal Welfare, Individualistic Ethics, and Inter-personal Comparisons of Utility," *Journal of Political Economy*, Vol. 63, No. 4 (1955), pp. 309–321.

Kemp, Murray, and Kew-Kwang Ng, "On the Existence of Social Welfare Functions: Social Orderings and Social Decision Functions," *Economica*, Vol. 43, No. 169 (1976), pp. 59–66.

———, "More on Social Welfare Functions: The Incompatibility of Individualism and Ordinalism," *Economica*, Vol. 44, No. 173 (1977), pp. 89–90.

Mas-Colell, Andreu, "The Recoverability of Consumers' Preferences from Market Demand Behavior," *Econometrica*, Vol. 45, No. 6 (1977), pp. 1409–1429.

Mera, Koichi, "Experimental Determination of Relative Marginal Utilities," *Quarterly Journal of Economics*, Vol. 83, No. 3 (1969), pp. 464–477.

Muellbauer, John, "The Political Economy of Price Indices," *Birkbeck Discussion Paper 22*, March (1974).

———, "Community Preferences and the Representative Consumer," *Econometrica*, Vol. 44, No. 5 (1976), pp. 979–1000.

———, "Testing the Barten Model of Household Composition Effects and the Cost of Children," *Economic Journal*, Vol. 87, No. 347 (1977), pp. 460–487.

Parks, Robert P., "An Impossibility Theorem for Fixed Preferences: A Dictatorial Bergson–Samuelson Welfare Function," *Review of Economic Studies*, Vol. 43(3), No. 135 (1976), pp. 447–450.

Phlips, Louis, *Applied Consumption Analysis*, North-Holland, Amsterdam (1974).

Phlips, Louis, and Richard Sanz-Ferrer, "A Taste-Dependent True Index of the Cost of Living," *Review of Economics and Statistics*, Vol. 42, No. 4 (1975), pp. 495–501.

Plott, Charles R., "Axiomatic Social Choice Theory: An Overview and Interpretation," *American Journal of Political Science*, Vol. 20, No. 3 (1976), pp. 511–596.

Pollak, Robert A., "The Theory of the Cost-of-Living Index," *Research Discussion Paper No. 11*, Research Division, Office of Prices and Living Conditions, U.S. Bureau of Labor Statistics (June 1971).

———, "Subindexes in the Cost-of-Living Index," *International Economic Review*, Vol. 16, No. 1 (1975a), pp. 135–150.

———, "The Intertemporal Cost-of-Living Index," *Annals of Economic and Social Measurement*, Vol. 4, No. 1 (1975b), 179–195.

———, "Habit Formation and Long-Run Utility Functions," *Journal of Economic Theory*, Vol. 13, No. 2 (1976), pp. 272–297.

———, "Welfare Evaluation and the Cost-of-Living Index in the Household Production Model, "*American Economic Review*, Vol. 68, No. 3 (1978), pp. 285–299.

———, "Bergson–Samuelson Social Welfare Functions and the Theory of Social Choice," *Quarterly Journal of Economics*, Vol. 93, No. 1 (1979), pp. 73–90.

———, "Group Cost-of-Living Indexes," *American Economic Review*, Vol. 70, No. 2 (1980), 273–278.

———, and Terence J. Wales, "Welfare Comparisons and Equivalence Scales," *American Economic Review*, Vol. 69, No. 2 (1979), pp. 216–221.

Roberts, Kevin, "Price-Independent Welfare Prescriptions," *Journal of Public Economics*, Vol. 13, No. 3 (1980), pp. 277–297.

Samuelson, Paul A., *Foundations of Economic Analysis*, Harvard University Press, Cambridge, Massachusetts (1947).

———, "Social Indifference Curves," *Quarterly Journal of Economics*, Vol. 70, No. 1 (1956), pp. 1–22.

———, "Arrow's Mathematical Politics," in S. Hook, ed., *Human Values and Economic Policy: A Symposium*, New York: New York University Press, (1967).

———, "Reaffirming the Existence of 'Reasonable' Bergson–Samuelson Social Welfare Functions," *Economica*, Vol. 44, No. 173 (1977), pp. 81–88.

———, and S. Swamy, "Invariant Economic Index Numbers and Canonical Duality: Survey and Synthesis, *American Economic Review*, Vol. 64, No. 4 (1974), pp. 566–593.

Scitovsky, T., "A Reconsideration of the Theory of Tariffs," *Review of Economic Studies*, Vol. 9, No. 2 (1941–1942), pp. 89–110.

Sen, Amartya K., *Collective Choice and Social Welfare*, San Francisco: Holden-Day (1970).

———, "Social Choice Theory: A Re-examination," *Econometrica*, Vol. 45, No. 1 (1977a), pp. 53–90.

———, "On Weights and Measures," *Econometrica*, Vol. 45, No. 7 (1977b), pp. 1539–1572.

The Treatment of "Quality" in the Cost-of-Living Index

1. INTRODUCTION

Products come in many varieties, varieties appear and disappear from markets, and prices change. This paper develops the implications of cost-of-living index theory for measuring the impact of these changes in availability and prices on household welfare. I examine an exhausting, although not exhaustive, number of alternative indexes. These indexes bear a strong family resemblance, since all begin with household preferences and compare the expenditure required to attain a particular indifference curve under two sets of constraints. The implications of this approach to index number construction depend on whether preferences are defined over goods or characteristics and on the nature of the constraints; this paper's principal message is the importance of choosing an appropriate specification for any particular application. Thus, I emphasize the diversity rather than the similarity of indexes corresponding to alternative specifications. The remainder of the introduction gives the flavor of the distinctions developed in the body of the paper and suggests some of their implications for the practical task of constructing index numbers.

The fundamental distinction is between the "goods approach" and the "characteristics approach": The goods approach treats each variety as a separate entity, while the characteristics approach focuses on attributes or characteristics of market goods.[1] Either approach can be used in conjunction with the conventional framework in which market goods are desired for their own sake, or the household production framework, in which goods are inputs into the production of desired commodities. Distinguishing between goods and characteristics approaches and between the conventional and household production frameworks yields four separate cases. In each of these cases, I distinguish between the "complete index"—indexes reflecting the effects of all availability and price changes on household welfare—and "subindexes" for particular products. I also distinguish between "exact indexes"—indexes taking full account of a household's ability to substitute in response to changes in relative prices and availability—and "bounds" which can be calculated with much less information about preferences.

This sixteenfold partition assumes that all characteristics approaches can

From *Journal of Public Economics*, Vol. 20, No. 1 (February 1983), pp. 25–53. Copyright © 1983 by North-Holland. Reprinted by permission of Elsevier Sequoia S.A.

be treated as one. In fact, there are many characteristics approaches, each reflecting a different specification of how characteristics and quantities enter the household's preferences. I discuss only two such specifications, "L-characteristics" and "H-characteristics." The L-characteristics framework is the model of "linear and additive" characteristics popularized by Lancaster; it adds up the characteristics contained in all varieties the household consumes and assumes that the total consumption of characteristics is all that matters. In the H-characteristics framework the household consumes, only a single variety of each product; it descends from the "heterogeneous" characteristics model proposed by Houthakker (1952).

Either characteristics approach can be formulated with a "continuous" or a "discrete" variety spectrum. A continuous variety spectrum implies that every variety is available in every period; a discrete spectrum permits new varieties to appear and old ones to disappear. Thus, the discrete spectrum is appropriate for analyzing the impact of changes in the availability of varieties on household welfare.

Cost-of-living index theory has implications for the practical task of constructing consumer price indexes in characteristics models, and provides a useful perspective from which to view the empirically oriented literature on "quality" and "hedonic indexes." However, when the theory's prescriptions diverge from our intuition or hedonic practice, we cannot automatically conclude that the defect lies with intuition or practice. I argue that it may reflect the limitations of the theory. In particular, theory's concern with a single household prevents it from recognizing the diversity of tastes and expenditure, and its focus on exact indexes and bounds leads it to neglect "approximations."

It is surprising that the implications of the cost-of-living index theory for measuring the effects of changes in prices and availability on household welfare have not been systematically treated in the literature on "quality change" and "hedonic indexes." This literature's strongly empirical orientation and the reluctance of investigators to adopt a particular theoretical framework for structuring their research and interpreting their findings probably explain why it was not. This reluctance might have been overcome if the theory seemed to yield simple prescriptions for index number construction, especially prescriptions broadly consistent with hedonic practice. Instead, however, it yields a proliferation of special cases which give the appearance of complexity. But diversity is not the same as complexity, and once an investigator chooses an appropriate specification for a particular application, theory yields relatively simple prescriptions.

The organization of this paper is as follows: In section 2, I discuss the goods approach to exact indexes, and in section 3, the two characteristics approaches. In section 4, I consider the goods approach to bounds, and in section 5, the two characteristics approaches. Section 6 examines the implications of the theory for actual index number construction and relates it to the literature on quality and hedonic indexes. Section 7 is a brief conclusion.

2. THE GOODS APPROACH: EXACT INDEXES

In this section I summarize the theory of the exact cost-of-living index in both its conventional setting and the household production framework, drawing heavily on Pollak (1978).

We denote the goods vector by X, the household's preference ordering by R, and the corresponding utility function by $V(X)$. The cost-of-living index is the ratio of the expenditures required to attain a particular base indifference curve under two price regimes. We denote the cost-of-living index by $I(P^a, P^b, X^0, R)$:

$$I(P^a, P^b, X^0, R) = \frac{E(P^a, X^0, R)}{E(P^b, X^0, R)}$$

where $E(P, X^0, R)$ is the "expenditure function," that is, the minimum expenditure required to attain the indifference curve of the goods vector X^0 from the preference ordering R in price situation P. The notation emphasizes that the index depends not only on "comparison prices," P^a, and "reference prices," P^b, but also on the choice of a base indifference map or preference ordering, R, and the specification of a base indifference curve, X^0, from that map.

According to the household production view, the household purchases "goods" on the market and combines them with time in a "household production process" to produce "commodities."[2] These commodities, rather than the goods, are the arguments of the household's preference ordering; market goods and time are not desired for their own sake, but only as inputs into the production of "commodities." To avoid further complicating an already complicated notation I shall ignore the role of time in household production and treat market goods as the only inputs into the production of commodities. We denote the n market goods by $X = (x_1, \ldots, x_n)$, the m commodities by $Z = (z_1, \ldots, z_m)$, the household's preference ordering over commodity vectors by R, and the corresponding utility function by $W(Z)$.[3] The household's technology is represented by a production set, T: the "output–input" vector $(Z, X) \in T$ if and only if the commodity collection Z is producible from the goods collection X. Unless explicitly stated to the contrary, constant returns to scale and/or the absence of joint production are *not* assumed, so there need not be a separate production function for each commodity.

The "commodity cost function," $C(P, Z; T)$, is defined as the minimum cost of producing the commodity bundle Z with technology T at goods prices P: $C(P, Z; T) = \min \sum p_k x_k$ subject to $(Z, X) \in T$.[4] The "expenditure function," $E(P, Z^0, R, T)$, show the minimum expenditure required to attain the indifference curve of Z^0: $E(P, Z^0, R, T) = \min C(P, Z; T)$ subject to ZRZ^0, where ZRZ^0 indicates that Z is "at least as good as" Z^0. The *constant technology cost-of-living index*, $\bar{I}(P^a, P^b, Z^0, R, T)$, is defined as the ratio of the expenditures required by a household with technology T and preferences R to attain a particular indifference curve under two price regimes:

$$\bar{I}(P^a, P^b, Z^0, R, T) = \frac{E(P^a, Z^0, R, T)}{E(P^b, Z^0, R, T)}.$$ 5

The *variable technology cost-of-living index*, $I(P^a, P^b, Z^0, R, T^a, T^b)$, reflects changes in the household's technology (i.e., from T^b to T^a) as well as changes in goods prices, and is defined by

$$I(P^a, P^b, Z^0, R, T^a, T^b) = \frac{E(P^a, Z^0, R, T^a)}{E(P^b, Z^0, R, T^b)}$$

The difficulty with treating each variety as a separate good in either the conventional or the household production framework is empirical rather than theoretical, and arises because the number of "goods" may be very large. When the number of goods is small—usually a few broad aggregates—it is possible to implement the theory and construct an exact cost-of-living index by specifying the functional form of the indirect utility function, estimating the parameters of the implied demand system, and calculating the exact index corresponding to these parameter estimates.[6] Unfortunately, treating each variety as a separate good requires us to deal with an unmanageably large number of variables; in the conventional framework it complicates estimation of preferences, while in the household production framework it complicates estimation of the technology. In either case, it does not permit us to estimate the parameters required to construct the exact index.[7]

In the theory of the cost-of-living index it is usually assumed that all goods are available in every period and that the household consumes some of every good in every price situation. These assumptions are often violated when products are available in many varieties, but relaxing them causes no serious difficulties. If a good is not available in a particular period, we treat its lack of availability as one of the constraints facing the household. The cost-of-living index is then the ratio of the expenditures required to attain a particular indifference curve under two alternative sets of constraints.[8] When a good is available but is not contained in the expenditure-minimizing market basket corresponding to a particular price regime, the expenditure function and the cost-of-living index are still unambiguously defined; corner solutions hold no terror for the modern economist.[9]

The empirical literature on quality is concerned with price indexes for particular products. From a theoretical standpoint, such indexes are "sub-indexes" of the "complete" cost-of-living index. The theory of subindexes in the conventional framework is developed in Pollak (1975a): The basic result is that if preferences are separable, then the "natural" subindexes constructed on the basis of the "specific" or "category" preference orderings are well-behaved cost-of-living indexes. If preferences are not separable, subindexes for categories (e.g., products), can still be defined, but they depend not only on the prices of the goods in the category but also on the quantities of goods in other categories. In the household production model, subindexes can also be defined, but these subindexes depend on the quantities in other categories unless both preferences and the household's technology are separable.

In this section I have examined the possibility of dealing with products which come in many varieties by treating each variety as a separate good. Although this provides a conceptual framework for dealing with both price changes and the appearance or disappearance of varieties, it does not provide a useful framework for index number construction because it requires us to deal with an unmanageably large number of goods. In the next section I examine models which avoid this defect by utilizing characteristics approaches.

3. THE CHARACTERISTICS APPROACH: EXACT INDEXES

Varieties embody characteristics, and characteristics are arguments of the household's preference ordering or its technology. These are the basic tenets of the "characteristics approach." In this section I describe the construction of exact cost-of-living indexes in two versions of the characteristics approach, one using Lancaster's "linear and additive" or "L-characteristics" and the other Houthakker's "heterogeneous" or "H-characteristics." I first describe their use in the conventional framework in which goods are desired for their own sake and then in the household production framework; I conclude with a brief discussion of subindexes.

The characteristics approach assumes that it is possible to identify the characteristics which matter to the household—that is, in the conventional framework, the characteristics which enter its preference ordering. These characteristics are taken to be objective and measurable properties of goods, not subjective perceptions or judgments reflecting the household's needs or aspirations.

The advantage of the characteristics approach is empirical rather than theoretical and can only be realized with relatively simple specifications of the way characteristics and quantities enter the household's preference ordering. Since even the most general characteristics approach is no more general than the goods approach, emphasis on tractable specifications is entirely appropriate. To facilitate estimation of preferences or technology, the characteristics approach must reduce the problem from one involving a large number of varieties, many of which are close substitutes, to one involving a small number of characteristics.

The L- and H-characteristics approaches, like all characteristics approaches, associate a vector of attributes with every variety and then make strong, simple assumptions about the way these attributes enter the household's preference ordering.

Although the L- and H-characteristics approaches are each special cases, most systematic discussions of characteristics have adopted one or the other. The L-characteristics approach captures the essence of the "diet problem":

Each good or variety (e.g., milk, oranges, hamburger) contains characteristics (e.g., vitamins, minerals, calories). "Quantity" and "quality" are directly substitutable for one another—a gallon of regular milk is equivalent to a half gallon of "supermilk" containing twice as much of each characteristic. The characteristics of different varieties are added together—the vitamins from milk to the vitamins from oranges—and the household is concerned only with its total consumption of each characteristic.[10]

The H-characteristics approach fits products which households purchase in only one variety, the "relevant variety."[11] Examples include toothpaste, laundry detergents, and beer, as well as apartments and most consumer durables such as refrigerators and washing machines. With nondurables the purchase of a single variety usually reflects the household's preferences; if the implied indifference curves are convex in the variety space they are linear. With durables the purchase of a single variety may reflect indivisibilities or transaction costs rather than preferences, but the analysis of such constraints is beyond the scope of this paper.

Either characteristics approach can be combined with a range of assumptions about the availability of varieties. I discuss two polar cases, the "discrete variety spectrum" and the "continuous variety spectrum." A variety spectrum is discrete if it contains a finite number of varieties; it is continuous if it contains a variety corresponding to every characteristics vector. With a discrete variety spectrum, new varieties can appear and old ones disappear; if there is a decrease in the diversity of varieties available—for example, if some varieties disappear from the market, no new ones appear, and the prices of varieties available in both periods remain unchanged—one would expect this to be reflected as an increase in the cost-of-living index of at least some households. With a continuous variety spectrum, the greatest possible diversity of varieties is available in every period. Thus, the discrete variety spectrum is the more natural one for analyzing changes in availability.[12]

The characteristics approach is formally equivalent to a household production model in which the varieties (goods) "produce" characteristics (commodities). With L-characteristics these vectors are combined by a linear and additive technology; with H-characteristics the characteristics vectors of different varieties are not combined at all, but preferences are such that the household always chooses to consume only one variety of each product.[13] The household production formulation identifies varieties independently of their characteristics (e.g., by brand or model). Thus, instead of regarding "quality change" as the disappearance of an old variety and its replacement by a new one, it views quality change as "technological change"—an alteration in the function transforming goods into characteristics—and measures its impact by the "variable technology cost-of-living index." The advantage of this interpretation is that we can draw on results from the household production literature. The disadvantage is that the characteristics approach differs significantly from other applications of the household production model, so that treating quality improvements as technical progress often conceals more than it illuminates.

Although the characteristics approach is formally equivalent to a household production model, it differs in three critical respects from standard applications of the household production model. First, the characteristics approach utilizes direct measures of the characteristics of varieties, while applications of the household production model typically utilize data on goods inputs but not on commodity outputs.[14] Second, since characteristics are objective and measurable attributes of varieties, the characteristics approach has no difficulty estimating household technology, while applications of the household production model often focus on problems associated with estimating household technology. Third, since characteristics are attributes of varieties and do not vary from one household to another, the characteristics approach corresponds to a household production model in which all households have identical technologies, while applications of the household production model usually permit the technology to vary from one household to another (e.g., better educated households are more efficient). In short, while we can speak of varieties "producing" characteristics, the process is not one of "household" production.

When the characteristics approach is used in conjunction with the household production framework — that is, when the varieties the household purchases are used to produce commodities such as "home-cooked meals" or "transportation services" — we can interpret the situation as a "two-stage" production process. In the first stage varieties produce characteristics and perhaps combine them according to a technology which is observable and common to all households; at the second stage, the household produces commodities from these inputs. In this case the variable technology cost-of-living index will reflect not only changes in the characteristics of goods, but all changes in the household's technology including, for example, those due to greater education. Although it is clearly desirable for a price index to reflect changes in the quality of goods, the desirability of it reflecting all changes in household technology depends on the purpose of the index.[15] Hence, when characteristics are superimposed on the household production framework, it is useful to maintain the distinction between the two stages, and to treat a "home-cooked meal" as a commodity the household produces with inputs of various foods whose characteristics include vitamins, minerals, and calories or "transportation services" as one whose inputs include automobile characteristics (e.g., horsepower, weight, length).[16]

3.1. L-characteristics in the Conventional Framework

In the L-characteristics model associated with a unit of good i is a *unit characteristic vector*, $\chi_i = (\chi_{i1}, \ldots, \chi_{iN})$ where N is the number of characteristics. The amounts of each characteristic obtained from different goods are added together and we denote the household's total consumption or use of the jth characteristic by ξ_j:

$$\xi_j = \sum \chi_{kj} x_k$$

and the corresponding vector by $\xi = (\xi_1, \ldots, \xi_N)$.[17] When L-characteristics are used in the conventional framework, the household's preference ordering, R^L, is defined over the N dimensional characteristics space.[18]

The *L-characteristics expenditure function* shows the minimum cost of attaining the indifference curve of ξ^0.

Definition. *The L-characteristics expenditure function*, $E^L(P, \xi^0, R^L)$, is defined by

$$E^L(P, \xi^0, R^L) = \min \sum p_k x_k$$

subject to $\xi R^L \xi^0$ where $\xi_j = \sum \chi_{kj} x_k$.

The *L-characteristics cost-of-living index* is the ratio of these expenditure functions.

Definition. The *L-characteristics cost of living index*, $I^L(P^a, P^b, \xi^0, R^L)$, is defined by

$$I^L(P^a, P^b, \xi^0, R^L) = \frac{E^L(P^a, \xi^0, R^L)}{E^L(P^b, \xi^0, R^L)}$$

The *L-characteristics cost function* shows the minimum cost of obtaining the characteristics vector ξ.

Definition. The *L-characteristics cost function*, $C^L(P, \xi)$, is defined by

$$C^L(P, \xi) = \min \sum p_k x_k$$

subject to $\sum \chi_{kj} x_k \geq \xi_j$.

The L-characteristics cost function is piecewise linear and homogeneous of degree one in the characteristics; this follows directly from the linear and additive way in which the characteristics contained in different goods are combined. Since the characteristics cost function is piecewise linear, it is not differentiable everywhere in the characteristics space; in particular, differentiability fails at points where the linear segments meet. Using the L-characteristics cost function, we can rewrite the cost-of-living index as

$$I^L(P^a, P^b, \xi^0, R^L) = \frac{C^L(P^a, \xi^{0a})}{C^L(P^b, \xi^{0b})}$$

where $\xi^{0a}(\xi^{0b})$ is the collection of characteristics which attains the indifference curve of ξ^0 at minimum cost at prices $P^a(P^b)$.

3.2 H-characteristics in the Conventional Framework

In the H-characteristics model, we denote purchases of the ith variety of product s by x_{si} and the corresponding unit characteristics vector by

$\chi_{si} = (\chi_{si1}, \ldots, \chi_{siN_s})$ where there are M products ($s = 1, \ldots, M$) and product s has N_s characteristics.[19]

If the variety spectrum is discrete, then the index i is an integer and we denote the number of varieties of product s by n_s; if the spectrum is continuous, then the index i can assume noninteger values. We denote the quantity of the "relevant variety" of a product s by x_s^* and the corresponding unit characteristics vector by χ_s^*. In the H-characteristics version of the conventional model, the household's preference ordering, R^H, is defined over the space $(\chi^*, X^*) = [(\chi_1^*, x_1^*), \ldots, (\chi_M^*, x_M^*)]$. As Davies (1974) and Muellbauer (1974b) point out, the requirement that the household consume only a single variety of each product can be derived from more basic assumptions which imply linear indifference curves in the variety space.[20] Alternatively, it can reflect an externally imposed constraint.

The *H-characteristics expenditure function* shows the minimum cost of attaining the indifference curve of (χ^{*0}, X^{*0}).

Definition. The *H-characteristics expenditure function*, $E^H[P, (\chi^{*0}, X^{*0}), R^H]$, is defined by

$$E^H[P, (\chi^{*0}, X^{*0}), R^H] = \min \sum_{v=1}^{M} \sum_{k=1}^{n_v} p_{vk} x_{vk}$$

subject to $(\chi^*, X^*) R^H (\chi^{*0}, X^{*0})$.[21]

The *H-characteristics cost-of-living index* is the ratio of these expenditure functions.

Definition. The *H-characteristics cost-of-living index*, $I^H[P^a, P^b, (\chi^{*0}, X^{*0}), R^H]$ is defined by

$$I^H[P^a, P^b, (\chi^{*0}, X^{*0}), R^H] = \frac{E^H[P^a, (\chi^{*0}, X^{*0}), R^H]}{E^H[P^b, (\chi^{*0}, X^{*0}), R^H]}$$

The *H-characteristics cost function* shows the minimum cost of obtaining the consumption pattern (χ^*, X^*), or one providing at least as much of every characteristic.

Definition. The *H-characteristics cost function*, $C^H[P, (\chi^*, X^*)]$, is defined by

$$C^H[P, (\chi^*, X^*)] = \min \sum_{v=1}^{M} \sum_{k=1}^{n_v} p_{vk} x_{vk}$$

subject to $\chi_{si} \geq \chi_s^*$ and $x_{si} \geq x_s^*$ for some i and for all s. When the variety spectrum is continuous the household can find varieties which correspond to any specified unit characteristics vector, χ^{*0}. However, when the variety spectrum is discrete, it is only by chance that an available variety will offer precisely the unit characteristics vector χ^{*0}, and, in this case, the H-characteristics cost function reflects the cost of the least expensive variety containing at least as much of every characteristic.[22]

Since each product is associated with a distinct collection of characteristics, the H-characteristics cost function is of the form

$$C^H[P,(\chi^*, X^*)] = \sum_{v=1}^{M} C^{Hv}(P, \chi_v^*) x_v^*$$

where $C^{Hs}(P, \chi_s^*)$ is the minimum cost of product s with a unit characteristics vector greater than or equal to χ_s^*. Hence, with a discrete variety spectrum, the H-characteristics cost function is a "step function," exhibiting discontinuities when changes in the specified characteristics vector cause the household to switch from one relevant variety to another. For example, if cars only are available with 100 and 200 h.p. engines, the cost associated with any specification less than 100 h.p. is the cost of the 100 h.p. model, while the cost of any specification between 100 and 200 h.p. is the cost of the 200 h.p. model. Like the L-characteristics cost function, the H-characteristics cost function is homogeneous of degree one in the quantities (the x's) but unlike the L-characteristics cost function, it need not be homogeneous of degree one in the characteristics. In the H-characteristics model there is a sharp distinction between doubling the number of units of a variety consumed and doubling the characteristics contents of each unit consumed, while in the L-characteristics model there is not.[23]

Using the H-characteristics cost function, the cost-of-living index can be written as

$$I^H[P^a, P^b, (\chi^{*0}, X^{*0}), R^H] = \frac{C^H[P^a, (\chi^{*0a}, X^{*0a})]}{C^H[P^b, (\chi^{*0b}, X^{*0b})]}$$

where $(\chi^{*0a}, X^{*0a})((\chi^{*0b}, X^{*0b}))$ is the consumption pattern which attains the indifference curve of (χ^{*0}, X^{*0}) at minimum cost at prices $P^a(P^b)$.

3.3. Characteristics in the Household Production Framework

The household production framework can be paired with either the L- or the H-characteristics approach. In the L-characteristics version of the household production model, the household's technology is represented by a production set, T^L. The output–input vector $(Z, \xi) \in T^L$ if and only if the commodity collection Z is producible from the characteristics collection ξ.

The *L-characteristics commodity expenditure function* shows the minimum expenditure required to attain the indifference curve of Z^0.

Definition. The *L-characteristics commodity expenditure function*, $E^L(P, Z^0, R, T^L)$, is defined by

$$E^L(P, Z^0, R, T^L) = \min \sum p_k x_k$$

subject to ZRZ^0, $(Z, \xi) \in T^L$, and $\xi_j = \sum \chi_{kj} x_k$, $j = 1, \ldots, N$.

The *L-characteristics constant technology cost-of-living index* is the ratio of the expenditure functions.

Definition. The *L-characteristics constant technology cost-of-living index,* $\bar{I}^L(P^a, P^b, Z^0, R, T^L)$, is defined by

$$\bar{I}^L(P^a, P^b, Z^0, R, T^L) = \frac{E^L(P^a, Z^0, R, T^L)}{E^L(P^b, Z^0, R, T^L)}$$

In the H-characteristics version of the household production model, the household produces commodities from H-characteristics. The household's technology is represented by a production set, T^H, and the output–input vector $[Z, (\chi^*, X^*)] \in T^H$ if and only if the commodity vector Z is producible from (χ^*, X^*).

The *H-characteristics commodity expenditure function* shows the minimum expenditure required to attain the indifference curve of Z^0.

Definition. The *H-characteristics commodity expenditure function,* $E^H(P, Z^0, R, T^H)$, is defined by

$$E^H(P, Z^0, R, T^H) = \min \sum_{v=1}^{m} \sum_{k=1}^{n_v} p_{vk} x_{vk}$$

subject to ZRZ^0, $[Z, (\chi^*, X^*)] \in T$, $\chi_{si} \geq \chi_s^*$, and $x_{si} \geq x_s^*$ for some i and for all s.

The *H-characteristics constant technology cost-of-living index* is the ratio of these expenditure functions.

Definition. The *H-characteristics constant technology cost-of-living index,* $\bar{I}^H(P^a, P^b, Z^0, R, T^H)$ is defined by

$$\bar{I}^H(P^a, P^b, Z^0, R, T^H) = \frac{E^H(P^a, Z^0, R, T^H)}{E^H(P^b, Z^0, R, T^H)}$$

3.4. Subindexes

Subindexes for groups of varieties can be constructed in both characteristics approaches and in both the conventional and the household production frameworks. I discuss subindexes with both L- and H-characteristics in the conventional framework, although H-characteristics are the dominant case in empirical applications.[24] Subindexes can be constructed for any collection of varieties, but it is especially interesting to consider subindexes for particular products, since this is the leading case in the empirical literature.

With L-characteristics I say that a group of varieties has "nonoverlapping" characteristics if no characteristic provided by any variety in the group is provided by any variety outside it. If a group of varieties has nonoverlapping characteristics, and if preferences are such that these characteristics are separable from the rest, then the subindex for the group is independent of the quantities of varieties in other groups. With overlapping characteristics or nonseparable preferences, the subindex for one group depends on varieties outside the group.

With H-characteristics, subindexes for products are unusual in that only one variety of each product is consumed under any price regime. Suppose, for example, that the commodity spectrum is discrete and that in the reference situation there is a unique relevant variety rather than a tie. Then small percentage changes in the price of the relevant variety cause equal percentage changes in the subindex, while small decreases in the prices of nonrelevant varieties have no effect on the subindex; furthermore, large price increases or the disappearance of nonrelevant varieties have no effect. Similarly, the appearance of a new variety does not affect the subindex unless it becomes the relevant variety. Thus with H-characteristics, the theory of the cost-of-living index has definite implications for constructing subindexes for particular products, but its prescriptions are not intuitively appealing; I return to this in section 6.

4. THE GOODS APPROACH: BOUNDS

Incomplete information about tastes and technology usually prevents us from constructing exact cost-of-living indexes, so we need indexes which require less information and which are upper bounds on exact indexes. The familiar Laspeyres index fulfils this need in the conventional framework, and the "goods Laspeyres index" and the "commodity Laspeyres index" do so in the household production framework. In this section I summarize some results on bounds on exact cost-of-living indexes drawing heavily on Pollak (1978).[25]

The familiar Laspeyres index, $J(P^a, P^b, X^b)$, is defined by

$$J(P^a, P^b, X^b) = \frac{\sum x_k^b p_k^a}{\sum x_k^b p_k^b}$$

where X^b denotes the collection of goods bought in the reference situation. The only information besides prices needed to construct the Laspeyres index is the collection of goods the household chose in the reference price-expenditure situation. It is well known that the Laspeyres index is an upper bound on the cost-of-living index based on the reference period tastes, R^b, evaluated at the reference period indifference curve, $X^b: I(P^a, P^b, X^b, R^b)$. Hereafter, allusions to the Laspeyres index as an upper bound should be understood as a shorthand for a longer and more precise statement which includes the specification of the base preference ordering and base indifference curve.

When products come in many varieties the Laspeyres index is simply the ratio of the cost at comparison prices to the cost at reference prices of the collection of varieties purchased in the reference period; this index is an upper bound on the corresponding exact index.[26] If any variety purchased in the reference period is unavailable in the comparison period, then the Laspeyres index is undefined, or, by convention, is infinite. Hence, when each variety is treated as a separate good the disappearance of a variety purchased in the reference period prevents construction of a useful Laspeyres index, since there is no legitimate way to replace one variety by another. At the very least, this implies that the exact index, which does permit substitutions, will play a more prominent role relative to the Laspeyres index when the "goods" are narrowly defined varieties rather than broad aggregates.[27]

The household production framework contains a richer set of bounding indexes than the conventional framework, since there is a different bounding index corresponding to each assumption about information availability. If we know nothing about the household's tastes or technology beyond what we can infer from the collection of goods it purchased in the reference situation, we can calculate the *goods Laspeyres index*, $\bar{J}(P^a, P^b, X^b)$:

$$\bar{J}(P^a, P^b, X^b) = \frac{\sum x_k^b p_k^a}{\sum x_k^b p_k^b}$$

This index is an upper bound on the constant technology cost-of-living index. If we know the household's technology and the collection of commodities it consumed in the reference situation, but not the household's tastes, then we can construct a better upper bound, the *commodity Laspeyres index*, $J(P^a, P^b, Z^b, T)$, which is defined by

$$J(P^a, P^b, Z^b, T) = \frac{C(P^a, Z^b, T)}{C(P^b, Z^b, T)}$$

The commodity Laspeyres index uses information about the household's technology to permit substitution among goods so that a fixed collection of commodities is produced at minimum cost; but like the traditional Laspeyres index, it does not permit any change in the commodity consumption pattern.

If each variety of each product is treated as a separate good, the goods Laspeyres index is subject to the same drawbacks as the Laspeyres index in the conventional framework: if a variety purchased in the reference situation disappears from the market, the index cannot be calculated. The commodity Laspeyres index is not subject to this defect, but its construction requires far more information; in particular, it requires knowledge of the household's technology. Furthermore, when the goods are narrowly defined varieties rather than broad aggregates, estimating household technology is difficult.[28]

Laspeyres-type bounds on subindexes are defined in the obvious way.

5. THE CHARACTERISTICS APPROACH: BOUNDS

In this section I consider bounds on the exact cost-of-living indexes in the four characteristics models discussed in section 3.

5.1. L-characteristics in the Conventional Framework

If all we know about preferences is what we can infer from the reference period consumption pattern, then the *characteristics Laspeyres index* is the best bound on the exact index. Construction of this bound requires more than the minimal information needed to construct the goods Laspeyres index, but much less than the exact index: In particular, we must know the characteristics content of all varieties and the reference period consumption pattern.

The *L-characteristics Laspeyres index* is the ratio of the minimum cost of the characteristics collection ξ^b at prices P^a to its cost at prices P^b, where ξ^b is the characteristics collection of the reference situation.

Definition. The *L-characteristics Laspeyres index*, $J^L(P^a, P^b, \xi^b)$, is defined by

$$J^L(P^a, P^b, \xi^b) = \frac{C^L(P^a, \xi^b)}{C^L(P^b, \xi^b)}$$

Theorem. The *goods Laspeyres index* is an upper bound on the *L-characteristics Laspeyres index*; and the *L-characteristics Laspeyres index* is an upper bound on the *cost-of-living index:*

$$I^L(P^a, P^b, \xi^b, R^{Lb}) \leqslant J^L(P^a, P^b, \xi^b) \leqslant J(P^a, P^b, X^b)$$

where ξ^b and X^b denote the consumption pattern of the reference situation.

Proof. The usual Laspeyres argument.

The L-characteristics Laspeyres index permits the substitution of one variety for another to attain the reference collection of characteristics at minimum cost. Hence, it is a better bound on the exact index than is the goods Laspeyres index, which represents the cost of purchasing the reference collection of varieties. Although both indexes reflect the cost of attaining the reference collection of characteristics, it is the L-characteristics Laspeyres index which reflects the minimum cost of doing so; formally, it is identical to the *commodity Laspeyres index* of the household production model.[29] The information requirements of the L-characteristics Laspeyres index are relatively modest. We must know which characteristics enter the household's preferences and the unit characteristics vector of each variety. Once the relevant characteristics have been identified, information about the characteristics contents of varieties could be obtained from manufacturers or *Consumer Reports.* The disappearance of varieties purchased in the reference period creates no difficulty, provided all characteristics they contained are present in available varieties.

5.2. H-characteristics in the Conventional Framework

With minimal information—knowing only the collection of varieties purchased in the reference situation—we can do no better than the goods Laspeyres index. In the H-characteristics framework, since only one variety of each product is consumed in each situation, the goods Laspeyres index reflects changes in the cost of a collection of goods in which each product is represented by a single variety. If one of these varieties is unavailable, the index is undefined, or, by convention, is infinite.

With additional information—knowledge of which characteristics enter the household's preferences and the characteristics content of each variety—we can do better. The *H-characteristics Laspeyres index* is the ratio of the minimum cost of the consumption pattern (χ^{*b}, X^{*b}) at prices P^a to its cost at prices P^b, where (χ^{*b}, X^{*b}) is the consumption pattern of the reference situation.

Definition. The *H-characteristics Laspeyres index*, $J^H[P^a, P^b, (\chi^{*b}, X^{*b})]$, is defined by

$$J^H[P^a, P^b, (\chi^{*b}, X^{*b})] = \frac{C^H[P^a, (\chi^{*b}, X^{*b})]}{C^H[P^b, (\chi^{*b}, X^{*b})]}$$

Theorem. The *goods Laspeyres index* is an upper bound on the *H-characteristics Laspeyres index*; and the *H-characteristics Laspeyres index* is an upper bound on the *H-characteristics cost-of-living index*:

$$I^H[P^a, P^b, (\chi^{*b}, X^{*b}), R^{Hb}] \leqslant J^H[P^a, P^b, (\chi^{*b}, X^{*b})] \leqslant J(P^a, P^b, X^b)$$

where (χ^{*b}, X^{*b}) and X^b denote the consumption pattern of the reference situation.

Proof. The usual Laspeyres argument.

Since the H-characteristics Laspeyres index permits some substitution of one variety for another, it is a better bound on the exact index than the goods Laspeyres, but the improvement is very limited. A variety purchased in the reference situation can be replaced only by a variety which "dominates" it—that is, one which contains at least as much of every characteristic. Under weak assumptions about markets, if one variety dominates another, then the better variety will command a higher price. Hence, the principal advantage of the H-characteristics Laspeyres index is that it provides a way to construct a bound when some varieties purchased in the reference period are not available.

6. THEORY AND PRACTICE

In this section I discuss the implications of cost-of-living index theory for the practical task of constructing consumer price indexes in characteristics models and its relation to the literature on "quality" and "hedonic indexes."[30] I use the word *theory* to designate the characteristics frameworks described above, together with their obvious generalizations.[31] Actual construction of price indexes in characteristics models can be decomposed into an "estimation stage" in which characteristics cost functions are obtained and a "composition stage" in which they are used to generate an index. Theory provides guidance for both stages, but there are two reasons why its prescriptions for the composition stage may be inappropriate. First, theory is concerned with a single household, while actual indexes may recognize the diversity of household tastes and expenditures. Second, theory has traditionally been concerned with exact indexes and their bounds, while actual indexes may be "approximations" rather than either exact indexes or bounds.

I use the phrase *hedonic approach* broadly, to encompass any empirically oriented procedure which uses characteristics, not as a precise technical term.[32] The hedonic approach is not an attempt to implement a particular theoretical framework, and, as one might expect, some applications coincide with the prescriptions of theory, while others do not. I interpret the *hedonic function* to be the empirical counterpart of the characteristics cost function— that is, a function showing the minimum cost of any collection of characteristics. The hedonic approach might be applied with L- or H-characteristics, or to the construction of complete indexes or subindexes. In practice, virtually all applications of the hedonic approach have been to single products, and virtually none have combined characteristics from different varieties.[33] Thus, the leading case is that of subindexes in the H-characteristics framework.[34]

The information used in hedonic analysis is severely limited; typically, the investigator knows the characteristics of each variety, its price in each period, and which varieties were consumed in the reference period.[35] This is not enough information to construct the exact index, but it is enough to construct the characteristics cost functions and the characteristics Laspeyres index; this index is the best upper bound on the exact index which can be obtained without additional information.[36]

The organization of this section is as follows: In section 6.1 I discuss the estimation stage, in which information about the prices and characteristics of available varieties is used to obtain the characteristics cost functions. Section 6.2 discusses the role of "implicit" or "shadow" prices of characteristics, a topic which overlaps the estimation and composition stages. In section 6.3 I discuss the composition stage, in which the estimated characteristics cost functions are used to generate a price index.

6.1. The Estimation Stage

The *hedonic function*—a relation between the prices of varieties and their characteristics—is an estimate of "the minimum price of any package of characteristics" [Rosen (1974, p. 37)] or "the constraint...to which the consumer is subject" [Triplett (1975b, p. 312)]. That is, the hedonic function is the empirical counterpart of the characteristics cost function. Theoretical restrictions on the form of the characteristics cost function are implied by the selection of a particular characteristics framework (e.g., discrete variety spectrum, H-characteristics in the household production model).

The choice between the conventional and household production frameworks determines the nature of the attributes which enter the characteristics cost function. Ohta and Griliches (1975, p. 328) assert that the appropriate characteristics are those which enter the utility function, those which yield utility per se. In the conventional framework this is correct, but the household production framework provides a rationale for characteristics which are "production relevant" rather than "utility relevant."[37]

According to Griliches (1971a, p. 5), the form of the hedonic function is an empirical matter. This is true in the H-characteristics framework with a continuous variety spectrum, but with a discrete variety spectrum, the characteristics cost function must be a step function.[38] Ohta and Griliches (1975, p. 326), describe the hedonic approach in terms which presuppose continuity of the variety spectrum without mentioning its crucial role: "What the hedonic approach attempted was to provide a tool for estimating 'missing' prices, prices of particular bundles not observed in the original or later periods." For example, consider an application to apartments using the H-characteristics framework. In this case the hedonic approach is a price collection procedure; instead of pricing an apartment with the reference period characteristics in the comparison period as "specification pricing" would require, one can use observations on apartments with other characteristics to estimate the characteristics cost function; evaluating the estimated characteristics cost function at the reference characteristics vector provides an estimate of how much an apartment with reference characteristics would cost in the comparison period.[39]

The validity of this procedure depends on the continuity or near continuity of the variety spectrum. The crucial underlying assumption is that apartments with the reference characteristics are available in the comparison period; when this assumption is satisfied, the usual hedonic regression provides an estimate of its rent. Proponents of the hedonic approach would argue that, for a given expenditure on data collection and processing, it provides a better estimate than specification pricing. In this application, however, the hedonic approach is merely a price collection procedure, not a conceptual framework for defining or constructing price indexes.

When the variety spectrum is discrete, the usual use of hedonic functions to estimate "missing" prices yields values which correspond to a hypothetical comparison price regime. Unless we wish to compare reference prices with such a fictitious price regime, the usual hedonic approach will yield misleading indexes.[40] It is only with a discrete variety spectrum that we can analyze changes in the diversity of varieties available: for a man who wears size $9\frac{1}{2}$ shoes, the knowledge that they are a linear combination of sizes 9 and 10 provides little comfort. Thus, while the usual hedonic approach may be suitable for analyzing changes in the prices of varieties, it cannot be used to analyze changes in their availability. From a practical standpoint, the issue is not whether the variety spectrum is continuous or discrete, but whether there are enough varieties available to make continuity an acceptable approximation. For example, apartments might be sufficiently continuous, while automobiles are not.[41]

6.2. Implicit Prices

Characteristics prices—"implicit," "shadow," or "hedonic" prices of characteristics—have traditionally played a major role in the hedonic approach. Indeed, Ohta and Griliches (1975, p. 325) identify the *hedonic hypothesis* with the use of implicit prices:

> The hedonic hypothesis assumes that a commodity can be viewed as a bundle of characteristics or attributes for which implicit prices can be derived from prices of different versions of the same commodity containing different levels of specific characteristics.

Nevertheless, it is essential to distinguish between the *hedonic approach* (i.e., any formulation which uses characteristics) and the *characteristics price approach* (i.e., formulations which rely on the implicit or shadow prices of characteristics), because the characteristics price approach is appropriate only in a very narrow range of cases and is likely to be misleading when applied outside this range.[42]

Characteristics prices are defined as the partial derivatives of the characteristics cost function. If the characteristics cost function is differentiable and homogeneous of degree one in the characteristics, then total cost can be written as the sum of the *characteristics prices* multiplied by the corresponding *characteristics quantities*. When we can write the characteristics cost function in this way, we can also write the exact cost-of-living index and the characteristics Laspeyres index in terms of characteristics prices.

Even when the characteristics cost function is differentiable and homogeneous of degree one, little or no simplification is achieved by introducing characteristics prices unless they are assumed to be constant. In general, characteristics prices (i.e., the partial derivatives of the characteristics cost function) are themselves functions whose values depend on the particular points in the characteristics space at which they are evaluated. If these characteristics price functions can be estimated, then the characteristics cost function can be calculated from them using Euler's theorem. However, estimating N characteristics price functions is no easier than estimating the characteristics cost function itself, and the use of characteristics prices does not generally yield better bounds on the exact index.[43]

In the L-characteristics framework, the characteristics cost function is homogeneous of degree one in the characteristics, but with a discrete variety spectrum, it is not everywhere differentiable. More specifically, the iso-cost curves are composed of linear segments; on each flat, the characteristics price ratio is equal to the slope, but at the vertices, they are undefined.[44]

In the H-characteristics framework, the characteristics cost function need not be homogeneous of degree one in characteristics; but unless it is it cannot be written as the sum of characteristics prices multiplied by the corresponding characteristics quantities, even when the differentiability condition is satisfied.[45] Hence, except in some very special cases, there is no direct way to reformulate either the exact cost-of-living index or the characteristics Laspeyres index in terms of characteristics prices. Furthermore, when the variety spectrum is discrete, the H-characteristics cost function is a step function, and since it is not differentiable at the points at which one variety replaces another, characteristics prices are undefined at these points and zero elsewhere.[46]

6.3. Composition

Theory offers a range of prescriptions for composing price indexes from estimated characteristics cost functions and other information. The choice of an appropriate prescription depends on the framework which is applicable, the information available, and the comparison to be made. The implications for index number construction of the choice between L- and H-characteristics, between the conventional and household production approaches, and between discrete and continuous variety spectra have already been discussed. Each of these choices is determined by the selection of an appropriate framework. The choice between the exact index and bounds, and the selection of a particular bounding index depends on the information available: in the conventional approach, to construct the exact index we must know the household's preferences, while in the household production approach we must know both its preferences and its technology. Finally, the choice between the complete index and a subindex for a particular product is determined by the purpose of the index. Thus, theory offers both a range of prescriptions for the estimation and composition stages of index number construction, and criteria for choosing among them. From the standpoint of empirical applications, the leading case is that of subindexes in the H-characteristics framework.

There are important cases, however, in which the indexes prescribed by the theory do not seem to reflect adequately changes in the availability and prices of varieties. Consider, for example, subindexes in the H-characteristics framework with a discrete variety spectrum. The exact subindex reflects only the price of the relevant variety of the reference situation, unless it is unavailable or unless variety prices have changed enough to displace it. Thus, increases in the prices of all nonrelevant varieties leave the exact subindex unaltered, and decreases leave it unaltered unless they are great enough to dethrone the relevant variety. The H-characteristics Laspeyres index is even less sensitive to changes in the prices of nonrelevant varieties, since the relevant variety of the reference period can only be replaced if it is unavailable, or if a variety containing at least as much of every characteristic is available at lower cost. An obvious defense of the theoretical indexes is that they are intended to reflect the impact of changes in availability and prices on the welfare of a particular household, and that they do precisely that. Such a defense concedes, as it must, that the theoretical indexes reflect only a narrow portion of the variety spectrum, but argues that this is appropriate for cost-of-living indexes. I find this defense unconvincing: It fails to recognize that the narrowness of the range of varieties represented in the theoretical indexes is a defect, and attempts instead to make it a virtue. In this case, I believe the intuition which rejects the prescriptions of theory is sound and that a more general theory of the cost-of-living index could provide a more suitable index.

A *group cost-of-living index*—an index which represents the preferences and expenditure levels of more than one household—would reflect changes in the availability and prices of varieties over a wider range of the variety spectrum than an index based on the preferences of one household. Traditional theory is concerned with the welfare of a single household, and the theoretical indexes discussed in this paper reflect this orientation. Group cost-of-living indexes have hardly been discussed. Muellbauer (1974a) considers what might be called the *average cost-of-living index*, a group index defined as the average of household cost-of-living index. Pollak (1980, 1981) investigates the *social cost-of-living index*, a group index based on a Bergson–Samuelson social welfare function.[47] A measure of the effect of availability and price changes which recognizes the diversity of preferences and expenditure levels underlying the spectrum of varieties in the marketplace must rest on a group cost-of-living index.[48]

A further source of dissonance between intuition and the prescriptions of traditional theory may be that intuition envisages an "approximation" while theory focuses almost exclusively on exact indexes and bounds. Approximations can be interpreted as combining assumptions about substitution possibilities which are less extreme and more plausible than those implicit in bounding indexes with stronger assumptions about information availability [see Samuelson and Swamy (1974, section VII) and Diewert (1976; 1981, section 6)].[49] For example, Irving Fisher's ideal index—the geometric mean of the Paasche and Laspeyres—is the exact cost-of-living index corresponding to the homogeneous quadratic utility function. Furthermore, one can argue that, for a large class of preference orderings, Fisher's ideal index provides a reasonable approximation to the exact index. Diewert (1976) formalizes this intuition. He terms a price index "superlative" if it is exact for some expenditure function and can provide a second-order differential approximation to an arbitrary twice differentiable expenditure function. Diewert shows that Fisher's ideal index is not the only superlative index; for example, the Törnquist price index is exact for the translog expenditure function.

Approximations for characteristics await development. While exact indexes measure the effects of the appearance or disappearance of varieties on a household's welfare, we usually lack the information needed to construct them. Laspeyres indexes, while requiring little information to construct, do not reflect the appearance of new varieties as long as the variety purchased in the reference period remains available.[50] Approximations may provide a channel between the Scylla of the full information requirement underlying exact indexes and the Charybdis of extreme ignorance underlying Laspeyres bounds.

7. CONCLUSION

This paper has examined the implications of cost-of-living index theory for measuring the impact of changes in the availability and prices of varieties on a household's welfare. These impacts can be analyzed using the "goods approach" or a "characteristics approach," but the latter provides a more useful foundation for actual index number construction. The precise implications of the characteristics approach depend on the specification of a particular characteristics model—that is, choosing between the L- and H-characteristics frameworks, between the conventional and household production approaches, and between discrete and continuous variety spectra. They also depend on the choice between complete indexes and subindexes and between exact indexes and bounds. Although theory provides some guidance for constructing characteristics cost functions, intuition about index numbers is sometimes sharply at variance with traditional theory which emphasizes exact indexes and bounds and focuses on the welfare of a single household. A more general theory of the cost-of-living index, one which considers the welfare of groups as well as single households and gives as much attention to approximations as to exact indexes or bounds, may provide a more satisfactory foundation for measuring the impact of changes in the availability and prices of varieties; but these are directions for future research.

NOTES

This research was supported in part by the United States Bureau of Labor Statistics, the National Science Foundation and the National Institutes of Health. It is a revision of Pollak (1975b). I am grateful to Barbara K. Atrostic, Hugh Davies, Stefano Fenoaltea, Franklin M. Fisher, Zvi Griliches, James J. Heckman, Linda Kalver, John Muellbauer, Thomas Ross, Paul J. Taubman, and Jack E. Triplett for helpful comments and discussion on various versions of this paper. Their suggestions have substantially improved it but I have not always followed their advice, and none of them should be held responsible for the views expressed.

1. These approaches also provide alternative frameworks for analyzing demand behavior, but their implications for demand analysis are beyond the scope of this paper.

2. The classic household production paper is Becker (1965). Also see Michael and Becker (1973) and Pollak and Wachter (1975).

3. Both here and in the traditional framework, I assume that the household's preference ordering over the commodity space is well behaved in the sense that it can be represented by a continuous utility function which is quasi-concave and nondecreasing in its arguments.

4. Throughout this paper, I use $\sum$ without an identifying index or limits of summation to mean $\sum_{k=1}^{n}$, a summation over all goods.

5. The household's preferences for commodities and its technology implicitly define a preference ordering in the goods space which can be used to define the *goods expenditure function* and the *goods cost-of-living index*. See Pollak (1978).

6. For a recent example of an index calculated in this way and references to the

literature, see Braithwait (1980). Such indexes might be callled "approximations" since they depend on the specified form of the indirect utility function as well as on the data from which they are estimated. However, they are not described as "approximations" in the index number literature, and I shall continue to refer to them as "exact indexes."

7. In section 4, I argue that treating each variety as a separate good also compromises the usefulness of the Laspeyres index.

8. We generalize the notion of a "price regime" to include the constraint that consumption of unavailable goods is zero, and adopt the convention that the price of a good which is not available is infinite. This enables us to code the information about lack of availability into the price vector. If the base indifference curve can be attained without positive consumption of the unavailable good, then the index is well defined. Otherwise, we conventionally describe the index as infinite. Fisher and Shell (1968, section IV) correctly point out that using the demand reservation price instead of an infinite price yields the same exact index and a better bound. The difficulty is that the demand reservation price depends on the household's preferences and is a function of all prices and the base indifference curve. When preferences are known, there is no advantage in using the demand reservation price to calculate the exact index. When they are not—the case in which bounds are relevant—we are unlikely to know enough about preferences to determine the demand reservation price. Thus, the superiority of the demand reservation price formulation depends on somewhat implausible assumptions about information availability.

9. The standard assumption of perfect divisibility can also be dropped, by treating the requirement that certain goods come only in integer quantities as an additional constraint. The notion of a price regime can be expanded to include indivisibility as well as availability constraints.

10. The approach is that popularized by Lancaster (1966a, b, 1971) and is often cited in the literature on quality and hedonic indexes.

11. The term *relevant variety* is from Davies (1974). Houthakker (1952) proposed a model in which the household consumes only one variety of each product, but his formal discussion is limited to the case of one characteristic. Theil (1952) discusses a multicharacteristics model in which the household may consume more than one variety of each product; he assumes that utility is a function of the number of units of each product consumed and their average characteristics content. Both Houthakker and Theil impose severe restrictions on admissible variations in variety prices. Models in which households consume only a single variety of each product have been refined and generalized by Muellbauer (1974b), Davies (1974), Rosen (1974), and Sweeney (1974). Muellbauer argues convincingly that the Fisher and Shell (1968) "simple repackaging" model should be interpreted in these terms, although he regards their model as distinct from Houthakker's because he emphasizes the latter's restrictions on price variations. Lancaster (1975) discusses what he calls "noncombinable" characteristics (essentially H-characteristics) but imposes a homogeneity assumption under which all households regard two units of variety i as equivalent to one unit of variety j if j contains twice as much of every characteristic as i.

12. One can often analyze such changes using a continuous variety spectrum by treating unavailable varieties as if they were available at very high prices.

13. Muellbauer (1974b) treats L-characteristics but not H-characteristics in terms of the household production model; Lucas (1975) is exclusively concerned with L-characteristics. Pollak (1978) originated as an attempt to establish the household production results needed to discuss "quality."

14. In characteristics models, one must first identify which characteristics are relevant, a problem I discuss in section 6.1. Pollak and Wachter (1975, pp. 273–276) emphasize the importance of observability and measurability of commodities in the household production context.

15. If the household's technology remains unchanged, the variable and constant technology indexes are identical. If the technology changes, the choice between these two indexes depends on what one is trying to measure.

16. Both of these commodities pose measurement problems which I ignore.

17. I use k as a running or dummy subscript for goods or varieties and i to designate a particular variety $(i = 1, \ldots, n)$. I use j to designate particular characteristics, $(j = 1, \ldots, N)$.

18. The usual monotonicity assumption, here and in the H-characteristics approach, implies that all characteristics are desirable, or at least that none are undesirable. When applied to characteristics which designate colors or styles, the meaning of this assumption is tenuous. In the household production framework, monotonicity implies that all characteristics are productive.

19. I use v as a running or dummy subscript for products; s to designate particular products; and si to designate particular varieties of particular products.

20. Even with linear indifference curves, a household might consume more than one variety, although there would exist an equally good consumption plan containing only one. Strictly speaking, we assume that the household consumes at most one variety of each product.

21. This notation presupposes a discrete variety spectrum; with a continuous variety spectrum, the second summation must be replaced by an integral. The most general case—a mixed, continuous-discrete variety spectrum—calls for a Stieltjes integral.

22. This definition presupposes that each characteristic is desirable.

23. The "combinable" characteristics model of Lancaster (1975) is a special case of the H-characteristics model in which quantity is directly substitutable for characteristics. Varieties are identified by their characteristic ratios, and doubling the characteristics content of a variety and halving the quantity of it which a household consumes leaves welfare unaltered. The implied characteristics cost function is homogeneous of degree one in characteristics.

24. The reader can easily extend the analysis to the household production framework.

25. Throughout this paper I discuss Laspeyres-type indexes and upper bounds, leaving the corresponding analysis of Paasche-type indexes and lower bounds to the reader.

26. The appearance of new varieties does not complicate construction of Laspeyres indexes, but the disappearance of old ones does.

27. This suggestion is reinforced by the intuition that substitution possibilities among varieties of a given product are greater than those among broader aggregates. If this is correct, then we would expect the Laspeyres index to lie closer to the exact index when the goods are broad aggregates and further from it when the goods are varieties which permit easy substitution.

28. When it is relatively easy to substitute one variety of a product for another in the household's technology, we would not expect the goods Laspeyres index to lie as close to the commodity Laspeyres index as it does when the goods are broad aggregates and technical substitution is more difficult.

29. Klevmarken (1977, p. 169) discusses this index, but it is not his "Laspeyres index."

30. I shall not discuss characteristics approaches to constructing other types of price indexes, quantity indexes, or to analyzing demand, supply, or market equilibrium.

31. These include, for example, more complex specifications of the way characteristics and quantities enter preferences.

32. This is consistent with Griliches (1971a, p. 4):

> The "hedonic," or, using a less value-loaded word, characteristics approach to the construction of price indexes is based on the empirical hypothesis (or research strategy) which asserts that the multitude of models and varieties of a particular commodity can be comprehended in terms of a much smaller number of characteristics or basic attributes of a commodity such as "size," "power," "trim," and "accessories," and that viewing the problem in this way will reduce greatly the magnitude of the pure new commodity or "technical change" problem, since most (though not all) new "models" of commodities may be viewed as a new combination of old characteristics. In its parametric version, it asserts the existence of a "reasonably well-fitting" relation between the prices of different models and the level of their various but not too numerous characteristics.

For example, see Ohta and Griliches (1975) and the papers collected in Griliches (1971b).

33. The diet problem is an exception, if it is considered an application of the hedonic approach.

34. In the L-characteristics framework with a continuous variety spectrum, the household consumes only one variety of each product. This is equivalent to the "combinable" characteristics model of Lancaster (1975) in which quantity is directly substitutable for characteristics.

35. Actually, knowing the objective and measurable characteristics of each variety is not enough; the investigator must identify which ones are relevant—that is, in the conventional framework, which characteristics enter household preferences.

36. The characteristics approach to price index construction can also be given a theoretical interpretation outside the cost-of-living index framework. For example, the work of Kravis and Lipsey (1971) on price indexes for electric generators can usefully be viewed against the theoretical framework for measuring producer prices described in Archibald (1975, 1977), or the discussion of the implicit GNP deflator in Fisher and Shell (1972). Triplett (1975a) provides a useful survey of treatments of quality in various price indexes.

37. Ohta and Griliches distinguish between "specification characteristics" (e.g., weight, horsepower) and "performance characteristics" (e.g., handling, ride) and argue that the logic of the hedonic approach favors performance characteristics over specification characteristics. It might be thought that the distinction between specification and performance characteristics corresponds to that between the household production and conventional frameworks; but Ohta and Griliches assume that the physical characteristics of a variety generate its performance characteristics without the aid of other inputs, so no "household" production is involved. Under their assumption, specification and performance characteristics constitute alternative sets of objective and measurable characteristics of the variety in question. Performance and specification characteristics imply identical exact indexes, but the Laspeyres index based on performance characteristics will be a better bound.

38. The L-characteristics framework is less likely to be appropriate, but it does

imply severe restrictions on the form of the characteristics cost function; it must be homogeneous of degree one, and, if the variety spectrum is discrete, piecewise linear in the characteristics. When the number of varieties is large, a differentiable function may provide a good approximation.

Rosen (1974, p. 37) claims that "a buyer can force (the characteristics cost function)... to be linear if certain types of arbitrage activities are allowed." But his argument appears to show only that the characteristics cost function is convex—that is,

$$C[\lambda \xi^* + (1 - \lambda)\xi^{**}] \leqslant \lambda C(\xi^*) + (1 - \lambda)C(\xi^{**}), \quad \text{for all } \lambda, 0 \leqslant \lambda \leqslant 1$$

and homogeneous of degree one in the characteristics.

Muellbauer (1974b, p. 988) points out that the commonly used semi-log form is not homogeneous of degree one, and hence is not compatible with the L-characteristics framework.

39. See Triplett (1971) for a thorough discussion of BLS pricing procedures and whether they lead to "quality bias" in BLS indexes.

40. Goods which are made to order can be treated as belonging to a continuous variety spectrum, because the fact that a particular variety was not produced in a particular period does not imply that it was not available, only that no one ordered it. If there were a posted price schedule, then the comparison period price of the base variety could be read off directly; the hedonic regression provides an estimate of the schedule. Electric generators, although not a consumer good, are an example of this use of the hedonic technique (see Kravis and Lipsey, 1971).

41. Sometimes one wants to compare a hypothetical price regime with a real one: for example, one might expand the Fisher–Griliches–Kaysen (1962) analysis of the cost of automobile model changes to include a theory of market behavior and predict the effect on new car prices (rather than production costs) of a hypothetical government regulation requiring automobile companies to produce only cars with the specifications of the average 1949 car each year since 1949. One could then construct a price index to compare this hypothetical price series with some reference price regime.

Barzel (1975), in a comment on Ohta and Griliches (1975), discusses the crucial role of their implicit assumption that the variety spectrum is continuous.

42. The discussion of characteristics prices is an application to index numbers of the analysis in Pollak (1978), since characteristics models can be viewed formally as household production models. More generally, Pollak and Wachter (1975) argue that the household production literature overemphasizes the role of commodity prices.

43. Muellbauer (1974b, pp. 982–983) and Klevmarken (1977) use characteristics prices to construct what they both call a "Laspeyres index," and show that it is not an upper bound on the exact index, except in very special cases. This observation argues strongly against their terminology.

There is one situation in which characteristics prices can sometimes be used to provide a better bound on the exact index, although more information is required than is usually employed in constructing hedonic indexes. The information required is the income-consumption curve in the characteristics space corresponding to the comparison price regime, and the procedure is essentially that developed in Pollak (1978, section V) in the household production context.

44. This assumes that there are fewer characteristics than varieties; if all individuals have identical preferences and equal total expenditure or homothetic preferences, then

all varieties will lie on a single flat. Lucas (1975, section I) emphasizes this point.

45. The characteristics cost function is homogeneous of degree one in the "combinable" characteristics model of Lancaster (1975).

46. Even if the characteristics cost function is not homogeneous of degree one, there are special cases in which the characteristics Laspeyres index can be written in terms of characteristics prices. These are analogous to the special cases discussed in Pollak (1978, p. 296) in the household production context.

There are two types of "characteristics prices" in the H-characteristics framework. The *total characteristics price* is the partial derivative of the H-characteristics cost function, $C^H(P, \chi^*, X^*)$; the *unit characteristics price* is the partial derivative of the *unit characteristics cost function*, $C^{Hs}(P, \chi_s^*)$. Implicit prices in the L-characteristics framework correspond to implicit unit prices, but it is sometimes possible to define analogues of implicit total prices. The foregoing objections apply to both types of characteristics prices.

47. Although these "aggregation" issues have received little attention in the theoretical literature, they have been recognized by those concerned with actual index number construction in the U.S. [see Gillingham (1974, pp. 251–252) and Triplett (1975a, pp. 65–66)] and the U.K. [see Prais (1959) and Nicholson (1975, but written in 1958)].

48. Muellbauer (1974b), Barzel (1975), and Lucas (1975) all recognize the inadequacy of the traditional "representative household" assumption.

49. Under this view, the line between approximations and exact indexes is ambiguous, since many approximations can be constructed by assuming that preferences belong to a particular class, and that enough information about demand behavior is available to identify a specific member of that class. Usually, estimation of exact indexes involves more data and more explicit stochastic assumptions than calculation of an approximation.

The distinction between bounds and approximations is not always made. For example, both Muellbauer (1974b) and Klevmarken (1977) use the term *approximation* to describe the "Laspeyres index" they construct using characteristics prices, and also to describe the Laspeyres index when it is an upper bound on the exact index.

50. The failure of the Laspeyres index to reflect changes in relative prices is universally understood. The treatment of new varieties and of substitutions induced by price changes are closely related, since new varieties can be treated as if they had infinite prices before their introduction.

REFERENCES

Archibald, Robert B., "On the Theory of Industrial Price Measurement: Input Price Indexes," Bureau of Labor Statistics, Working Paper No. 48, 1975.
———, "On the Theory of Industrial Price Measurement: Output Price Index," *Annals of Economic and Social Measurement*, Vol. 6 (1977), pp. 57–72.
Barzel, Yoram, "Comments on Automobile Prices Revisited: Extensions of the Hedonic Hypothesis," in Nestor E. Terleckyj, ed., *Household Production and Consumption, Studies in Income and Wealth*, No. 40, National Bureau of Economic Research, Conference on Research in Income and Wealth, New York: Columbia University Press (1975), pp. 391–398.
Becker, Gary S., "A Theory of the Allocation of Time," *Economic Journal*, Vol. 75 (1965), pp. 493–517.

Braithwait, Steven D., "The Substitution Bias of the Laspeyres Price Index: An Analysis Using Estimated Cost-of-Living Indexes," *American Economic Review*, Vol. 70 (1980), pp. 64–77.

Davies, Hugh, "The Consumer's Choice among Qualities of Goods," Discussion Paper No. 26, Department of Economics, Birkbeck College, University of London, mimeographed, 1974.

Diewert, W. E., "Exact and Superlative Index Numbers," *Journal of Econometrics*, Vol. 4 (1976), pp. 115–145.

_____, "The Economic Theory of Index Numbers: A Survey," in Angus Deaton, ed., *Essays in the Theory and Measurement of Consumer Behaviour in Honour of Sir Richard Stone*, Cambridge: Cambridge University Press (1981), pp. 163–208.

Fisher, Franklin M., Zvi Griliches, and Carl Kaysen, "The Costs of Automobile Model Changes since 1949," *Journal of Political Economy*, Vol. 70 (1962), pp. 433–451.

Fisher, Franklin M., and Karl Shell, "Taste and Quality Change in the Pure Theory of the True Cost-of-Living Index," in J. N. Wolfe, ed., *Value, Capital and Growth: Papers in Honour of Sir John Hicks*, Edinburgh: University of Edinburgh Press, (1968), pp. 97–139.

_____, "The Pure Theory of the National Output Deflator," in *The Economic Theory of Price Indices*, New York: Academic Press (1972), pp. 49–113.

Gillingham, Robert R., "A Conceptual Framework for the Consumer Price Index," *Proceedings of the Business and Economic Statistics Section, American Statistical Association* (1974), pp. 246–252.

Griliches, Zvi, "Introduction: Hedonic Price Indexes Revisited," in Zvi Griliches, ed., *Price Indexes and Quality Change*, Cambridge, Massachusetts: Harvard University Press (1971a), pp. 3–15.

_____, ed., *Price Indexes and Quality Change*, Cambridge, Massachusetts: Harvard University Press, 1971b.

Houthakker, H. S., "Compensated Changes in Quantities and Qualities Consumed," *Review of Economic Studies*, Vol. 19 (1952), pp. 155–164.

Klevmarken, N. Anders, "A Note on New Goods and Quality Changes in the True Cost-of-Living Index in View of Lancaster's Model of Consumer Behavior," *Econometrica*, Vol. 45 (1977), pp. 163–173.

Kravis, Irving B., and Robert E. Lipsey, "Price Competitiveness in World Trade," New York: National Bureau of Economic Research, 1971.

Lancaster, Kelvin J., "A New Approach to Consumer Theory," *Journal of Political Economy*, Vol. 84 (1966a), pp. 132–157.

_____, "Change and Innovation in the Technology of Consumption," *American Economic Review*, Vol. 56 (1966b), pp. 14–23.

_____, *Consumer Demand: A New Approach*, New York: Columbia University Press, 1971.

_____, "Socially Optimal Product Differentiation," *American Economic Review*, Vol. 65 (1975), pp. 567–585.

Lucas, Robert E. B., "Hedonic Price Functions," *Economic Inquiry*, Vol. 13 (1975), pp. 157–178.

Michael, Robert T., and Gary S. Becker, "On the New Theory of Consumer Behavior," *Swedish Journal of Economics*, Vol. 75 (1973), pp. 378–396.

Muellbauer, John, "The Political Economy of Price Indices," Birkbeck Discussion Paper No. 22, 1974a.

_____, "Household Production Theory, Quality and the 'Hedonic Technique'," *American Economic Review*, Vol. 64 (1974b), pp. 977–994.

Nicholson, J. L., "Whose Cost of Living?" *Journal of the Royal Statistical Society*, Series A, Vol. 138 (1975), pp. 540–542.

Ohta, Makoto, and Zvi Griliches, "Automobile Prices Revisited: Extensions of the Hedonic Hypothesis," in Nestor E. Terleckyj, ed., *Household Production and Consumption, Studies in Income and Wealth*, No. 40, National Bureau of Economic Research, Conference on Research in Income and Wealth, New York: Columbia University Press (1975), pp. 325–390.

Pollak, Robert A., "Subindexes of the Cost-of-Living Index," *International Economic Review*, Vol. 16 (1975a), pp. 135–150.

————, "The Treatment of 'Quality' in Demand Analysis and the Cost-of-Living Index," mimeographed, 1975b.

————, "Welfare Evaluation and the Cost-of-Living Index in the Household Production Model," *American Economic Review*, Vol. 68 (1978), pp. 285–299.

————, "Group Cost-of-Living Indexes," *American Economic Review*, Vol. 70 (1980), pp. 273–278.

————, "The Social Cost-of-Living Index," *Journal of Public Economics*, Vol. 15 (1981), pp. 311–336.

Pollak, Robert A., and Michael L. Wachter, "The Relevance of the Household Production Function and its Implications for the Allocation of Time," *Journal of Political Economy*, Vol. 83 (1975), pp. 255–277.

Prais, S. J., "Whose Cost of Living?" *Review of Economic Studies*, Vol. 26 (1959), pp. 126–134.

Rosen, Sherwin, "Hedonic Prices and Implicit Markets: Product Differentiation in Pure Competition," *Journal of Political Economy*, Vol. 82 (1974), pp. 34–55.

Samuelson, Paul A., and S. Swamy, "Invariant Economic Index Numbers and Canonical Duality: Survey and Synthesis," *American Economic Review*, Vol. 64 (1974), pp. 566–593.

Sweeney, James L., "Quality, Commodity Hierarchies, and Housing Markets," *Econometrica*, Vol. 42 (1974), pp. 147–167.

Theil, H., "Qualities, Prices and Budget enquiries," *Review of Economic Studies*, Vol. 19 (1952), pp. 129–147.

Triplett, Jack E., "Quality Bias in Price Indexes and New Methods of Quality Measurement," in Zvi Griliches, ed., *Price Indexes and Quality Change*, Cambridge, Massachusetts: Harvard University Press (1971), pp. 180–214.

————, "The measurement of Inflation: A Survey of Research on the Accuracy of Price Indexes," in Paul H. Earl, ed., *Analysis of Inflation*, Lexington, Massachusetts: D.C. Heath and Company Lexington Books (1975a), pp. 19–82.

————, "Consumer Demand and Characteristics of Consumption Goods," in Nestor E. Terleckyj, ed., *Household Production and Consumption, Studies in Income and Wealth*, No. 40, National Bureau of Economic Research, Conference on Research in Income and Wealth, New York: Columbia University (1975b), pp. 305–323.

The Treatment of the Environment
in the Cost-of-Living Index

1. INTRODUCTION

The purpose of this paper is to consider the treatment of environmental variables in the cost-of-living index. The issue is central to the theory of place-to-place comparisons, as well as to the treatment of such obvious environmental variables as air and water pollution and the variations in the availability of services provided by governmental units without user charges. Seasonal variations in tastes, if they reflect seasonal variations in the environment, can also be treated in terms of the framework proposed here.

2. NOTATION

We let x_i denote consumption of good i and X the corresponding consumption vector: $X = (x_1, \ldots, x_n)$; p_i denotes the price of the ith good and P the price vector: $P = (p_1, \ldots, p_n)$; ε denotes the vector of environmental variables which enter the utility function. The environmental variables may be characteristics of the environment in a narrow sense (e.g., temperature, rainfall or levels of air or water pollution) or they may be goods provided by the government without user charges. The distinction between the ε's and the x's is that the former have prices associated with them, while the latter do not. That is, the difference between the environmental variables and the goods has to do with the way they enter the constraints rather than their intrinsic character or the way they enter the household's preference ordering. To compare a situation in which a particular service is provided by the government with a situation in which the same service is provided privately requires us to treat the same variable as an ε in one situation and an x in the other.

3. PREFERENCES: TWO POSSIBLE APPROACHES

There are two possible models of environment-dependent preferences. The first—the *conditional* approach—assumes that the objects of choice are commodity vectors (X) and that the preference ordering over the commodity space depends on the state of the environment (ε). We denote a preference ordering of this type by $R(\varepsilon)$, and we interpret the statement, $X^a R(\bar{\varepsilon}) X^b$, to mean that X^a is at least as good as X^b according to the preference ordering corresponding to the environment $\bar{\varepsilon}$. The second approach to environment-dependent preferences—the *unconditional* model—assumes that the objects of choice are goods–environment pairs (X, ε). Under this approach the individual's preference ordering, R, reflects his ordering over alternatives such as (X^a, ε^a) and (X^b, ε^b). We interpret that statement, $(X^a, \varepsilon^a)R(X^b, \varepsilon^b)$, to mean that the goods–environment pair (X^a, ε^a) is at least as good as the goods–environment pair (X^b, ε^b).[1]

4. THE CONDITIONAL APPROACH

The conditional preference ordering does not permit comparisons of alternative price–environment situations; it only allows comparisons of alternative price situations on the basis of a given state of the environment. Corresponding to the conditional preference ordering, $R(\varepsilon)$, is the conditional expenditure function, $E[P, X, R(\varepsilon); \varepsilon]$, which shows the minimum expenditure required to attain the indifference curve X of the preference ordering $R(\varepsilon)$. In many cases the expenditure function itself provides a complete answer to the cost-of-living question being asked, and construction of a cost-of-living index is unnecessary. Traditionally, however, the cost-of-living question has been answered by an index defined as the ratio of two expenditure functions. The *conditional environment-dependent cost-of-living index*, $I[P^a, P^b, X, R(\varepsilon); \varepsilon]$, is defined by

$$I[P^a, P^b, X, R(\varepsilon); \varepsilon] = \frac{E[P^a, X, R(\varepsilon); \varepsilon]}{E[P^b, X, R(\varepsilon); \varepsilon]}$$

This index is the ratio of the expenditure required to attain the indifference curve of X under two price regimes. The comparison is based on a particular state of the environment; in effect, the index compares the price vectors P^a and P^b on the assumption that the environment is held fixed. One would expect the value of the index to be sensitive to the environment which is specified, but the choice of a base state of the environment, like the choice of a base indifference curve, must be dictated by the purpose for which the index is being constructed.

The conditional environment-dependent cost-of-living index is not an index which compares alternative price–environment situations, but a systematic way of comparing alternative price situations when such comparisons depend on the state of the environment. Hence, the resulting index is essentially the same as the subindexes discussed in Pollak (1975).

The conditional Laspeyres index is defined in the obvious way, and is an upper bound on the conditional environment-dependent cost-of-living index where the base environment is the environment of the reference period and the base indifference curve is the reference period indifference curve.

The conditional preference ordering does not permit comparisons of situations in which the state of the environment differs. Any welfare comparison in which the alternatives involve different states of the environment requires statements of the form "(X^a, ε^a) is at least as good as (X^b, ε^b)," and this type of statement cannot be made on the basis of the conditional preference ordering. If we calculate the ratio

$$\frac{E[P^a, X, R(\varepsilon^a); \varepsilon^a]}{E[P^b, X, R(\varepsilon^b); \varepsilon^b]}$$

and find that its value is unity, we cannot infer that the individual is indifferent between the price–environment situations (P^a, ε^a) and (P^b, ε^b). We can only conclude that the expenditure required to attain the indifference curve of X of the preference ordering $R(\varepsilon^a)$ is the same as that required to attain the indifference curve of X of the preference ordering $R(\varepsilon^b)$. But since the conditional preference ordering does not permit us to compare the individual's welfare in situations in which the environment differs, this comparison has no welfare significance.

5. THE UNCONDITIONAL APPROACH

The unconditional preference ordering does permit us to compare alternative price–environment situations. Corresponding to the unconditional preference ordering is the unconditional expenditure function $E[(P, \varepsilon), (X^o, \varepsilon^o), R]$ which shows the minimum expenditure required to attain the indifference curve of (X^o, ε^o) of the preference ordering R. In many cases, the expenditure function provides a satisfactory answer to the cost-of-living question, and construction of the cost-of-living index is unnecessary. The unconditional cost-of-living index is defined as the ratio of the unconditional expenditure functions. To compare the price–environment situation (P^a, ε^a) with (P^b, ε^b) using the base indifference curve (X, ε), the unconditional cost-of-living index, $I[(P^a, \varepsilon^a), (P^b, \varepsilon^b), (X, \varepsilon), R]$, is defined by

$$I[(P^a, \varepsilon^a), (P^b, \varepsilon^b), (X, \varepsilon), R] = \frac{E[(P^a, \varepsilon^a), (X, \varepsilon), R]}{E[(P^b, \varepsilon^b), (X, \varepsilon), R]}$$

The unconditional cost-of-living index is essentially the same as the cost-of-living index under a regime of straight or quantity rationing.

To discuss the properties of the unconditional cost-of-living index, we first examine the properties of the unconditional expenditure function. (a) The unconditional expenditure function is homogeneous of degree one in prices: $E[(\lambda P, \varepsilon), (X^o, \varepsilon^o), R] = \lambda E[(P, \varepsilon), (X^o, \varepsilon^o), R]$ for all $\lambda > 0$. That is, if prices double, expenditure must double to allow the individual in the environment ε to attain the indifference curve of (X^o, ε^o). (b) The unconditional expenditure function is an increasing function of prices: if $P^{a'} \geqslant P^a$, then $E[(P^{a'}, \varepsilon), (X^o, \varepsilon^o), R] \geqslant E[(P^a, \varepsilon), (X^o, \varepsilon^o), R]$. (c) If we adopt the convention of measuring environmental variables as "goods" rather than "bads," then the unconditional expenditure function is a decreasing function of the environmental variables:

if $\varepsilon^{a'} \geqslant \varepsilon^{a}$, then $E[(P, \varepsilon^{a'}), (X^{\circ}, \varepsilon^{\circ}), R] \leqslant E[(P, \varepsilon^{a}), (X^{\circ}, \varepsilon^{\circ}), R]$. This result is essentially a restatement of the measurement convention, and has no independent substance; furthermore, if some individuals regard a particular environmental variable as a "good" while others regard it as a "bad," then different measurement conventions will be required for different individuals. Hence, this convention should be used with caution.

The properties of the unconditional cost-of-living index follow directly from its definition as the ratio of unconditional expenditure functions. In particular,

P∗1 $I[(P^{a}, \varepsilon^{a}), (P^{b}, \varepsilon^{b}), (X, \varepsilon), R] = 1/I[(P^{b}, \varepsilon^{b}), (P^{a}, \varepsilon^{a}), (X, \varepsilon), R]$

P∗2 $I[(\lambda P^{a}, \varepsilon^{a}), (P^{b}, \varepsilon^{b}), (X, \varepsilon), R] = \lambda I[(P^{a}, \varepsilon^{a}), (P^{b}, \varepsilon^{b}), (X, \varepsilon), R]$

P∗3 If $P^{a'} \geqslant P^{a}$, then $I[(P^{a'}, \varepsilon^{a}), (P^{b}, \varepsilon^{b}), (X, \varepsilon), R] \geqslant I[(P^{a}, \varepsilon^{a}), (P^{b}, \varepsilon^{b}), (X, \varepsilon), R]$

P∗4 If $\varepsilon^{a'} \geqslant \varepsilon^{a}$, then $I[(P^{a}, \varepsilon^{a'}), (P^{b}, \varepsilon^{b}), (X, \varepsilon), R] \leqslant I[(P^{a}, \varepsilon^{a}), (P^{b}, \varepsilon^{b}), (X, \varepsilon), R]$

It is instructive to consider situations such as that postulated in P∗4—that is, situations which differ with respect to the environment but not with respect to prices, to emphasize that the unconditional cost-of-living index permits the comparison of alternative environments. The unconditional cost-of-living index need not equal unity when $P^{a} = P^{b}$, because of the role of the environment in the index. In particular, if $P^{a} = P^{b}$ and $\varepsilon^{b} > \varepsilon^{a}$, then expenditure on goods in the comparison situation must be larger than in the reference situation to make the individual indifferent between them.

To generalize the Laspeyres index theorem to the unconditional cost-of-living index appears to require such stringent assumptions as to make it almost useless. The appropriate generalization seems to be the following: Suppose that the state of the environment ε^{a} is unconditionally at least as good as ε^{b}, in the sense that for all X, $(X, \varepsilon^{a}) R(X, \varepsilon^{b})$. It follows immediately that $(X^{b}, \varepsilon^{a}) R(X^{b}, \varepsilon^{b})$, and, hence $E[(P^{a}, \varepsilon^{a}), (X^{b}, \varepsilon^{b}), R] \leqslant \sum p_{k}^{a} x_{k}^{b}$. Dividing both sides of this inequality by reference period expenditure yields a generalized version of the Laspeyres theorem. The difficulty is that it rests on the extremely strong assumption that the comparison state of the environment is unconditionally at least as good as the reference state, an assumption which is unlikely to be satisfied when the environment has many dimensions. Under the convention that environmental variables are "goods," this condition will clearly be satisfied whenever $\varepsilon^{a} \geqslant \varepsilon^{b}$.[2]

NOTES

This research was supported in part by the U.S. Bureau of Labor Statistics and the National Science Foundation, but neither they nor the University of Pennsylvania should be held responsible for the views expressed.

1. We assume that the conditional environment-dependent preference ordering $R(\varepsilon)$ can be represented by a utility function $U(X; \varepsilon)$. The semicolon indicates that the

preference ordering represented by the utility function is conditional on ε, and does not represent a preference ordering over (X, ε). We assume that the unconditional environment-dependent preference ordering can be represented by a utility function $U(X, \varepsilon)$. The comma in place of the semicolon indicates that the preference ordering represented by this utility function is a preference ordering over goods–environment pairs (X, ε). If the conditional utility function $U(X; \varepsilon)$ represents the conditional preference ordering $R(\varepsilon)$, then so does the conditional utility function $V(X; \varepsilon)$, defined by $V(X; \varepsilon) = F[U(X; \varepsilon), \varepsilon]$, where F is monotonically increasing in its first argument. If the unconditional utility function $U(X, \varepsilon)$ represents the unconditional preference ordering R, then so does the unconditional utility function $V(X, \varepsilon)$ defined by $V(X, \varepsilon) = F[U(X, \varepsilon)]$ where F is a monotonically increasing function; furthermore, these are the only utility functions representing the unconditional preference ordering R.

2. It is also possible to construct an unconditional cost-of-living index using shadow prices. To do so, one first defines the expenditure functions in terms of the shadow prices. The appropriate shadow prices for the environment, however, are not those corresponding to the consumption patterns of the reference or comparison situations. Instead, we must first calculate the consumption pattern which minimizes the cost of attaining the indifference curve of (X, ε), in the price environment situation (P^a, ε^a); the shadow prices corresponding to this consumption pattern are used to calculate the expenditure function for the reference situation. Similarly, the expenditure function in the comparison situation is calculated on the basis of the consumption pattern which minimizes the cost of attaining the indifference curve of (X, ε) in the price–environment situation (P^b, ε^b). The ratio of these expenditure functions is the shadow cost-of-living index.

The objection to defining the unconditional cost-of-living index in this way is that there is no straightforward interpretation of the resulting index in terms of compensation. That is, the shadow cost-of-living index does not answer the cost-of-living question.

Consumer Durables
in a Cost-of-Living Index

The treatment of consumer durables in a cost-of-living index is difficult for a number of reasons, many of them unrelated to "durability." The most fundamental problems arise because consumer durables cannot be treated in a one-period framework and because the multiperiod framework is intractable even without durables. In a multiperiod world, the cost-of-living index reflects changes in the wealth required to attain a given indifference curve. The intertemporal utility function reflects future as well as present consumption, and the multiperiod cost-of-living index reflects changes in future as well as current prices. A multiperiod formulation automatically deals with "savings" by explicitly recognizing the future consumption which it is intended to provide.

The introduction of durables into a multiperiod model requires no alteration in the utility function, unless the household derives utility from the ownership of goods as well as from their use. This is a possibility which should be investigated, but in the following discussion I assume that households own durables solely to enjoy the flow of services they provide, and not because they derive satisfaction from ownership.[1]

The construction of a multiperiod cost-of-living index requires no special assumptions about preferences, the absence of frictions, or the existence of perfect markets in consumer goods. It does, however, require other assumptions: (1) *perfect foresight*. Unless we are prepared to deal explicitly with uncertainty, we must assume it away. (2) *perfect capital markets*. Unless we are prepared to deal with multiple budget constraints involving inequalities, we must assume that capital markets are perfect—only if households can borrow and lend without limit at a single rate can we define "wealth." (3) Finally, the construction of a multiperiod cost-of-living index requires data on future prices, and, since there are few futures markets in consumer goods, these prices cannot be observed. In principle, multiperiod cost-of-living indexes could be constructed if we knew how expected prices were related to current prices; thus, an increase in the current price of eggs would influence the index not only directly, but also through its effect on expected egg prices. With our present knowledge of the formation of expectations, a cost-of-living index based on a model of price expectations should not be taken seriously. To summarize: A multiperiod cost-of-living index requires data on future prices as well as current prices, and hence it is not practical; this negative conclusion holds even in a world without cosumer durables.

Since a multiperiod cost-of-living index is impractical, we now examine the conditions under which it is possible to construct a meaningful one-period cost-of-living index in a multiperiod world. To construct such an index, it must be possible to associate both a cost and a measure of utility with consumption in a single period.

We can associate a measure of utility with consumption in a single period if and only if the intertemporal utility function is weakly separable when consumption is partitioned by periods; in this case there exist one-period utility functions which are themselves arguments of the intertemporal utility function. The separability of the intertemporal utility function is a necessary condition for the construction of a one-period cost-of-living index because it is only in this case that we can associate a measure of utility with consumption in a single period without regard to consumption in other periods.

We can associate a cost with consumption in a single period if and only if the intertemporal budget function is strongly separable when consumption is partitioned by periods. This terminology is new and requires some explanation. In a one-period world there is a budget function, $B(x_1,\ldots,x_n)$, which associates a cost with every consumption plan. The budget constraint is given by $B(x_1,\ldots,x_n)-\mu \leqslant 0$, where μ denotes income, and, under the assumption that the household can buy as much as it likes at market prices, we have $B(x_1,\ldots,x_n)=\sum_k p_k x_k$. Under other assumptions, however, the budget function takes a more complicated form. For example, in cases of monopsony or quantity discounts, the budget function is of the form $B(x_1,\ldots,x_n)=\sum_k \beta^k(x_k)$, and the marginal and average cost of a good vary with the quantity consumed. In the case of tie-in sales, the marginal cost of a good depends on the quantities of other goods consumed, and it is not clear what is meant by "average cost." From these examples, it appears that in a one-period world little of real importance is lost by focusing on the linear budget function, $\sum_k p_k x_k$. But in a multiperiod world, this is not the case.

In the multiperiod world, we can associate a cost with consumption in each period if and only if the intertemporal budget function is strongly separable: $B(X)=\sum_t B^t(X_t)$. Both common sense and casual observation suggest that the budget function is not separable, and that the marginal cost of the services of a durable in one period depends on the quantity of those services consumed in another. Because of setup and moving costs, this would be true even in a world with perfect rental markets and no transaction costs, such as sales taxes or legal fees.

Instead of beginning with the case of perfect rental and secondhand markets, we begin with the opposite polar case of no rental or secondhand markets. In such a world, the only way to enjoy the services of a durable is to purchase it. There is no way to allocate the cost of the services of a durable among periods. The utility maximization problem will generate shadow prices for the services of the durable in each period, but these shadow prices clearly depend on planned consumption in other periods. Thus, there is no way to associate costs with consumption in a single period.

Most of the difficulties associated with consumer durables—both in demand analysis and in the cost-of-living index—are reflections of the complexity of the budget function, and, in particular, of its lack of separability. In a frictionless world—a world with no moving or setup costs—there are two cases in which an unambiguous cost is associated with consumption in a single period: the cases of perfect rental markets, and perfect capital and secondhand markets.

In a frictionless world with perfect rental markets, there is an unambiguous cost associated with the use of a durable for a single period. Whether or not markets are perfect, the *marginal household* will be indifferent between renting a house, car, or other durable and owning it; after all, this is what makes it the marginal household. In a frictionless world with perfect markets, *all households* will be indifferent between renting and owning.[2] In such a world, the rental is an unambiguous measure of the cost to the household of the services provided by the durable; if we observe a 10 percent increase in house rents, we may conclude that there has been a 10 percent increase in the cost of housing services to homeowners.[3]

Similarly, in a frictionless world of perfect capital and secondhand markets, each household is indifferent between continuing to own its present house and the alternative of selling it and buying another (or buying it back). Under these conditions, the difference between the purchase price of a durable and the present value (at the market rate of interest) of the secondhand price that the used durable is expected to bring at the end of the period is an unambiguous measure of the cost to the household of the services provided by the durable. However, in the absence of futures markets the expected price of the used durable cannot be observed directly.

The capital markets in which consumers can borrow and lend and the secondhand markets for consumer durables are generally thought to be extremely imperfect. The imperfection of capital markets may be adduced from the difference between borrowing and lending rates, and imperfections in secondhand markets from the discrepancy between buying and selling prices. Houses and automobiles are the two consumer durables for which the capital–secondhand market approach appears most promising, and a satisfactory treatment of these durables would be of value even if it could not be extended to refrigerators, washing machines, or clothing. But those who argue for an approach based on secondhand markets ought to do so in terms of a model which recognizes that buying and selling prices differ.

To summarize: it is possible to construct a meaningful partial cost-of-living index if the intertemporal utility and budget functions are separable. In a frictionless world, the budget function is separable if either rental markets or capital and secondhand markets are perfect. Whether preferences are separable is an empirical question which has not yet been systematically investigated. But we do not live in a frictionless world, and casual observations suggest that the budget function is not separable; this effectively precludes construction of a meaningful one-period cost-of-living index.

Although a one-period cost-of-living index cannot be constructed, it may still be possible to construct a cost-of-living index for nondurables and services. The conditions under which such an index can be constructed follow immediately from our earlier discussion: It must be possible to associate a measure of utility and a cost with the consumption of nondurables and services in a single period. That is, in the intertemporal utility function, nondurables and services in a single period must be separable from both durables in the period and from all consumption in other periods. This is a different separability condition than the one required for a one-period cost-of-living index, and, although this condition is not logically stronger, it seems to me less plausible. Although I suspect that nondurables and services are not separable from durables in a single period, this is an empirical question which should be investigated. The restrictions which must be satisfied by the budget function, however, seem quite plausible: The cost of nondurables and services must be independent of current consumption of durables and all consumption in other periods. I believe that the Bureau should give serious attention to constructing a cost-of-living index for nondurables and services.

NOTES

This research was supported by a contract from the Bureau of Labor Statistics, U.S. Department of Labor.

1. It is frequently claimed that people buy prestigious cars for reasons unconnected with their desire for transportation services, but this is not the issue. The question is, would they be indifferent between a rented Cadillac and one they own: the neighbors need never know.

2. If households derive utility from owning as well as using the services of durables, the rental approach fails even in a frictionless world; no one would rent.

3. Even if we could show that the rental was an upper bound on the cost of owning, we could not infer that changes in the rental were an upper bound on changes in the cost of owning.

Mortgage Interest Rates in the CPI*

There are two levels of problems associated with the treatment of mortgage interest rates in the CPI. At a fundamental conceptual level any treatment of interest rates should be rationalized in terms of a model which deals explicitly with intertemporal allocation. The traditional analysis underlying the cost-of-living index and the Laspeyres price index ignores intertemporal allocation, but it cannot be ignored if we are to have a theoretically satisfactory treatment of either home ownership or consumer durables. Unfortunately, as I have argued elsewhere, a satisfactory treatment of them also depends on generalizing the usual model to take account of transactions costs and "frictions" such as "set-up" and moving costs.[1]

It is useful to distinguish objections to the treatment of mortgage interest rates based on fundamental conceptual grounds from those which accept the framework of the CPI and criticize within that context. Within the CPI framework there are two possible objections. To distinguish between them, suppose that house prices have always been and remain constant, and consider a once and for all increase in the mortgage interest rate. Suppose that the initial rate, say 4 percent, had prevailed for so long that all outstanding mortgages were initially at that rate; if the mortgage interest rate remains unchanged at its new rate, say 8 percent, for a sufficiently long time, then all outstanding mortgages will eventually be at 8 percent. Of course, there will be a transition period during which those who obtained mortgages before the increase will continue to pay 4 percent while those with more recent mortgages pay 8 percent.

There are two comparisons we can make: (1) a comparison of the situation before the increase with the long-run situation when all the 4 percent mortgages have disappeared and everyone has an 8 percent mortgage; (2) a comparison of the initial situation with the situation 1 year later, a situation in which some people have the old 4 percent mortgages while others have the new 8 percent ones. There is no ambiguity about the magnitude of the long-run increase in the interest rate, so any objection to the long-run behavior of the index must reflect dissatisfaction with the weight which the index assigns to mortgage interest rates. Most of the criticism of the treatment of mortgage interest rates in the CPI has focused on the behavior of the index during the transition period when 4 percent and 8 percent mortgages coexist.

*This research was supported by a contract from the Bureau of Labor Statistics, U.S. Department of Labor.

Although I have some doubts about the appropriateness of the long-run behavior of the index and believe that the weight associated with mortgage interest rates should be reconsidered, I shall focus on the transition period.

The CPI treatment of the transition is abrupt and simple: the index reflects the full long-run impact of any change in mortgage interest rates in the period in which the change occurs. If all mortgages were immediately refinanced at the prevailing interest rate, this treatment would certainly be appropriate. But in a world in which old mortgages are not refinanced immediately, the current CPI treatment exaggerates the impact of a change in mortgage interest rates on the index population during the transition period. A gradual adjustment of the index to its long-run value has strong intuitive appeal.

To be clear on the implications of the CPI treatment of the transition, it is useful to examine the time path of the index corresponding to a different scenario of interest rate behavior. Suppose that all mortgages were initially at 4 percent, that the rate increased to 8 percent, remained there for one period, and then returned to 4 percent. The current CPI treatment would abruptly increase the CPI to the long-run value corresponding to the 8 percent rate—the value it would attain if 4 percent mortgages disappeared and all outstanding mortgages were at 8 percent—and then, after one period, abruptly decrease it to its previous level. Our argument in the last paragraph suggests that the impact of this interest rate scenario on the index population would be more accurately represented by an index which showed a smaller initial increase and then gradually returned to its initial level.

A logically similar problem, but one with fewer extraneous complications, arises in the treatment of long-term leases on houses or apartments. Consider a world in which all apartments are rented on 5-year leases. The calculation of the appropriate weight is much simpler in this case than in that of mortgage interest rates, so the long-run treatment is less in doubt. In the short run, during the transition from one level of rents to another, those with leases obtained before the increase will be paying a lower rent than those with more recent leases. If the purpose of the index is to reflect the effect of price changes on the welfare of an index population which includes both those with new leases and those with old leases, the treatment which permits a gradual adjustment of the index to its long-run level is appropriate.

The appropriateness of any particular treatment of mortgage interest rates depends, of course, on the purpose of the index. For example, if we redefine the index population to include only those who buy houses in the current period, then an abrupt transition is appropriate. More importantly, if the purpose of the index is to provide an indication of the success of monetary or fiscal policy in influencing the prices of consumer goods and services, it is necessary to focus on those prices which reflect current market forces. The point here is not that some prices adjust more rapidly than others to market forces and that rapidly adjusting prices should be given a heavy weight in such an index, although this view has some merit. The point is that even if some people have agreements (leases and mortgages) which permit them to pay prices which differ from current prices, an index intended to reflect current market forces should use current prices. The fact that current prices differ from average prices paid by consumers is interesting but irrelevant.

NOTES

1. See Robert A. Pollak, "Consumer Durables in a Cost-of-Living Index," Submitted to the Bureau of Labor Statistics in May, 1970.

The Treatment of Taxes in the Consumer Price Index

The proper treatment of taxes in a price index depends on the type of index one is constructing and that, in turn, should depend on the purpose which the index is to serve. The Stigler committee concluded, "A constant-utility index is the appropriate index for the main purposes for which the Consumer Price Index is used" (p. 52). In the light of subsequent theoretical work, the term "cost-of-living" index is more appropriate.

In this paper I shall assume that the CPI is intended to be a cost-of-living index, and I shall consider the appropriate treatment of taxes within that framework. It is generally recognized that a decision to make the CPI a cost-of-living index would have significant implications for the treatment of substitutions induced by changes in relative prices. It is less widely appreciated that it would also have implications for many other problems, including the treatment of taxes. A major advantage of such a decision is that it would provide a consistent framework within which to evaluate alternative treatments of a variety of problems. This is true even if the procedure which is theoretically correct is not feasible—as is now the case with substitutions induced by relative price changes. The use of the cost-of-living framework would permit sensible and consistent choices among the "second-best" procedures which are feasible.

This paper discusses the treatment of taxes in a cost-of-living index. To the extent that it is possible, I shall assume away other problems associated with the construction of a cost-of-living index. In particular, I say nothing about the treatment of substitutions induced by changes in relative prices, new goods, quality changes, or changes in tastes, and very little about consumer durables or goods and services provided by the government.

In section 1, I consider the treatment of taxes in a one-period world; in section 2, their treatment in a multiperiod world without consumer durables; and in section 3, their treatment in a multiperiod world with consumer durables. A summary and a list of recommendations are presented in section 4.

1. TAXES IN A ONE-PERIOD WORLD

In a one-period world, the cost-of-living index approach provides fairly explicit guidance on most issues which arise in constructing price indexes. To avoid complications unrelated to taxes, I assume that tastes do not change and that the individual's preferences are of the fixed coefficient type. This avoids the problems associated with substitutions induced by changes in relative prices. I choose as the base indifference curve the one corresponding to the base-year consumption pattern. Under these assumptions—provided there is no government and no taxes—the Laspeyres index coincides with the cost-of-living index. We now examine the implications of introducing government and taxes.

1.1. Sales and Excise Taxes

Suppose that the only taxes are sales and excise taxes, and that the government provides consumers with no goods or services. Under our assumption about preferences, the cost-of-living index reflects the cost of the collection of goods and services consumed in the base period; hence, sales and excise taxes associated with the purchase of goods and services should be included in the index.

This does not mean that we must redefine "price," narrowly defined, and taxes. But whether we use the word "price" to refer to the sum of prices and taxes is a definitional problem without substantive implications.

1.2. Consumption Taxes

Now suppose that the government imposes a "consumption tax."[1] That is, instead of filing an income tax return, everyone is required to file a "consumption tax return" in which he reports his consumption of each good and service during the past year; his tax liability is then determined from a tax table which gives the tax rate applicable to each commodity.[2]

From the standpoint of a cost-of-living index, a consumption tax is part of the cost of consuming the base-period collection of goods and services. Hence, consumption taxes should be reflected in the index.[3]

1.3. Goods Provided by Governments

The proper treatment of goods and services provided by governments— whether they are sold to consumers or provided without charge—has little to do with the proper treatment of taxes.

From the standpoint of the cost-of-living index, goods which consumers buy from the government are no different from goods which they buy from the private sector. Thus, postage stamps, bridge tolls, and government-supplied electricity and water should be treated just as if they were provided by the private sector. From the standpoint of a cost-of-living index, the cost to the government of supplying these goods and services is irrelevant. The cost-of-living index reflects the perspective of the household, not that of the government or of society as a whole.

The proper treatment of government goods and services for which there is no explicit user charge is much more difficult, and is beyond the scope of this paper. The most straightforward way to avoid these problems is to assume that the quality and availability of "free" government goods and services does not change over time. This assumption allows us to discuss the construction of a price index which treats taxes properly without having to deal simultaneously with the treatment of government goods and services.[4]

1.4. Income Taxes

The cost-of-living approach to the construction of a price index implies unique solutions to many problems. It does not, however, imply a unique treatment of income taxes. Instead, there are two treatments of income taxes which fall within the cost of living framework. The "expenditure cost-of-living" (ECOL) index measures changes in the amount one must spend to consume the base-period collection of private goods and services. The "income cost-of-living" index (ICOL) measures changes in the income one must receive (before taxes) to be able to consume the base-period collection of private goods and services. Each of these indexes answers a sensible question within the cost-of-living framework. It is incorrect to argue that the expenditure concept is more traditional than the income concept. The theory of index numbers has traditionally ignored such real-world problems as taxes, and in a one-period world without taxes, ECOL and ICOL coincide.[5]

If the consumer's income tax liability is independent of the goods and services he consumes and of his sources of income, then the ICOL can easily be computed from the ECOL and a tax schedule.[6] If income tax liability depends on the goods and services he consumed (e.g., if there are tax "credits" for medical expenses or state sales taxes), then the computation of the ICOL must take account of the tax credits implied by the base-period consumption pattern. If the tax liability depends on the sources of income, then computation of the ICOL requires a specific assumption about the sources of income. For example, income taxes might depend on the industry or sector in which income is earned, or on the occupation of the worker.[7]

2. TAXES IN A MULTIPERIOD WORLD WITHOUT DURABLES

In this section I discuss the treatment of taxes in a multiperiod world without consumer durables. Even without new goods, quality change, taste change, government, or taxes, such a world is remarkably intractable. From a theoretical standpoint, future goods must be treated in the same way as present goods. Thus, the multiperiod analogue of the collection of goods and services is a life-time consumption plan specifying the amount of each good to be consumed in each period. The multiperiod analogue of the cost-of-living index is an index which measures changes in the wealth required to permit an individual to follow such a plan. To compute this index one would have to know not only the life-time consumption plan, but (1) all present and future prices and (2) all present and future interest rates.[8]

We need a theoretical basis for constructing a one-period index in a multiperiod world. The assumption which enables us to separate consumption behavior in one period from all other periods is called "weak separability."[9] I also assume that within each period, the individual's preferences are of the fixed coefficient type. This avoids the problems associated with substitutions induced by changes in relative prices and guarantees that the index will be of the fixed weight type. Finally, I assume that the individual's preferences are the same in the current period as they were in the last period.[10] I choose as the base indifference curve the one corresponding to the base-year consumption pattern.

Under these assumptions, the ECOL index can be computed just as it was in a one-period world. The treatment of sales taxes, excise taxes, consumption taxes, and goods purchased from the government is the same as in section 1. Goods provided "free" by the government are assumed constant.

The construction of the ICOL index is more difficult than the ECOL index because, in a multiperiod world, it must deal with both income taxes and saving. I begin with the treatment of saving, and then consider income taxes.

Even under our strong assumptions about preferences, "savings" decisions are affected by expectations of future prices and interest rates.[11] If we are to construct an analogue of the one-period ICOL in a multiperiod world, we must somehow "solve" the savings problem. The only tractable procedure I can imagine for dealing with this problem in a computable price index is to treat "real savings" (i.e., money savings divided by a price index) as part of the base-period collection of goods and services. I do not know what assumptions about preferences and expectations are needed to justify this procedure, although I intend to work on this question.

Thus, in a multiperiod world without income taxes, the ECOL is given by

$$\text{ECOL} = \frac{\sum_k p_k^1 q_k^0}{\sum_k p_k^0 q_k^0}$$

and ICOL is given by

$$\text{ICOL} = \frac{\sum p_k^1 q_k^0 + (\text{ECOL})S^0}{\sum p_k^0 q_k^0 + S^0}$$

where p's and q's denote prices and quantities and S^0 denotes saving in the base period. Factoring out ECOL yields

$$\text{ICOL} = \frac{\text{ECOL}\left[\dfrac{\sum p_k^1 q_k^0}{\text{ECOL}} + S^0\right]}{\sum p_k^0 q_k^0 + S^0}$$

and since

$$\frac{\sum p_k^1 q_k^0}{\text{ECOL}} = \sum p_k^0 q_k^0$$

this implies ICOL = ECOL. Thus, if we treat "real saving" as part of the market basket, then, in a world without income taxes, the income cost-of-living index is the same as the expenditure cost-of-living index.

In a world with income taxes, the income cost-of-living index and the expenditure cost-of-living index are no longer identical, but calculation of the ICOL from the ECOL is relatively simple. If income taxes are independent of the sources of income and disposition of income, then one has only to calculate from the tax schedule the before-tax income required to leave the individual with enough after-tax income to buy the base-period collection of goods and services, including "real saving." If taxes depend on the sources of income (e.g., if the first $100 of dividend income is treated differently from wage income), then specific assumptions about sources of income must be made. Allowance must also be made for any dependence of tax liability on the consumption pattern.

3. TAXES IN A MULTIPERIOD WORLD WITH DURABLES

The major difficulty in constructing a cost-of-living index in a world with consumer durables and taxes is the treatment of consumer durables, not the treatment of taxes. As in a multiperiod world without consumer durables, the heart of the problem is to find a sensible way to reduce a multiperiod problem to a one-period problem. The added difficulty is that consumer ownership of durable goods provides another link between the present and the future.

I shall assume that a way to treat consumer durables in a world without taxes has been found. In particular, I assume that it is possible to identify a "cost" or "price" with the flow of services provided by a durable. If this cannot be done, then one cannot construct an index which includes durables.

Taxes associated with the ownership or use of consumer durables are consumption taxes. Hence, these taxes should be reflected in the cost-of-living index. Whether this is done by incorporating taxes into the "cost" or "price" of the flow of services, or whether taxes are added in separately is of no consequence.

Calculation of the ICOL index with consumer durables is essentially the same as without them. The only difference is that adjustments must be made for the tax treatment of durables (e.g., the deductibility of real estate taxes and mortgage interest payments).

4. SUMMARY

While the consumer price index serves a variety of needs, it appears that most of those needs would best be served by a cost-of-living index. Therefore, I recommend that the CPI be made a cost-of-living index.

There are, however, two legitimate "cost-of-living indexes," the expenditure cost-of-living (ECOL) index and the income cost-of-living (ICOL) index. The former measures changes in the after-tax income required to consume a base-period collection of goods and services while the latter measures changes in the before-tax income required. For purposes of computing the ICOL index, "real saving" is considered part of the base-period basket. I recommend that both the ECOL and the ICOL be published.

Construction of either the ECOL or the ICOL requires a satisfactory measure of the flow of services provided by consumer durables and the cost of these services. Further work on the treatment of consumer durables is necessary before this will be possible. Because of the difficulty of treating consumer durables, I recommend publication of an expenditure-type cost-of-living index which includes consumer durables.

There is a clear need for a price index suitable for place-to-place comparisons, both for analytical purposes and in connection with such policy issues as national welfare standards and revenue sharing. Indeed, much of the pressure for the development of an index which includes income taxes is due to a concern with the differential treatment of localities which use income taxes and those which use sales or property taxes. This concern is often based on a misunderstanding of the nature of the CPI, which is not appropriate for place-to-place comparisons, but it is indicative of the need for an index which can be used to make place-to-place comparisons. Therefore, I recommend that an index suitable for place-to-place comparisons be developed.

The treatment of goods and services provided "free" by governments is even more crucial in making place-to-place comparisons than in making comparisons over time. The problems involved are extremely difficult, but place-to-place comparisons require the measurement of differences in services provided by governments. Therefore, I recommend that further work be done on the problem of treating government services.

Recommendations

1. Make the consumer price index a cost-of-living index.
2. Publish both an "expenditure cost-of-living" index and an "income cost-of-living" index.
3. Do further work on the treatment of consumer durables.
4. Publish an expenditure-type cost-of-living index excluding durables.
5. Develop a price index suitable for place-to-place comparisons.
6. Do further work on the treatment of "free" government services.

NOTES

1. I argue in section 3 that real estate taxes and automobile registration fees are consumption taxes.

2. The consumption tax might be based on consumption measured in physical units or in dollars; for our purpose, it makes no difference.

3. As in the case of sales and excise taxes, it makes no substantive difference whether we redefine "price" to include these taxes; regardless of how we define "price," the cost-of-living index should reflect consumption taxes.

4. Technically, under this assumption government goods and services can be absorbed into the parameters of the utility function.

5. In a multiperiod world, the ECOL and ICOL may differ because of saving. In a one-period world, all after-tax income is spent, so income taxes are the only possible cause of divergence.

6. If the tax liability depends on the demographic characteristics of the consumer (e.g., age, sex, marital status, number of children) then computation of the ICOL requires specific assumptions about these characteristics.

7. In a one-period world, there is little scope for discussing differential treatment of dividends and labor income.

8. In such an index, a price increase which was expected to be permanent would have a much greater impact than a price increase which was expected to be temporary.

9. Technically, I assume that the intertemporal utility function is a "tree."

10. Technically, I assume that branch utility functions are identical.

11. And in an imperfect world with uncertainty and transaction costs, by the entire menu of financial assets available.

Index